CLASS, STATE, AND STRUGGLE IN NEPAL

Writings 1989–1995

Class, State, and Struggle in Nepal
Writings 1989–1995

STEPHEN LAWRENCE MIKESELL

MANOHAR
1999

The following publishers have generously given permission to republish in the same or altered form the copyrighted works by the author: 'First Aid for the Nation: Health Professionals and the Movement', Copyright 1990, by *Media Nepal.* 'Comparative Study of South Asian Caste and Mediterranean Citizenship in the Development of the State', Copyright 1991, by Centre for Nepal and Asian Studies/Tribhuvan University. 'Up-Country Bazaar and Changing Forces', Copyright 1992 by Himal Association. 'The Local Government Law and Participatory Democracy: A Comparison of Opposites', Copyright 1992, by the Nepal Law Society. 'A Critique of Levi's Urban Mesocosm Thesis', Copyright 1993, by Centre for Nepal and Asian Studies/Tribhuvan University. 'Democratizing the University', Copyright 1993, by *The Kathmandu Post.* 'Mercantilism and Domestic Industry', Copyright 1990, and 'Afro-American Sociology and Nepali Social Science', Copyright 1993, by Department of Sociology/Anthropology, Tribhuvan University–Kirtipur.

First published 1999

© Stephen L. Mikesell 1999

ISBN 81-7304-267-5

Published by
Ajay Kumar Jain for
Manohar Publishers & Distributors
2/6, Ansari Road, Daryaganj
New Delhi 110002

Printed at
Rajkamal Electric Press
B35/9, G.T. Karnal Road Industrial Area
Delhi – 110 033

For Aidan Southall

Contents

Illustrations

Acknowledgements

THE PRODUCTION of a book is always a social effort, even when written in isolation, since the writer is her or himself a social product. It is rare that it is not also a collective effort as well, for which I can only make a few of the acknowledgments due. Foremost I wish to acknowledge the working class individuals in the villages and cities of Nepal who have been the most generous with the least to be generous by, who have always treated me with kindness and without condescension, and who have given me the most insight and helped me keep my feet on the ground throughout all my work in Nepal. For their influence in my theory and practice, their unreserved criticism, and their generous encouragement and support, I wish to acknowledge Professors Aidan Southall (Wisconsin) and Mathura Shrestha (Institute of Medicine), Keshav Gautam (Society for Participatory Cultural Education), Surendra Pande (Communist Party-UML), Baburam Bhattarai (United People's Front), Hisila Yami (Prayana Woman's Pariwar), Nirmal Tuladhar (Centre for Nepal and Asian Studies, Tribhuvan University), Renu Sharma and Tara Upreti (Foundation for the Solidarity and Development of Women), Anil Bhattarai (Ajammari Bio-intensive Agriculture Farm), Dr. Anna Lou Dehavenon (Action Research Project on Hunger, Homelessness and Family Health), Professor Rojer Nance (Birmingham) and my brother-in-law Kiran Shrestha who was instrumental in aspects of my work. I want to gratefully acknowledge the generous assistance of Santa Bahadur Nepali in my work with Dalits in Bandipur, Ram Kumari Deula with sweepers in Bhaktapur, and Padma Tuladhar and Suchita Tuladhar with merchants in Kathmandu.

I wish to acknowledge the Department of Anthropology and Sociology and the Centre for Nepal and Asian Studies at Tribhuvan University in Kirtipur for generously providing official affiliation at different stages of my work and apologize to them for the inconvenience that this affiliation sometimes caused with the university's top-heavy and parasitic bureaucracy. Particular thanks go to the anthropologist Dr. Om Gurung and linguist Nirmal Tuladhar for their staunch support in doing this, and the kindness, interest, and professional conviviality—as well as criticism—shown me by the faculty and staff in both these departments who are too many to list here. Also appreciation is due to my journalist friends and colleagues in *Himal Magazine* and the late *Everest Herald*— particularly my kind co-editor, Narod Wagle, who taught me how to write an editorial—for taking me much more seriously than I deserved as a journalist and allowing me to interact in their busy, and oftentimes noisy, sphere.

For their generous support of various stages of my research and writing, I wish to acknowledge the assistance of grants from the Joint Committee on South Asia of the Social Science Research Council and the American Council of Learned Societies with funds provided by the Ford Foundation and the National Endowment for Humanities, the United States Educational Foundation Fulbright-Hays Doctoral and Post-Doctoral Research Abroad Programs, and the Wenner-Grenn Foundation for Anthropological Research. The usual disclaimer holds that nothing of what is written here should be seen as reflecting the views or policies of any of these organizations.

And finally but foremost, I wish to express my gratitude to my partner in craziness, Jamuna Shrestha, for her support, including much of the typing of the manuscript, and a great variety of other assistance, and to my daughters Rhitu and Ritika Shrestha who have always been a source of great energy, affection, and the most honest and severe criticism.

STEPHEN MIKESELL

CHAPTER 1

Introduction

I CAME TO Nepal on 8 June 1989 to continue research left off two years earlier on the relationship of the merchant bazaar to the development of classes and the state within the context of the global development of commerce and industry. This earlier research focused on merchants of Bandipur, a two-hundred year-old bazaar town in the hills of west-central Nepal. Having identified the bazaar merchants as agents of the expansion of the circulation of industrial capital into the up-country markets of hill Nepal, I intended to shift the focus of my study to the villagers' and industrial workers' experience of this process. Events, however, added another dimension to my work. Even as I was fitting myself back into my wife's extended family and struggling over research arrangements with the national university's Research Division chief (who was demanding a major share of my research grant and his assignment to my payroll), the Nepali Communist Party (Marxist-Leninist) was secretly laying plans to unite the chronically divided opposition in a political movement to force the government to end a three-decades-old ban on political parties. The resulting 'Democracy Movement' lasted from 18 February to 10 April 1990. Besides ultimately forcing the king to suspend the constitutional article outlawing political parties, the movement led to the disintegration of the layered series of patronage-based representative councils known as the 'Panchayat System', widely seen as the source of the corruption plaguing the country. The coming months and years led to the drafting of a new constitution; formation of, elections to, and machinations of a new two-tiered parliament; rewriting of the local government law and elections to local councils; strikes and street demonstrations by opposition parties against the government; and, early in 1996, the initiation of a Maoist guerrilla war by the 'people's war' faction of the Communist Party.

Already at the time of my earlier research it was clear that some sort of uprising was imminent. The rural direct producers were suffering pervasive bondage rooted in the long history of landlord and commercial expansion represented in the state-building process. The Panchayat System, sustained and supported by foreign state, superstate, and multinational corporate ingress, had added unprecedented bureaucratic growth, which was erupting like a cancer atop the earlier forms of inequality and eating away at villager autonomy and control over the production process. New forms of appropriation introduced new appropriating groups and elaborated the old ones: the palace, landowners, bureaucrats, contractors, administrators, business owners, international businesses, and a whole new cadre of intelligentsia, both domestic and foreign. The newly emergent groups clamoured for a larger share in the political process and its spoils. They placed themselves as leaders of a democracy movement presenting itself as a general liberation of the oppressed classes, but their interest was in reorganizing the benefits of the state without disturbing its exploitative and oppressive character. Once the door had been pried open sufficiently wide for them to stick their feet in, they shut down the movement before the disenfranchised masses could also enter and make their own claims on the state and society.

I observed both sides of this equation during and after the movement. In the days before the movement, I taught the mostly urban students in the graduate campus of the national university while doing research among villagers and factory workers in the Chitwan. On 18 January 1991 I sat under the canopy set up for foreign observers in the compound of the supreme leader of the Congress Party, Ganesh Man Singh, where thousands of people listened to the leaders of the Nepali Congress and Indian Janata Dal and Socialist parties announce 18 February as the first day of the movement. I observed in the days leading up to the movement the government frantically truck in paid participants to counter-rallies, with their speeches by Panchas and royalty, and begin a rain of terror in the countryside and campuses. In the past, selective police terror had caused people to cringe alone in their houses; now, widespread terror drove people together and emboldened them. During the first week of the movement I sat cross-legged in my house with a middle-aged man disparaged as 'the Left Doctor' by the police as he coordinated medical students and doctors and shouted directions into the telephone for defense against the police and armed *goondas* breaking into people's houses in Bhaktapur. In five days our phone registered 800 calls. During the relative lull in the weeks following the initial outbreak of the movement, I sipped tea on the clay floor of a smoky shanty outside Narayanghat with villagers too terrified to speak due to police jeeps roaming from village to village in search of young men. In the seventh week the whole country erupted in general protests. I sat with lawyers and engineers who sipped Johnny Walker with first secretaries of Western embassies and the reporter from the *New York Times* as military trucks brimming with green-clad police rumbled past. On 6 April I was knocked down as a crowd of a quarter-million people fled before the 'Crack! Crack!' of military gunfire in the city centre. From inside a packed house we watched a soldier crouch and shoot dead a youth dancing defiantly in the middle of the street and that night we listened to military trucks haul away the bodies of the young. After three days of martial law, the king and selected representatives from the opposition arrived at an agreement to end the movement, sending the population jubilantly into the streets celebrating what was being heralded as the 'advent of democracy'. This though the 'minimal settlement' represented by the agreement had reversed nearly all the demands raised by the movement.

After the movement, the leaders became ministers, the lawyer advocated lucratively for the Nepali Congress party against the Communists, the engineer headed a multi-billion dollar dam project, and the dead became 'martyrs'. Landlords continued to pressure the Chitwan peasants for debts, and factory workers in the government textile factor in Hataunda found their unions split along party lines and no longer able to organize against managers who continued to siphon off profits for their personal benefit. A first-year college student whose village parents had used all their resources to finance his education flunked his exams because he had been fighting 'the revolution' while apolitical students took high marks and headed for further study and professions. I went to villages as anthropologist for the Ministry of Health to look at why the health system was failing the poor. I showed how substantial change in health required basic social and political changes, and with a new, popularly-oriented minister, we thought that they could be effected. But the ministers fell into the same old circuit of seminars, embassy parties, commemorations, dedications, and other fickle forms of notoriety that accompany position, while a sophisticated and far more experienced bureaucracy continued to protect and expand its self-interest. To pick up money to finance my own work and keep my family, I edited collections of mediocre seminar papers on law, health, the environment and the economy. Foreign organizations and agencies found familiar ground by funding seminars. A procession of gradually fattening new 'democrat' ministers with their flag-waving black automobiles and military guards majestically inaugurated these seminars, from which they rushed home to watch themselves on Nepal TV. I gathered that we were the bottom of a food chain of sorts: the higher your status the closer you get to Geneva, New York and Washington. The catered food of the five star hotels was as greasy as the seminars were tedious, so I extracted myself from the seminar circuit and redoubled my work with village-based organizations, continuing editing to make a living. In 1996 I took a job as features page editor in the *Everest Herald*, a start-up national daily newspaper initiated by journalists disenchanted with the *Kathmandu Post*, which had become politically partisan to the Congress Party. I learned a lot about newspapers but found the power of the pen illusory. Sometimes we received a threatening phone call from a ministry or embassy which disapproved of an angle of our story, but otherwise I felt the medium was ineffectual because the urban dwellers and foreign embassies who read the paper had too much to lose to effect substantial change, even on a personal level.

This again confirmed a growing sense of mine that real, substantial change could only evolve from the direct producers themselves. The urban and foreign elites' status and benefits committed them too deeply to the exploitative structures of society built up over the preceding decades and centuries. House servants, imported alcohol, computers, cars, name-brand imports, grotesque 'modern' cement houses, and the notoriety of being on TV: these things enslave them as much as their own enthrallment of the villagers through rent, usury, high fees, inflation, and corruption. The difference is that their bondage is rewarded with the jealous adulation of their relatives and members of their social class and recognition by foreign agencies and officials, while the toiling villagers are despised for their life of labour which provides the urban dwellers with their sustenance and comfort. Furthermore, in the short-term at least, they receive international subsidies and payoffs to support their lifestyle and can shut out the social and environmental unraveling of the country with high brick walls and police protection or, if life becomes too difficult, flee the country, while the direct producers must bear the costs.

Because they immediately suffer the consequences and due to their direct involvement in the production process and close dependence on the natural environment, the peasants and workers are positioned to understand how their livelihood depends directly upon sustaining the community and natural environment. A number of us realized that significant contribution to their struggle (which ultimately affects everyone's well-being) could not be done on an abstract level or as members of a vanguard, but by throwing one's lot in with them. Living and working alongside of them, putting our children into their schools, and working with them to make their community as good as we could wish for our children, but on their terms. I was privileged to work alongside some people trying to do this, in part at least. Like me they had their social contexts and were pressured by demands and obligations that kept us from always seeing the path straight.

The papers in this volume are all written as part of my own struggle to see the path straight. They aim to identify the social class arrangement of the country and how these class dynamics have sprung from and been subsumed within larger spheres of interaction. I sought to expose the flawed premises given to the interpretations of the 'Democracy Movement' and show that the implementation of formal democratic institutions has little to do with democracy if the direct producers are kept from engaging directly within the political process. I asked questions of the nature of people's bondage and exploitation and sought ways to bring the direct producers into the political process through changing the ways of producing, thinking, interacting, and relating to each other and to nature. This book is divided into several sections reflecting different periods of my development and the various issues I was addressing from 1989 to 1996.

Part I, 'Exegesis on Method' consists of three critical studies of Nepali social science. Chapter 2, 'My Apperception', written initially as part of the introduction for this book, lays out the framework of my analysis in the context of my graduate and post-graduate work. It starts with my growing dissatisfaction with nineteenth century culture theory and the framework of understanding it has imposed on the people of Nepal (and elsewhere in the commercial and financial colonies of the world) and follows my discovery of an approach that locates the subject of history in human self-creation.

This lays the way to an open-ended view of the world confronting us as a social product that not only makes humans but can be remade by them. I developed Chapter 3, 'Historical Materialist Method and Analysis of Culture in Nepal', from a series of lectures I gave to graduate students at the Kirtipur Campus of Tribhuvan University in a course designated 'conflict theory'. This work stems from my return to Marx's and Engels' *German Ideology*, and Marx's 'Introduction' to the *Grundrisse*, his section on production in *Capital*, and his notes to his ethnographic readings late in life in *The Ethnological Notebooks of Karl Marx*, to understand the materialist method and apply it to Nepal's situation. Some of the themes introduced in the previous chapter are more thoroughly developed, beginning with a critique of the tendency of the anthropology of Nepal to start with the apparently concrete, immediate categories, such as the village community or population, as the object of analysis which are themselves contingent upon other categories and conditions presupposed but omitted from the inquiry by the anthropologist. In contrast, I further develop the idea of how Marx located the premise of his subject in human creative activity, or 'production', with the aim of eliminating contingency and proceeded from there. Such a perspective allowed me to locate the village community in Nepal within much larger historical and regional, even global, frameworks. Chapter 4, 'Unlocking Submerged Voices: Afro-American Scholarship and Nepali Social Science', a paper originally read at the first Sociological and Anthropological Conference in Nepal, argues that a particular dominant discourse of European social science has been transferred to Nepal, whereas suppressed discourses within western social science, in this case that of African-American sociology, have been eliminated. Yet this suppressed discourse perhaps speaks more to the situation of the bulk of Nepal's people, who are rural and poor, because they and the American working class are confronting the same forces of political-economic and cultural domination experienced by America's disenfranchised groups. This work extended from my own first introduction to the so-called Black sociology, particularly the impassioned writings of W.E.B. Du Bois, a towering visionary who sought to link up the understanding and struggle of colonized peoples throughout the world with that of the divided American working class.

Part II, 'The Democracy Movement and its Aftermath', developed directly out of my experience leading up to, during and following the 1990 Democracy Movement in Nepal. Chapter 5, 'Social-History of the Jaana Andalan: A Critical Analysis', which also started as a part of the introduction to this book but took a life of its own, presents a history of the 1990 Democracy Movement in Nepal and subsequent developments up to 1998 from a historical materialist perspective. It attempts to place the movement within the long history of state and class development within Nepal and offer an alternative direction of political development. Chapter 6, 'Health Workers and the Movement', written during the summer of 1990, describes the role that health workers played in accelerating and publicizing the movement. In retrospect, this work, which was based on my close contact with doctors and nurses during and immediately after the movement, reflected an overly optimistic appraisal both of the role of the intellectuals in the movement, particularly doctors, and the dimensions of their radicalism. If I were to rewrite this now, I would discard the notion of the possibility of intellectuals serving as a vanguard for a long-term movement that could provide any sort of substantial alternative to the trajectory of development, a.k.a. commercialization, that is occurring now. Western oriented, economically privileged, out of touch with their people, most are simply too much a product of commercialization and consequently organically committed to it. Chapter 7, 'The Interim Constitution and Transition to Democracy in Nepal', read at the South Asian Meetings in Madison, Wisconsin, in December 1990, sums up the struggle that took place around the writing of the new constitution following the movement. Its import is that the process of writing the constitution was characterized by demobilization of the movement and a retreat from its demands, to the extent that the production of the new constitution turned into an exercise in eliminating any sort of popular, democratic discussion rather than engendering it— despite the constitution's claim to being 'democratic'. The main purpose of this demobilization was to allow a compromise between the landed property and commission agent forces represented in the old regime and the new emergent ones consisting of an alliance of bureaucracy, domestic mercantile capital, and international finance. The paper criticizes the Communist Parties, which were calling for an interim constitution and constituent assembly, for not taking the initiative in implementing their demands independent of the actions of the rest of the ruling class. In retrospect their failure to do so came from their leadership's confusion of obtaining government office, articulated in the majority position of *baudaliya jaanabad* 'multi-party' democracy, with revolutionary struggle. I wrote Chapter 8, 'The Local Government Law and Participatory Democracy: A Comparison of Opposites', just prior to the institution of the new local government law. It shows further how the constitutional and legal processes were being used to suppress the extension of real democracy to the bulk of Nepal's people, despite the 'democratic', 'participatory' rhetoric being used. It compares Nepal's experience to those of the Workers Party of Brazil and the Squatters Movement in Chile in order to illustrate the pitfalls of the 'democratizing struggle' and offers some alternatives to overcoming them. Chapter 9, 'Charisma and its Routinization', is a previously unpublished piece developed out of my continuing disillusionment with the dominant majority (and for that matter the equally rigid minority) position within the Communist Party (United Marxist Leninist), represented by its General Secretary Madan Bhandari and, after his death in 1993, Madhav Nepal, which I saw as using mass politics for short-term political objectives rather than long-term building of a solid Communist movement. Referring to the sociologist Max Weber's *Economy and Society*, this piece observes how the charisma imparted by the act of struggle of the oppressed has been taken over as a personal quality by the leadership and used for consolidating and legitimating their own power over the party while disempowering and dismantling the party's organizational base. Chapter 10, 'Democratizing Tribhuvan University', which extended from my own experience teaching at the national university of Nepal and was published in the national newspaper, *The Kathmandu Post*, observes that the national university is being destroyed by centralized bureaucratic control and the tendency of the government in power to treat it as a sinecure for its cadres and hangers-on. I advocate devolving control over the university from the government and the bureaucracy to its faculties rather than attempting the centre-directed, heavily foreign-aid-financed changes embarked upon by the Vice Chancellor.

Part III, 'South Asia, Nepal and Strategy Following the People's Movement', consists of three pieces that I wrote for the journal *Jhilko* ('Spark', named after the newspaper of the Russian Bolshevik party), the intellectual organ of the Revolutionary International Movement affiliated Communist Party–Masal ('Torch'). These three pieces (chapters 11–13) criticize the theoretical understanding of the situation of Nepal's countryside and the dominant political orientation of the Communist movement. During the fall of that year I found myself drawn into the warm, humid, overcrowded meeting room of the French Cultural Centre in Kathmandu in which intellectuals from all spectra of the opposition, anticipating the coming social movement, argued over the nature of exploitative relationships in the countryside. Only later did I see these discussions, which seemed too often to be a splitting of hairs, as part of the jockeying of various elements of the different 'banned' political parties for their place, as leaders, in the coming political movement and the struggle over the agenda that would provide the means for them to take this place—a 'war of position' as opposed to 'war of movement', in Gramsci's terms. These maneuvers necessarily took the form of highly theoretical discussions, as any indication of political intentions would have brought quick reprisals by the Home Ministry and its police force, as happened in another meeting at Tribhuvan University. Solicited in part possibly to discredit other viewpoints being expressed in this seminar, I wrote a series of articles for *Jhilko*. I doubt that my main purpose—to show that political transformations cannot lead to revolutionary transformation of society without being preceded by cultural transformation—garnered much sincere interest. I indicated possible strategies for widely involving villagers in the political process and challenging the trend of shifting ever greater powers into the state. Such a path, though ultimately liberating for everyone, would have seemed threatening to intellectuals who conceived themselves as heirs to the policies of centralization and self-aggrandizement of Lenin or Nehru. Mine was the social scientist's conceit: thinking that I was the analyst of society when in fact I had been caught up in its currents and assigned to purposes I little understood. Although I was unaware of this overtly at this time, it contributed to my growing disquiet that little could come from writing for an audience of intellectuals on the subject of turning over power to the working classes, even among the Left. Despite their rhetoric, their's is a different agenda.

Chapter 11, 'Marx's Ethnological Notebooks, Feudalism in Asia, and Strategy in Nepal' (Mikesell 1990a), aimed at critiquing the Nepal Communist movement's dogmatic Comintern strategy of first overthrowing the feudal elements as the main enemy and then overthrowing the capitalists in the belief that capitalism would lay the path to socialism. I argue that this was an opportunistic misreading of history which would serve to consolidate and extend the already existing hold of capital over the countryside, since Nepal was not feudal but already subsumed by international capital. I develop a theme addressed by Stein (1977, 1980) and Fox (1971, 1973, 1977) in their critique of mainstream South Asia scholars for applying the European historical periodization to South Asian history, emulating the high, 'legitimate' history imparted from colonial Europe, when what is needed is the generation of history from the regional perspective and experience. Chapter 12, 'The Class Basis of the Movement: Historical Origins and Present Significance', was written immediately following the political movement of 1990 and aimed to build upon the perspective introduced by the previous article by laying out actual strategic steps that could be taken. I further developed my critique of the application of European categories and showed the manner of development of the community and state in terms of the subordination of previously 'segmentary states', which organized themselves in terms of kinship and coordinated social power by *inclusion* of groups within a community, by states based on patriarchal private property, which accumulated social power through building ranked, aristocratic societies based on *exclusionary* principles. Chapter 13, 'The Next Step: Cultivating the Roots of Rebellion', produced after the movement during the period of the interim government and perceiving the lack of programme or initiatives among the Left, tried to develop alternative strategies to those of the Nepali Left through direct involvement of the direct producers in the political process. This and the other works in this section all aim to counter the elitist and exclusionary vanguardist principles which, in the tradition of Nehru, Lenin, Stalin, and Mao due to the proclivities of the intelligentsia, dominate Socialist and Communist theory and practice in Nepal.

Part IV, 'Bandipur Bazaar', reproduces two articles developed from my work on the merchant bazaar in west-central Nepal, where I did my dissertation research. Both aimed at challenging the mainline view of the Nepali countryside as having remained isolated from regional and global processes until recent years. Chapter 14, 'Up-country Bazaar and Changing Forces' uses the history of Bandipur as a particular example of processes of market penetration and general expansion of the domination of commodity relations over the countryside through the length of the middle hills over the last two-hundred years. Chapter 15, 'Mercantilism and Domestic

Industry in West-Central Nepal', looks particularly at examples of documents kept by the merchants of Bandipur as important sources of historical material for understanding the history of processes taking place in the countryside. Nepali historiography has relied primarily upon official records, religious manuscripts and various kinds of engravings in copper plates and stone tablets for its documentation. This piece argues that the merchant's records, including debt vouchers, ledgers, letters and factory records, provide an intimate written documentation of not only merchant activity in the bazaars but of the peasantry through record of their relationships with the peasants. The records of the last two-hundred years are particularly important because this is the period in which the merchants became agents of the expansion of industrial capital into up-country markets and through this expansion became a significant subaltern class force within the state, to eventually emerge as partners in the political control of the state. This work suggests that anthropologists utilize personal records of provincial merchants, scribes, and official figures in Nepal in order to provide historical depth to ethnographic research in place of the presumption of an ahistorical or mythical-historical countryside that has previously characterised the major part of ethnographic work.

The works in the final Part V, 'Critique of Theory and Practice in Nepal', address various issues in the anthropological theory of Nepal and the subcontinent. Chapter 16, 'A Comparative Study of South Asian Caste and Mediterranean Citizenship in the Development of Classes and the State', observes that the usual treatment of caste places it in the same order of abstraction as class, leading to a tendency to treat caste as being mutually exclusive from class and understandable only in its own terms. I argue that the class that is usually compared with caste is that of industrial capitalist society in which commodity relations dominate. When class is treated generically in terms of distribution of people and products within the production process, caste becomes understood as an aspect of the reproduction of class relations. The Western category which should be compared to caste of the Indian subcontinent should be not class but citizenship. Comparison should be made first not between the contemporary developed forms, but with their initial forms and the imperatives that they were first created to deal with in the Ancient world. When we look at their respective emergence, caste and citizenship both arose to address a similar problem of the rise of private property and transformation of the state brought about by the Neolithic Revolution. Due to different conditions of the expansion of these new class relations, the two categories developed upon and elaborated different elements of the lineage-based organizations which preceded them. As ideology, they both have developed and persisted up to the present day, but with very different content and purposes than in the past. Proper analysis of caste requires identifying this content. In today's world—in which social life is increasingly falling under, and struggling against, a global regime of commerce and finance—caste and citizenship must be understood in terms of this regime.

Although Chapter 17, 'A Critique of Bhaktapur as Urban Mesocosm', originally appeared as a review of Levi's (1992) monumental study of ritual in the Kathmandu Valley city of Bhaktapur, its underlying purpose was to critique a major tendency of much of the foreign ethnography in Nepal to treat contemporary culture and life as being in essence unchanging and understandable in terms of rituals and their associated texts. Based on the analysis of ritual and symbols, Levy argues that the city of Bhaktapur is simultaneously a 'middle universe' between the household and the larger universe (South Asia? the globe?) and an intermediate stage between the first pristine city and the subsequent industrial one. I argue against being able to understand urban society purely in terms of ritual, particularly in light of my own documentation of the historical experience of the Bhaktapur merchants and their relationship to the countryside and the state, which contradicts many of the key assumptions made by Levy. Levy's separation of the domestic sphere from civil society and the state fails to recognize the manner that the household reproduces the larger society and consequently that the state penetrates into the household. The portrayal of Bhaktapur as a transitional stage is equivocal. Such an approach of locating the present in some unchanged past finds its precedence in the late eighteenth and early nineteenth century British colonial proposition that the people of the subcontinent were still in a feudal past and it was the role of the East India Company to bring them up to the British present (Bernard Cohn 1996). This project, which actually was little more than a scholarly justification for subjugation of the people and general looting of the subcontinent, required objectifying the people of the subcontinent in terms of this supposed past. This objectification included among other things imposition of a legal code retrieved from ancient texts, separation of selected artifacts of material life from their living contexts and depositing them in museums for proper reinterpretation, establishment of universities and schools based on the British model of education, creation of a sterile, 'objective' history removed from the context of the active interpretive life of the people, imposition of dress codes that fit these preconceptions, and transformation of local scholars into collectors and compilers of local knowledge for the British who then decided upon the manner of organization, categorization, interpretation and the uses given to the knowledge.

PART I

Exegesis on Method

CHAPTER 2

My Apperception

WHEN I FIRST visited Nepal in 1980 my studies in anthropology predisposed me to conceive of the country in terms of a population divided into many different groups, each with its own unique culture which could be studied apart from the whole in its own terms. Each of these cultural groups was identified either by common language or by common caste, and it was assumed that the people of each different language or *varna* had their own way of life with its characteristic underlying ideas, complexes of symbols, rituals, adaptations to the environment, ways of relating together and doing things, and forms of perceiving and experiencing the world, all of which could be positively known through empirical observation of any sample community or local group of individuals or even of a single individual or 'informant' belonging to the population. These cultures, furthermore, were seen as all being encompassed more generally within national and regional traditions such that they were presented together in area studies as the 'Peoples of Nepal' or 'Peoples of South Asia', under the assumption—according to the accepted divisions of the world—that this larger geographically defined collectivity of cultures shares a similar essence and can also be known on its own terms. This approach to comprehending populations follows from the culture concept in anthropology as formulated by the nineteenth century founder of anthropology, the British colonial administrator Edward Tylor, who conceived culture as being the 'whole' of a people's material and non-material life.

During my first foray into graduate-level anthropology from 1977 to 1981, I engaged in fieldwork in Endicott, Washington, a town in the US Northwest which had been settled by German-Russian immigrants in the last part of the nineteenth century and the beginning of the twentieth. I grew increasingly uncomfortable with the culture concept, not only because it failed to provide a unifying vision of a common human life and effort but, when taken within the long-term historic and prehistoric records, the notion of separate and isolated development of different peoples with their own different cultures *contradicts* humankind's characteristic intercourse between populations and fluidity of practices and ideas. The German-Russians of Eastern Washington, who had originally fled the war-ridden Palatinate region of Germany for Russia at the invitation of Tsar Katherine in the eighteenth century and then migrated to North and South America in the face of heavy industrialization, agrarian reforms and rising anti-German sentiments of the late nineteenth and early twentieth centuries, and who by the 1970s had essentially evaporated as a separate cultural population or community, seemed to exemplify this fluidity.

In that study I had already realized that understanding a group of people required some sort of alternate, historical framework of analysis, as it was their experience and what they had done with that experience that made their culture. But lacking other frameworks of understanding, I continued to force the townspeople's historical experience into a culturalogical understanding, particularly in terms of John Bennett's application of the concept of 'opportunity costs' to people's choices between different cultural adaptations in the face of changing historical circumstances.[1] This resulted in the meaningless truism that people chose to do things and make choices because these choices were adaptive to whatever historical circumstances I identified. The millions of dead strewn along the way of course never become informants. In retrospect, the problem of migration and transformation of the Russian-Germans in the United States and Russia had more to do with the history of the development of the relations of land, labour and capital in Europe and the United States and the changing class relations that this embodied, starting with the feudal upheaval and peasant wars in eighteenth century Germany, the simultaneous pushing back of the Tartars and opening up of vast lands for colonization in the south of Tsar Catherine's Russia, the consolidation of capital and growth of monopoly capitalism in late nineteenth century Europe and the United States, movement of international banks into Russia and differentiation of the Russian peasantry in the late nineteenth century, and the railroad building and capitalization of agriculture in the twentieth century United States. Much of what I identified as characteristically Russian-German turned out to be the general experience first of European peasantry and then of American farmers, and I would have understood what was happening far better through an analysis of particular processes instead of trying to search for a unique cultural pattern or adaptation—something that, predisposed by my discipline, I had assumed but not tested. Such analysis would have given tremendous insight into the forces that led to the Russian revolution and placed these in comparative perspective with American agriculture, an important task. However, this required knowledge of a dynamic motive force of history (which cultural analysis fails to provide) and of a relationship of subject and object in human life that is not contingent upon other methodically excluded factors.[2]

Before I had thought this through, I followed this research experience with my first visit to Nepal. In Nepal, the pursuit of culture studies had led to the accumulation of a large number of monographs on the 'cultures' of Nepal, described as such.[3] Such studies were an important step in the development of the anthropology of the region, some of it quite interesting and curious in its own right, because in addition to making detailed, intimate descriptions of people's lives and thought as apprehended by the experience and thought of anthropologists and providing a critique of the current conceptions of the world, particularly that only the 'Western' way of life and perceptions were valid, it laid out a record of the development of anthropology's self understanding of and confrontation with the world. By setting out and objectifying that self understanding and describing the confrontation in minute though generally bewilderingly detail, these works provided the material for critical reflection on and change of not only this understanding of the world but the social practice giving rise to this understanding. I have been slow to develop an appreciation of this dialectic myself, which has led much of my work to treat these culture studies somewhat stridently, even though I too am participating in this process.

The culture concept starts by making certain universal assumptions about human life without first demonstrating whether they are true or universally valid, and then it extends these assumptions in particular studies to confirm and magnify itself. The main assumption is that unique and separate cultures exist which determine the forms

of community and individual life of specific populations of people
enjoying their own more or less autonomous existence. Each cultural
population is in turn assumed to be defined by a shared language
or, in South Asia, caste, such that all individuals born to the same
native tongue or caste fall into the same culture group. Since culture
is determinative, all the members of a linguistic or caste group are
expected to share the same basic patterns of consciousness and be
driven by the same normative imperatives. Thus observations of any
individual or collection of individuals (such as a village) from among
the population or 'cultural group' defined in this way can be used
to describe and confirm the existence of this culture. Thus the
tautology that cultures determine linguistically or caste delimited
populations and linguistic or caste-delimited populations define
cultures.

Turning to the determination of culture groups in Nepal, language
at first appears to be a valid defining element because it would seem
that common language facilitates communication among members
of the same linguistic group while providing a barrier to communication with individuals of other linguistic groups. Similarly, caste
strikes the anthropologist, especially the Westerner, infused with the
ideal of equality and what Durkheim called the 'cult of the
individual', as being a rigid structure with a concrete existence which
bounds people and restricts interaction and communication.
Nevertheless, there is and always has been not only a pragmatic
flexibility and flux in caste, but an immense communication and
close interdependence between peoples of different languages and
castes in Nepal—certainly much more than between most
suburbanites and ghetto dwellers of the reputedly egalitarian, anti-
caste United States or, for that matter, between the power elite and
the rest of the US population. Many people are typically bi- or tri-
lingual, and due to ubiquitous labour migration from hill villages into
urban areas and to other countries, especially India, individuals may
spend most of their adult lives among people speaking languages
other than their mother tongue. Although the rulers and their
intellectual sycophants, who flattered themselves with genealogies
tracing their ancestry to high-caste descendants of Indian princely
and aristocratic lineages (which finds its counterpart today in
diplomas and certificates) tried from the mid-nineteenth century to
legislate inflexibility into caste in order to sustain their family
positions in the state and society against the growing demands of

emergent mercantile and bureaucratic-servitor classes, as well as the ever-present moral outrage of the direct producers against the brutality of their oppression. Legislation and ruling class pretensions aside, caste never enjoyed as much recognition or played the same role in Nepal as it did in colonial and post-colonial India, where the British regime took it over and formalized it as a sociological paradigm and a legally sanctioned norm, and where elements within the nationalist successor regime continue to fan it to preserve or extend their interests.

While both language and caste may participate in the various divisions and processes of society, it is a mistake to allow these to define the object or scope of the study. When language or caste is assumed as the concrete, determining instance of culture, the object and extent of inquiry and the framework in which the observations are comprehended are already defined prior to the study. Designation of language and caste as independent variables furthermore ignores the manner that other factors, such as social class, control over labour, state administration, formal educational institutions, national and international advertising, media, trade and finance facilitate or limit interaction and experience. It denies the creative essence of culture in that people do not merely receive culture but through their lives extend their own interests and simultaneously *produce* and *reproduce* it, their social relations, and thereby particular forms of family, community and state. The commonality of producing and reproducing culture has struck me as being more significant than the fact that there are many particular ways that people go about this production—even as this variety is a result of this production-reproduction. Variety, which provides the means for humans to grapple with the limitless situations and problems offered by our universe, only becomes a problem and threat for groups attempting to centralize power and impose a dull uniformity in the name of progress. Both language and caste are themselves cultural products created by human intentional activity, and to assume that they are the concrete, determining instance of culture denies their character as themselves social products and excludes other possibilities prior to knowing the object. Caste and language must themselves be treated as dependent upon other, prior historical variables involved in their production and explained as such, something that cannot be done solely through empirical observation.

In 1980 I lacked alternative frameworks of understanding, and mainstream anthropology, denying the existence of an historical subject and its own subjective participation in history in its emulation of objective science, could at best only provide this framework in bits and pieces which I was unable to tie together. Yet I did perceive in my first visit to Nepal that real life is not so straightforward and logical as I had been led to believe by the ethnographies I had read. These tend, forgivably, to neatly reduce people's lives into particular explanatory frameworks according to the prior commitments of their authors and, from a scientific perspective, *less* forgivably, to exclude the possibility of alternative explanations and fail to emphasize the contingent and tentative character given to all knowledge, recognition of which is so central to science. Influenced perhaps by the revolution in thought and philosophy introduced by the theory of relativity, anthropology did recognize the relative character of the researcher's own way of looking at the world. This supposedly was corrected with an idea called 'cultural relativism' in which all cultures were presented as equally valid in their own terms. However, what was not established—as is required in physics—was identifying the manner in which observed frames of reference where separated from the larger one of science, if they were (something which cannot be assumed a priori), or that the perceptions of difference (of 'otherness', in the current postmodern rubric) and the significance given to them may themselves be products of the anthropologist's own standpoint.

Nor did cultural relativism, or for that matter the recent 'reflexive approaches' which have come to criticize the un-self-critical objectivity of previous earlier anthropology, extensively question the standpoint of the researcher as a social being, his/her way of life, and the state of the world that this life and research were contingent upon. Few even now question the global inequalities of distribution, the nature of academia and its role in this global distribution, the anthropological endeavour, the institutional context of anthropology and other social sciences generally, and the orientation towards career advancement and professional status as an important motivation behind research and publishing. Little is said of the waste incurred by militarism, the private motor car as the premier means of transport, the commodity basis of social relations, the political organization of the anthropologist's 'own' society, and many other aspects of life which the anthropologist takes for granted in his/her research activity and life as an anthropologist and citizen. These continue to be taken as givens, remaining largely excluded from the purview of the anthropological enterprise. Most critique and reflexivity have remained on a personal level or at the level of technique and field method, detached from the anthropologist's core being, rather than extending back to this social context. Whereas colonialism (or neocolonialism), for example, has come under criticism (Asad 1973), the way of life and general values that it extends from and represents remain mostly untouched. The implication is that colonized peoples should be able to live the same life as the colonizers and not that such a life depends upon colonialism, militarism, consumerism, wasteful production, poisoning and raping the earth, extending rapacious bureaucracy, breaking up indigenous communities, and sending Nepali girls to Bombay brothels—all of which are totally unsustainable from both ecological and social perspectives. Using what it understood as scientific objectivity, anthropology has systematically isolated the object of knowledge from the anthropologist's own institutional, professional and general social context—including 'the field' as part of this social context—thereby separating the act of knowing from its object. This reductionist science is indeed an inversion of the scientific method as it was practiced in the pre-commercial era and as it continues to be practiced by villagers and in indigenous communities worldwide, which seeks to uncover how the act of knowing shapes and colours the way things are known and, moreover, how this act is a part of what is known.

In my first trip to Nepal, poorly trained and unprepared, I stayed six weeks in a village of Gurung speaking people in the district of Lamjung some 100 km north-west of Kathmandu, where I observed intense interaction, communication, and interdependency between Gurung speakers and people of different groups in the locality. My doubts grew over the relationship of language to particular cultural totalities. Obviously, with many of the men as veterans of the first and second wars and others currently in the British and Indian armies; with the villagers going to the Newar merchants in Khudi Bazaar at the bottom of the hill for imported clothing, batteries, salt and other goods; with many villagers becoming involved in the hotel business that has been emerging with the growth of tourism; and with a general shift of villagers downhill to roadside bazaars and to the cities: these villagers were living very much a part of something much bigger than the local village and language group, and it seemed inconceivable that they could be known merely by describing the village. It was also pointed out to me by my research assistant Sher Bahadur Gurung, who was far more capable than me, that *these* Gurungs who lived on the east end of what was known as the Gurung 'culture area' had for centuries had little interaction with the communities belonging to the same linguistic population in the west, and indeed one found the Gurung language of the other virtually unintelligible, leading them to communicate in Nepali instead.

Furthermore, groups of the same linguistic and caste groups from divergent parts of the 'Gurung area' had experienced quite different histories of incorporation into the state and commerce. I also observed that people of the same linguistic group could experience vastly different situations in society, which put them into different social settings and statuses. In this same high mountain village there were sheep herders and farmers, whereas to the south in the Mahabharat foothills Gurung villages are interspersed among those of Magar speaking people, all of whom necessarily practise agriculture without the supposedly normative Gurung pastoral component of the high mountain villages. All these groups furthermore intensely interact with local Newar merchants and various kinds of administrators, and many of the members of their population are administrators, shopkeepers, students, school teachers, urban wage labourers, politicians and on and on. Many of them even go to the merchant bazaar in the festival season where they display their 'traditional' dances to much wider audiences than just their own language speakers while shopping for goods imported from all over the world. Many natives of Gurung-speaking villages have spent most of their lives in the British army; other Gurungs have been born and raised outside Nepal. Retirement to urban centers such as Pokhara and Kathmandu can be said to be normative for successful individuals. Many others have moved down to the plains along the Indian border and scattered among people speaking other languages and practicing all kinds of livelihoods. Others have obtained advanced education and are teaching in the university, enjoying international fellowships, seminars and exchanges, or are working for foreign agencies. Some have emigrated to Europe, the United States or elsewhere to do everything from working in department stores, running hotels and restaurants to teaching in universities.

Yet ethnographies tended to ignore all these activities and experiences as irrelevant and see the mountain area as the 'pure' Gurung area in which the people pursue survivals of a primeval pastoral life which they originally brought from Tibet. The structure of the society and the historical traditions, however, locate different origins for different groups even from among the same so-called culture group, such that the people were not really 'purely' one group from the start. These different origins are expressed, for instance, in terms of different strata of clans, each with its own historical origins assigned to it and mythological explanations for its position within both the local and the larger national hierarchies. Some pursuits, such as hiring labour for colonial and neo-colonial armies, have been presented as essentially Gurung characteristics—an 'addiction to arms' is the oft repeated phrase of the eighteenth century British resident Kirkpatrick regarding the Gurungs and certain other similar 'martial races'—even though this pattern is clearly a product of the recent colonial conquest of the subcontinent and is shared by many other groups labelled as 'martial races' (nobody currently calls the many poor young people in the United States who are being forced into the army by the recent deindustrialization there a 'martial race'; furthermore, as the Gurungs were fighting in an unending series of European conflagrations engulfing the entire world, it seems that the Europeans are the real martial race, recreating the rest of the world's peoples in their own image). For the colonists, the advantage of recruiting these highlanders was that they were aloof from the strife and antagonism ensuing from colonial rule and thus made disinterested or 'loyal' soldiers. Presently, recruitment into the military and similarly the mass 'forced draft' brothelization of hill women into sex labour not only serves as a pressure valve by removing some of the population from hill societies rigidified by exploitation, but it regiments and binds the energy of these 'surplus' peoples, thereby suppressing the immense tensions and anger building in the countryside and dampening the possibility of rebellion and positive change in the region. On the side of the clients of the brothels, the sex trade shunts young men's social powerlessness and market-created dissatisfaction into brothel consumption, just as militarization and creation of straw enemies from historical brothers and sisters such as Pakistan vis-á-vis India distracts the population. If the Nepal and Indian governments fail to act decisively on the sex trade, it is not due merely to their ambivalence. Other characteristics, when they no longer fit the anthropologist's preconceptions or prejudices, are interpreted as being either impure versions of or total departures from a pristine Gurung culture. Finally, many of the attributes specified as definitive of this one culture enjoy widespread practice by other groups in the area—for example, environmental adaptations, production practices, labour processes, and religious rituals and institutions— and thus cannot be the defining criteria of particular cultures. They should rather be understood in terms of more general relations and history of the region and their place in the larger picture.

In 1981 the money and prestige of an international development consultancy in Nepal drew my graduate advisor away from the university (putting into practice an earlier counsel of his that the motivation for anthropology should be 'income'), so I transferred, belatedly, to the University of Wisconsin. In my first term there, Aidan Southall, well known for his work in Africa and as one of the founders of urban anthropology, introduced me to Marxist anthropology, particularly the French structuralist version of the Marxism of Louis Althusser which had been brought to the discipline by anthropologists such as Lionel Terray, Claude Meillassoux, Maurice Godelier, David Seddon and others. Aidan Southall, whose approach is so catholic and his learning so thorough that it is difficult to classify him as either Marxist or structuralist, had criticized the concept of tribe, which had been heavily worked in both Africa and India, as being a product and tool of colonial imagination and not the objective analytic category that it is made out to be by anthropology (a position which pitted him against Marshall Sahlins, who had set up 'tribe' as an evolutionary stage in the development of human organization and a generic type for comparative purposes; this produced an interesting tension between us and Sahlin's Chicago students). Southall saw the term tribe as the attempt of colonial administration to impose the ideology of the modern nation state onto the peoples who historically had organized themselves much more inclusively according to very different class relations than given by the modern-day usage of the term state (Southall 1956, 1984a, 1988). The modern state divides and excludes people from the means and fruits of their labour, where the early state sought to concentrate human labour and effort through inclusion in terms of the metaphor of kinship. The modern usage of the concept 'tribe', which also differs greatly from the original ancient Roman usage of this Latin term, served to facilitate the subordination of peoples to colonial administration and thereby to the present globally dominant financial-industrial-mercantile-bureaucratic interests represented by it.

Although eighteenth and nineteenth century British residents in Kathmandu had applied the term 'tribe' to the relatively autonomous non-Hindu groups, who they disparaged for their 'barbarian' culture as opposed to the 'civilized' one of the high Hindu religion, it was never taken over by the rulers of Nepal—who chose instead to categorize the people constitutionally in terms of different *varna* and *jati*. Tribe thus never came into anthropological parlance in Nepal. With the general opening of Nepal's communities to anthropologists following the 'Democracy Revolution of 1951', anthropologists took over caste as an analytic category and called both Hindu and non-Hindu linguistic populations 'culture groups'. The application of the idea of culture group to those same populations in Nepal which had earlier been referred to as tribes derives from a common ideological connotation and agenda shared with Nepal's ruling groups who the foreigners were forging alliances with. In contrast, none of the pre-industrial political and social groupings were aligned according to the current cultural groups. If there is a current *Nepali* national unity, it is a product of forcible imposition of central administration and Nepali language, and the consensus, if not unity of interests, of the various elements making up the indigenous, regional and international ruling class that has emerged as the product of the colonial project.

In Wisconsin, the Althusserian Marxist approach encouraged us to focus on the structures of relations underlying these categories and seeing the categories as determined by them. I remained unhappy about the even more confusing jargon and abstract mental gymnastics of much of the Marxist anthropological writing. This seemed to be an inversion of Marx, who emphasized precise, concrete thinking. Whereas these works were difficult because they verged on obfuscation, the difficulty of Marx's work was due to the complexity of his subject and his attempts to understand life and thought in all its dimensions as clearly as possible. Marx premised culture and society on human creative effort—that is, 'production'—with the key being in the relations between people and with things involved in this process of creation and recreation (see Chapter 3), whereas Marxist anthropology in its Althusserian version located the subject in structures represented in the relationships between categories. Thus it began already with an abstraction. Many of the various structures were simply being traded for old worn-out concepts without changing the essential way that these concepts were being used. 'Social formation' was used in place of society; 'forces of production' for technology, technique, and technical knowledge; 'relations of production' for social relations; 'mode of production' for the manner that social relations were combined with particular techniques; and 'superstructure' referred to ideological and legal structures. Transforming these terms into formal analytic categories which denoted structures tended to impose rigid boundaries onto the real world in terms of separate entities isolated from each other, making it difficult to identify the interrelatedness and unity that characterizes all things in the world (and universe). It is no surprise then that the relationships, or 'articulation' (implying interaction of separately existing things), of structures became the problem, although structures, as the way that people order and link their relations in the world and with people, are products of human activity, or labour, and thus human activity should have been the problem—which indeed Marx poses as his starting point in his presentation of the historical materialist method in *The German Ideology*.

This approach could not get beyond what was experienced as being the only reality, and it continued to assume that there was an objective world—structures—that not only determined human life but could be known outside of and separate from the knower. Merely that the anthropologist *can* engage in knowing the subject—say, villagers in Nepal—indicates a relationship with the subject engaged through the anthropologist's activity, and thus analysis must encompass this relationship and the activity. That the anthropologist's inquiry and scientific analysis and presentation goes according to his or her own agenda and priorities oftentimes formulated in the academy prior to the research indicates that many conditions are assumed by this relationship. These must be uncovered as part of the research: otherwise knowledge remains contingent on what is left unsaid. Location of the subject in structures, furthermore, left no essential role for history—although for Marx, time, along with intentionality or will, is an essential element of life, and thus life cannot be understood except as historical, along with relation to human interests. Like functionalist anthropology, which always looked for explanations of behaviour in terms of some sort of utilitarian purpose, from either a psychological or societal perspective, Althusserian Marxism became a formal exercise in relating together various structures of a predetermined nature. It did not bring to question the basic manner that we comprehend ourselves and our world and how we relate to it, which is the aim of science, and it did not overcome the contingency in thought and existence that occurs by failing to do so. To overcome this contingency is difficult, because it requires not just changing the way we think about things, but our relationship to what we are thinking about.

When I first read *Capital* in 1981 during my first semester at Wisconsin, I discovered it to be far more clear and simple in its exposition than the so-called Marxist anthropology, or indeed other subfields of anthropology which treat particular spheres of human activity in isolation—such as economic or political anthropology—and thus the analysis in *Capital* to a large degree starts out where these leave off. Its complexity was in its subject, not exposition, and it was far more thorough and methodical in its development of concepts than I was accustomed to in anthropology. I was excited by understanding the inner workings of exchange, the creation and accumulation of value, money, the labour process, and capital as a historical complex of relationships used for appropriating and accumulating social surplus. Yet my sense of the method of *Capital* as an essentially different way of comprehending the world remained undeveloped due to my lack of understanding of the underlying philosophical perspectives and the social context in which Marx had undertaken his analysis. This had its counterpart in my similar lack of understanding of anthropology's social context (whose origins were contemporaneous with Marx's writing of *Capital*) and philosophical basis, except in what I had gained from the inadequate exposition of Marvin Harris's (1968) *The Rise of Anthropological Theory*—inadequate because I could not perceive in it how anthropological theory was a product of and participated in the more general history of social development.

In the winter break following my first semester at Wisconsin, my colleague Hermina DeSota and myself isolated ourselves and read and discussed, sentence by sentence, 'Forms of Property that Preceded Capitalist Production' from Marx's outline for *Capital*, the *Grundrisse*. The *Grundrisse* lays bare the foundation of *Capital* on Marx's Hegelian philosophical framework. The 'Forms of Property' in particular have been used by the Marxist anthropologists of the Althusserian school as a key framework for applying a Marxian understanding to anthropology. It identifies what Marx calls three basic forms of property—Asiatic, Ancient, and Germanic—which have provided the historical premises of society in different periods and places in history. DeSota and I came up with a somewhat different understanding of the chapter than that given it by the Althusserian school of Marxism. The Althussarian school, following Stalin, emphasized progressive evolution of the underlying structures of relationships in society which it saw represented by each of these forms of property, or 'modes of production', as they called it. We saw Marx's aim as not so much one of identifying the historical development of the structure of society as locating the development of the subject of history and the manner that this historical subject produced and reproduced, and in the process, transformed itself. Subsequently, in reading Hegel's *Philosophy of History*, I saw that Marx's scheme basically reproduced Hegel's categorization of world history in terms of the Oriental, Greek, Roman and German worlds. The difference being that Marx located the subject of history not in Hegel's 'Idea', of which the different 'worlds' were merely the manifestation of its emergence in history (realized most fully in the German bureaucratic state), but in the manner that the urban community in different times and places initially based itself upon the land and that the relationship in land, industry and commerce which emerged from this base mediated the relationships and consciousness of individuals.

The Althusserian interpretation of Marx and, even more dogmatically, the Stalinist one, called these forms of property different 'modes of production', or essential configurations of the structure of relations between technology ('forces of production') and human relations ('relations of production'), for which all historical societies ('social formations') were manifestations. In reading Marx closely, one sees in contrast that he treated these different forms as the initial premises upon which different urban civilizations supposedly first established themselves and which, depending upon the extent of their social development at the time, shaped the character of their subsequent development. He saw various inherent limitations and possibilities in each of these forms, but not in the direct determinative sense given them by the structuralists. The social subject consisted of individuals, as shaped by these relations, and society developed out of their active production and reproduction of their relations through their lives' activities, or labour. Reproduction, he pointed out, was simultaneously *new* production. Human life thereby is not *merely* a replication of already existing relations and cultural forms; it is an extension of human will and intentionality, according to the extent of the individual's consciousness and the social forces at hand to carry it out. Existing dominant groups in society attempt to sustain the relations in which they are dominant by bending the willful activity of other groups to their own purposes and preventing them from putting to use their growing capability or exercising their consciousness given them by the production of new relations and ways of conceiving the world extending out of the productive-reproductive process. This leads to a contradiction between what is possible and the relations which allow people to realize these possibilities—in other words, between need, always socially defined, and the satisfaction of those needs. As emergent groups associated with the new social forces prevailed over ever increasing spheres of social life, the new relations representing their will and intention 'subsumed', or incorporated into their own movement and development, the old. Political revolution, when it occurred, followed when this subsumption was well progressed and the emergent groups were already positioned to take control of political power through widespread control of human activity (called under capitalism the labour processes), social life and culture (Gramsci's 'hegemony'). Thus the reference to historical materialism in graduate school in terms of the euphemism 'conflict theory' was a misnomer, because conflict played a relatively small role in Marx's scheme, which instead emphasized human self creation, represented in the dialectical duality production-reproduction. Many revolutionary Marxists also saw capture of state power—politically or militarily—as the most direct path to revolution without realizing that social and cultural transformation must by-and-large precede it. This was by no means an innocent mistake as it justified grab of the institutions of power without devolving meaningful control to the working classes.

My background in ethnography predisposed me to look critically at the Hegelian framework given to the historical development of society. This is especially true of the Asiatic form of property, known as the 'Asiatic Mode of Production' by the structuralists, which was based less upon historical or ethnographic data than on European attribution of a despotic character to the Mughal court, propagated by the British according to their colonial objectives and developed to high level of abstraction, and thus fantasy, by German thinkers. Marx's attempt to fit the materialist world history into the Hegelian framework seemed to deny his own assertion that the initial premise of history is the real life of living individuals.

Nevertheless, Marx's central thesis in his dialectical understanding of history is valid: that empirically observed forms of society and life each have their specific historical preconditions and premises which confront people of subsequent periods, not only as the limiting conditions of human life, but as the means for humans to actively engage with these conditions and remake them anew. The premises of social life, because they themselves are historical products (natural as well as social), are not immediately given by empirical observation but must be discovered and understood by analysing the historical antecedents of the current forms of activity. Thereby the study no longer locates the premise in seemingly concrete categories given *a priori* by the discipline according to its own premises—the linguistic or caste population—but makes the premises of the study something that has to be discovered through the analysis according to the nature of the object of the study itself. This breaks the circular logic of the culture concept, allowing inquiry to be no longer a process of confirming predetermined categories but of developing our intellectual appropriation of the subject and our relationship to it according to its own being. This must be a continually expanding and inclusive project as each set of premises is peeled away and previously unanticipated and more inclusive relations, and possibilities for ourselves as social beings, are uncovered.

The generation of knowledge itself must be seen as a product of historical process, and since the act of knowing implies a relation to the subject, the process of knowing must also fall within the purview of the inquiry. In his *Ethnological Notebooks,* a project of his last three years of life, Marx seemed to be in a process of superseding the general Hegelian schema[4] and seeking to discover the actual historical premises being disclosed by ethnography and how these developed.[5] He critically appropriated the ethnographic studies appearing at the time, discarding many of the propositions such as Bachoven's (1861) 'mother's right', Phear's (1880) interpretation of India as a feudal society, and Morgan's positioning the development of the family prior to that of the clan, as examples.[6]

This awareness of the need to uncover the historical premises of social life—and thereby of ethnography—led me from 1985 to 1987 in my dissertation research in Nepal to attempt a departure from descriptive monographic village studies characteristic of Nepali ethnography. Rather than presume the existence of some form of a community which can be known positively as a social whole on its own terms as the object of study, I set out to uncover the historical premises of the community and understand how people subsequently developed these premises through their lives and activity. I tried not to make premature presumptions about the boundaries or nature of community. My only assumption could be the observation that there is one world, from which it follows that there must be what H.G. Wells (1951) calls a 'universal history'. The various divisions that people throw between themselves or by which one group of people sets itself over another, be they cultural, ethnic, class, caste, racial or national, cannot be accepted beforehand as givens explainable in their own terms but must be analyzed according to this universal history. My previous readings and study predisposed me towards this global perspective:[7] this included, besides Marx (who emphasized in the *German Ideology* that life must be understood according to the full extent of people's relations, social and material), Luxemburg's (1951) study of accumulation and imperialism, Baran's (1957) and Frank's (1966, 1979) development of dependency theory, Wallerstein's (1974) world system theory, and Wolf's (1982) retrieval of the history of the colonized and their colonization, to say nothing of Southall's (n.d., 1997) own global study of the rise and development of the city worldwide, all of whom took a global rather than national view. In this way I hoped to understand the real extent and content of community as it is given by history. I chose to focus on the merchant community in Nepal because I knew that industrial capital initially extended into up-country communities through commercial relations. I proposed that by studying the merchant community the actual machinery and process whereby this came about could be retrieved and analysed.[8]

I took up a study of Bandipur Bazaar, a 200-year-old merchant community astride the Mahabharat range of foothills of the Himalaya, on a trade route between the Gangetic plain and the villages of the valleys and ridges of the high Himalaya. Like similar merchant communities throughout the length of the middle hills, Bandipur had been founded and settled by Newar merchants migrating out of the urban settlements of the Kathmandu valley into the length and breadth of the new kingdom at the time of the wars of conquest of the late eighteenth and early nineteenth centuries. This period coincided with the onset of industrial capitalism, and while the establishment of these communities premised itself upon the pre-existing forms of commerce and local production, their growth and development became intimately tied to the career of industrial capitalist penetration into the subcontinent. By studying the activities of the merchants, I found that the actual content of the community and the ultimate purpose of people's activities have greatly changed, and even by the 'Democracy Revolution' of 1951, which enthnographers generally treat as the watershed of change in the society,[9] community life, production, commerce, and also cultural and ideological forms had become subsumed to the circulation and valorization of industrial commodities, even though immediate relations seem to have sustained forms and representations that do not fit the formal image of industrial capitalist relations. Industrial capitalism took over pre-existing forms and relations of trade and production and turned them to extending the circulation of industrial capital into the remotest areas of Nepal. Through this process, which I later found to have paralleled developments in other up-country regions of the subcontinent, the merchants gradually extended their sway over distribution in the countryside and their cultural hegemony as a class, taking over the previously existing forms of domination and displacing or merging into the position of the previously hegemonic ruling classes which had earlier subordinated the community.

Due to this incorporation of people into the circulation of industrial commodities and the subordination of local relations to commodity relations generally, and thereby the purposes and logic of capitalist industry, I found that the interaction between people in Nepal was not confined to the cultural categories in which they have been generally empirically apprehended by descriptive ethnography. Rather, their immediately observable forms had to be apprehended in terms of the full extent of their relations. These relations drew them into interaction with groups of different castes and languages. They put them into relationships with factory workers in India, Japan, and the United States which have grown increasingly significant as time progressed, not only for the Nepali villagers but, as is now becoming painfully evident with the so-called restructuring and the deindustrialization of Euro-American and Japanese industry, for the industrial and intellectual workers in those countries as well. I found that the interaction between groups and across regions had greater effective power over people than that of the cultural ideas within groups, which usually are treated as the primary determinative element in cultural analyses. These relations, furthermore, provide content to these cultural ideals such that the ideas of particular 'cultures' are largely a product of this interaction and thus have to be understood in terms of it.

Finally, as anthropology and the other social sciences are products of the same processes subordinating the community in Nepal, the social scientist's role in the process must also come under scrutiny. I have been addressing this in part by trying to understand the manner that social science and social scientists have been participating in the process, both in particular instances and in terms of the general theoretical perspective and assumptions discussed above. Neither my suburban upbringing, which inculcates a sense of responsibility that extends only as far as it does not require acknowledging and changing the premises and conditions of my existence, and the anthropology curriculum, which in the name of objectivity develops its students for detached academic reflection, prepared me for this task. This led me to enter into it with a great deal of naiveté, causing me to commit many errors, both of commission and omission. The nine years which encompass the writings of this book have been a time of working these things out and trying to figure out how I would go about leading my life, something that continues to frustrate, intrigue and challenge me.

NOTES

1   A concept drawn from investment economics, 'opportunity cost' had a certain comfortable universality about it, because it was itself the underlying rationale of the dominant arrangement of human interaction and distribution of labour and wealth, yet it was neither a theory nor did it explained anything.

2   Since I wrote this I have come to know that John Bodley (1997) is productively engaged in just such a study in the same Palouse hills that I did my Russian German work, and furthermore is giving it a scope that seeks to encompass the whole of *Homo sapiens*' experience in both time and space.

3   Examples of this genre include *The Sherpas of Nepal* (Fürer-Haimendorf 1964), *The Newars* (Nepali 1965), *The Magars of Banyan Hill* (Hitchcock 1966), *Le Gurungs* (Pignede 1966), *The Gurungs of Nepal* (Messerschmidt 1976), *Sherpas through their Rituals* (Ortner 1978), *The Himalayan Woman* (Jones and Jones 1976), and *The Peoples of Nepal* (Bista 1987).

4   Although it remained in specifics, such as the quote that I have taken in Chapter 16 ('A Comparative Study of South Asian Caste and Mediterranean

Citizenship in the Development of Classes and the State') that caste is the 'fossilization' of certain attributes of kinship.

5   A project also taken up by Southall in a very similar and much more finished fashion in his book *The City in Time and Space* (1997).

6   Engels, using Marx's notes, made the mother right central to his thesis in *Family, Private Property and the State*, but in this and many other key aspects, Engels went against Marx's own intention, leading Raya Dunayevskaya to say that Engels had let down Marx's bequest of this project to him.

7   This perspective differs profoundly from the current 'post-modern' emphasis on globalization, which is basically about what is perceived as a globalization of international capital. This is paradoxical because capital by definition was global from the start. Marx treated the human project as a global one—indeed as the essential character of *Homo sapiens*. What he saw in capitalism was that the division of labour was being extended worldwide, which would allow the development for the first time of a general world historical consciousness of the working classes.

8   This is not to recognize that the study could start anyplace, as the 'part contains the whole', in the words of Lukács.

9   See Chapter 5 for more extensive discussion of the role of the 1950–1 insurrection as not revolution but transfer of state power.

CHAPTER 3

Historical Materialist Method and Analysis of Culture in Nepal

ANTHROPOLOGICAL analysis in Nepal has generally proceeded on the assumption that the people of Nepal are divided into a number of cultural groups (more recently 'ethnic' groups) defined either by shared language or common caste or both—thus Newar language and Newar culture and Gurung language and Gurung culture, or Brahman caste and high caste culture, and so forth. This follows the designation of the same groups as 'tribe' and 'caste' by the British, who then proceeded to attach normative traits on the basis of reports by authoritative informants who received their authority from caste status and official position (Kirkpatrick 1811; Hamilton 1919; Hodgson 1871). As the British never extended their colonial administration directly to Nepal, this early use of the word tribe also never entered into official parlance in the country, but the categorization of people according to language, caste or both has from early on shaped all subsequent ethnography. It also received a legal status in the Nepal Muluki Ain (Legal Code) of 1854 (Höfer 1979), which ranked the different linguistic groups in terms of a caste hierarchy. Subsequent to Höfer's translation, a number of ethnographies have referred to this legal code as providing the textual ideal or template of people's cultural self-understanding. In recent years categorization within the caste framework has been inverted, but preserved and thus further mythologized, in terms of the designation of a *jaana jati* 'people's *jats*' by intellectuals from among various language groups in attempt to create an indigenous people's nationalist movement against what they perceive as the source of their oppression—the Hindu high-caste conquest, domination, and oppression of the country's 'indigenous' peoples—

without addressing the class divisions within these groups or participation of individuals from among them in this oppression in the household, community, marketplace and state. Ethnography acknowledges the various state organizations—both the early pre-Hindu states and the Rajput 'little kingdoms'—as well as the present capitalist state, but they are taken on their own terms and, except in their associated rituals, treated largely as epiphenomena, especially since they seemed to have arisen on totally different principles from these concrete cultural populations.

It does seem logical to start with various kinds of population, such as culture group, caste group and ethnic group, as they seem to be concrete objects that can be positively known. On the assumption that all the members of a linguistically defined population share similar cultural patterns and that culture is determinative of normative behaviour, ethnographers have generally chosen a village or city (or a city quarter) as a representative sample from which observations can be generalized to the population as a whole. *Which* particular village is chosen is usually justified in terms of the questions to be asked of it and the prior assumptions brought to the study. The village or, in urban studies, the city is assumed to represent a self-contained totality which can be known through empirical participant observation and interpretive analysis of one or more years' cycle of life. Indeed, each structure—family, clan, village, culture group, and nation state—is commonly seen as being encapsulated within the next larger structure and analysed as a relatively autonomous entity in its own terms or in interaction with the whole without losing its essential autonomy. Village society is pictured as basically undifferentiated, and observations of village life are assumed to be normative for the village as a whole in the manner that the village is normative for the population. If differentiation is apprehended, it is usually presented in terms of immediate culturally or constitutionally given patterns, such as caste, clan or forms of patronage. Culture and life ways are assumed to have been largely timeless and unchanging (i.e. 'traditional') until Nepal opened its borders to foreigners and started large-scale 'development' in 1951. Components such as caste or clan seen to represent this past life are treated as continuing to be determinative, while entities such as political parties (especially the widespread Communist and labour movements), ubiquitous labour migration, including widespread forced participation of central hill women in sex labour, the absorption of hill labour into regional markets and the vast transformations this has already brought, and other elements which do not fit preconceived notions have for the most been methodologically excluded as unimportant to the ideal conceptions of culture. Similarly, certain kinds of ideas, such as Hindu or Buddhist religious ideas, were seen as overwhelmingly determinative, while popular media, advertising, education, and various forms of secular ideas are not dealt with on equal footing, if at all. The result of this normative approach to culture has been that the ethnographic literature on Nepal has produced a large body of village studies focusing on different cultures, but little attempt has been made to render these cultures within the context of larger, current historical and geographical contexts—as a product of people's activity as well as determinative of behaviour.

The problem with starting with a population, says Marx in the 'Introduction' to his *Grundrisse* (1973), is that it is a 'chaotic conception' which presupposes the nature and character of the object prior to knowing it. Analysis always leads from this 'imagined concrete' towards more simple concepts to 'a few determining abstract, general relations', such as environment, clan and kinship, household patterns, caste, and symbols. Together these categories are seen as making up systems of behaviour and ideas which conceive the whole as consisting of many complex determinations which also tend to confirm the original assumptions made about the whole— what it encompasses, its extent, and so on. Analysis starts with the series of encapsulated entities [family, lineage group, sub-caste (chiefdom), culture group (tribe), nation state] and ends by constituting them with 'facts' derived from empirical observations. Historical development of each succeeding level is seen as a stagewise process of introducing increasingly complex categories, first of the family or domestic group, then the clan, caste, then prehistoric 'little kingdoms', and finally the 'unified' state. Each preceding simpler category is treated as existing more or less autonomously within the subsequent more complex one, allowing it to be treated as a survival of previously autonomous forms, despite the existence of transcendent relations, and dealt with largely on its own terms.

This movement of the simple abstract to the predetermined concrete, from kinship and family relations to clan and then village, urban community and finally culture group, is the way that the ethnographer appropriates his or her own experience as a scientific observer and turns it into a description of people's lives as something concrete. This movement of simple to the complex has been framed as an evolutionary sequence (Sahlins and Service 1960) extending from the clan through the tribe, chiefdom and state. But this is not the process whereby the concrete world comes into being. Simple ethnographic categories, such as those of relations within the domestic or lineage group, presuppose a population. This population is not the abstract one assumed prior to the analysis, such as 'culture group' or 'society', but 'a population producing in specific relations; as well as a certain kind of family, or commune, or state, etc'. The simple categories 'can never exist other than as . . . abstract, one-sided relation[s] within an already given, concrete living whole'. The development of the whole provides the categories with an 'antediluvian existence', whose character, composition and extent, as well as the relation of the ethnographer and his science to it, can only be determined in relation to this 'already given, concrete living whole'—not a preconceived one (Marx 1973:101).

Within this concrete whole a specific form of production predominates over others, and as it expands to subsume increasing areas and spheres of activity, 'its relations assign rank and influence to all others'. In precapitalist society, for example, particular forms of rent will refer to all kinds of product from the land. Rent in parts of South Asia in turn was represented in terms of *jat* and *varna*, which ranked people's relations to land in terms of concepts of *dharma* and *karma*, which in turn had many concrete determinations in society quite different than those which have come to predominate with the spread of industrial capitalism. Other categories that predominate presently had a more limited and specialized existence. The commodity, for instance, was once limited just to trade of excess goods, controlled by a small group of specialists, and restricted to limited spheres of activity, such as the merchant bazaar. Furthermore, it too was coloured with relations in land and categories of caste. With the increasing domination of industrial capital throughout the world, all kinds of activity have increasingly become oriented towards commodity relations and characterized by commodity relations themselves. No longer is the commodity limited to particular forms or specialized spheres within society. Consequently, the commodity has been taking the form of the most general abstraction encompassing all other categories of social life.

The starting point for analysis must be the most general category of the epoch, which extends from the predominant form of production. It cannot start with categories having their own specialized existence, otherwise the analysis will remain contingent upon the more general category and the manner that the relations represented by it have subsumed the less general one. Furthermore, study of what Tyler calls 'survivals' of earlier cultural forms and societies which have supposedly persisted into the present is misplaced, because what seems to be survival has become distorted and been made one-sided by subsequent development and can only be understood from the standpoint of the currently existing social whole. This, however, does not mean a reduction of everything down into the predominant category. To establish which category predominates requires identifying the nature of the social whole. This involves seeking out the premises assigned to the object of study, its nature and content. These premises are to be found in the 'real individuals, their activity and the material conditions under which they live, both those which they find already existing and those produced by their activity'.[1] This is to be contrasted with the tendency of the social sciences to start with certain disciplinary givens, for example anthropology starts with Tyler's creed that the object of study, culture, 'is the whole', which has been further specified by Geertz as the ideas that people have of their culture; or the macro-economist assigns the unit of analysis to the nation state. In both instances the nature of the object of study is already defined prior to the study.

The anthropologist's presence in the situation being described furthermore implies relationships with his or her object, thus the anthropologist is necessarily a part of what is being described. This relationship always presupposes and shapes our appropriation of the people studied by our study. The anthropological categories which frame the study and its presentation in terms of notions of scientific objectivity, and the presumptions made by these categories, predispose the ethnographer to see the object in terms of leading a separate existence from his or her own. As anthropological research was itself a product of the spread of capitalism and the colonial encounter, this objectivity has led ethnographers to omit the colonial or successor regime situation from the picture, except in formal terms. Yet when the colonial and successor regimes forcefully refashion and uphold the village situation by utilizing political patronage and controlling national finance, laws, police, military and election machinery,[2] it seems that this is part of the problem of research as well. In omitting the colonial and successor situation, the anthropologist also omits the institutional framework of the anthropological endeavour: the national agreements facilitating research, the government protection supplied to the researcher and his/her project, the orientation towards tenure and professional status, the requirement to publish or perish, the state and corporate underwriting of the university, foundations and funding, the involvement of the state and corporations in the fieldwork setting, the commitment of the researcher to academia or to corporations hiring him over those of the people studied, and so forth. The omission of these factors is on the same order as that of the physical scientist who omits observations because they failed to support his hypothesis.

Understanding built on such analysis obviously remains contingent upon what has been left out or not encompassed by the researcher's questions or is currently incomprehensible. The scientific method always assumes that all understanding is contingent upon possible future observations and experience and thus always tentative and relative. This is not the sense of contingency introduced by post-modernism, which invalidates any sort of positive analysis and thereby makes all interpretations valid. Rather it is due to the historical character of human activity.

BACK TO MARX

Analysis bent upon understanding must seek to uncover the presuppositions implied in our categories and contained within the relations referred to by them. This requires establishing premises which make minimal assumptions about the subject.[3] Since the object of analysis is the product of human historical activity, the minimal condition is that people 'must be in a position to live in order to be able to make history'.[4] Life of real people of course takes certain historical forms whose nature or what they encompass cannot be assumed beforehand. This must be established through analysis of the empirical conditions, and the assumptions made about them must be included within the purview of this analysis.

The premise that people must be in a position to live leads to the condition that human life has certain requirements or needs which have to be satisfied: 'life involves before everything else eating and drinking, a habitation, clothing and many other things' or 'material life itself' (Marx 1983:30). Thus the history that people make must first of all be a history of *satisfying the needs* of life—of meeting the initial condition posed by life. Just as life has various historical forms, needs also take their own corresponding forms. These become more complex and diffuse as society grows more complex. Thus in village Nepal it would be insufficient simply to describe local agricultural practices when villagers spend half the year engaged in agricultural labour in India or when members of the family have migrated to Saudia Arabia or Korea for work, as currently characterizes the Nepali village; their needs and the needs imposed for reproducing village life are tied up with those of production, circulation and reproduction of monopoly capital and global capitalist society.

Needs are satisfied through production, which, by satisfying the conditions following from the initial premise, *affirms* that premise. Production is purposeful activity, or labour, in which people engage to

appropriate the materials of nature in a form adapted to [their] own needs. . . . At the end of every labour process, a result emerges which had already existed ideally. Man not only effects a change of form in the materials of nature; he also realizes . . . his own purpose in these materials. And this is a purpose he is conscious of, it determines the mode of his activity with the rigidity of a law, and he must subordinate his will to it. (Marx 1977:284)

That an 'ideal' exists as the determining purpose of activity makes it easy to assume that the ideas or their mediating symbols constitute the material world. This has led many anthropologists, indeed whole branches of anthropology, to analyse society and culture solely in terms of ideas, ritual and symbols. People's ideal conceptions, however, arise according to the conditions of their existence, which itself is a product of previous activity; thus study of society solely in these terms must necessarily remain laden with contingency. This is *not* economic determinism or reductionism, as is often made of this perspective. Ideas and institutions *do* orient and determine human life, but always as the products of previous activity and according to the conditions provided by it. Only when ideas are looked at in isolation from the historical context given by previous human activity do they seem in themselves to be constituting the material world.

Production is a double relationship, encompassing three simultaneous 'aspects or . . . moments' (Marx and Engels 1983:30–1). The first aspect 'is the production of the *means* to satisfy these needs, the production of material life itself' (ibid., emphasis added).[5] The second aspect is that in producing the means for satisfying the initial needs people simultaneously create new needs.[6] Whereas the production of means is the 'affirmation' of the initial premise (in order to live people must produce the means for satisfying the needs of life), it is simultaneously the negation of this premise: as the means to satisfy needs become available, people no longer have the same needs and new ones will arise. Thus Marx identifies the dialectical dynamic of history at the very core of human life and activity; artifices explaining process and change are unnecessary. Production not only satisfies the conditions of life, it changes them as well.

The third aspect of production is that by producing the means to satisfy the needs of life people also produce life. They produce and reproduce themselves, as individuals and as social beings engaged in certain forms of intercourse, as members of particular forms of organization of this intercourse—family, clan, state, super-state.[7] Initially, simpler forms of relationships were the only relationships, and society could be analysed in terms of them. But 'when increased needs create new social relations and the increased population new needs' (Marx and Engels 1983:31), the more complex forms of relationships subordinate or 'subsume'[8] the simpler ones, which then can then no longer be understood in their own terms. 'They must then be treated and analysed according to the existing empirical data' (ibid.).[9] This returns to the point made above, that the village—or family, culture group, or nation state—can be understood not in its own terms but only according to the full extent of relations as defined by the participation of people in the production and reproduction of life; I refer to this perspective in my critique of Levy's reduction of the city into three autonomous spheres—urban microcosm, mesocosm and macrocosm (see Chapter 17).

The three aspects of production described above simultaneously '*appear* as a double relationship' (ibid., emphasis added). On the one hand is a *natural relationship* of the labour process between humans and the means of production,[10] which includes (1) the *objects* of human labour, meaning the materials that are worked into products for consumption,[11] (2) the *instruments* of labour, meaning both (a) things or complexes 'of things which the worker interposes between himself and the object of his labour and which serves as a conductor, directing his activity into that object . . . making use of the mechanical, physical and chemical properties of some substances in order to set them to work on other substances as instruments of his power, and in accordance with his purposes'[12] and (b) 'in a wider sense . . . all the objective conditions necessary for carrying on the labour process . . . [which] do not enter directly into the labour process, but without them it is either impossible for it to take place, or possible only to a partial extent'[13] (Marx 1977:285–6). On the other hand is a *social relationship*, 'by [which] we understand the co-operation of several individuals, no matter under what conditions, in what manner and to what end'.

Marx and Engels (1983:31) referred to the former as the 'mode of production, or industrial state', and to the latter as the 'mode of co-operation, or social state' (later simply 'relations of production'— Marx 1977:175n).[14] Because all aspects of human society arise from human creative activity or production, it is this dual relationship which is the foundation of social and ideological forms generally.[15] The word 'appear' emphasized in the first sentence of the previous paragraph implies that this double relationship is a surface 'presence' ('one-sided immediate unity') which contains some underlying dynamic grasped through its motion, not its appearance. 'To treat this surface process . . . as only nominally important, is to fail in grasping the whole. . . . However, to remain on the surface and become enraptured by "the immediacy of its being" is to fall into "pure illusion"' (Nicolaus 1973:31). Althusser and Balibar's (1970) emphasis on the 'structures' of the means of production, relations of production and forces of production, rather than on production as creative process, is an example of such an 'illusion', which unfortunately has coloured anthropology's appropriation of the materialist approach; furthermore, even at a superficial level, they mixed up the priority of relationship of these categories (see Mikesell 1992).

The previously produced means of production and products, along with the socially developed individual[16] and practical or scientific knowledge, provide the capacity to produce, the 'productive powers of labour'.[17] These productive forces are 'an acquired force, the product of former activity'. The productive forces are the basis of human history in that each succeeding generation finds at hand the accumulated productive forces of previous generations, conditioning how individuals apply their practical energy, their labour.[18] It follows then that a

specific mode of production . . . presupposes a given level of social productive forces and their forms of development as its historical precondition: a precondition which is itself the historical result and product of a preceding process and from which the new mode of production proceeds as its given basis; that the production relations corresponding to this specific, historically determined mode of production—relations which human beings enter into during the process of social life, in the creation of their social life—possess a specific, historical and transitory character; and, finally that the distribution relations essentially coincident with these production relations are their opposite side, so that both share the same historically transitory character. (Marx 1959:878)

Although, as products of human labour, the productive forces 'are *organs of the human mind which are created by the human hand*, the objectified power of knowledge' (Marx 1986:92), their historical social character leads these forces to confront individuals as a power alien to them and working to subject individuals to particular social interests. These material and social products of labour not only put at people's disposal immense creative capability for producing and reproducing themselves and their social relations (and thereby these forces as well) in complex intercourse with others, they determine the specific character of society and the manner in which individuals and groups participate. Confronting humans as a great power, the productive forces seem to have an independent existence all their own rather than being something created and recreated by humans. This is the *alienated existence* of human beings in which they are controlled by their own products.

How does this alienated existence come about? The productive forces not only consist of natural and social relationships; the latter contain the former as a 'socialized nature' (Marx and Engels 1883:27–30). Once humans harness nature, it ceases to exist separately from human relations. This social character of the relations of production takes form in a certain division of labour which arises with the expansion of the productive forces, the rise of new needs, and population growth. The division of labour is simultaneously given in the 'unequal distribution, both quantitative and qualitative, of labour and its products, hence property: . . . the power of disposing the labour power of others. Division of labour and private property are, moreover, identical expressions: in the one the same thing is affirmed with reference to activity is affirmed in the other with reference to the product of the activity' (ibid.:34).[19] From the perspective of the individual, distribution appears as a social law; and from that of the society, 'almost as a pre-economic fact'—environmental adaptations, conquest, revolution, myth and symbolic activity, law, etc.—preceding production to determine the individual's position within the system of production and the character of the society, respectively. It is an easy step then to identify distribution as being constituted outside of and prior to production (as handled in economics or in functionalist or symbolic anthropology, for example). But this appearance derives from the origin of distribution in the mode of production and the production relations as a product of previous epochs.[20]

Meillassoux (1978c:161) thus is mistaken when he locates social distribution in consumption and attributes it to arising out of the seasonal cycle. This frames distribution according to the self-understanding of capital, which justifies distribution in terms of a 'putting up of capital' at the start of the productive cycle and receiving the proper reward at the end of it. In reality, distribution does not arise out of the seasonal cycle but through the course of the development of production, and it can only be fully understood through the development of production. The unasked question in Meillassoux's case is the origin of the inequality that allowed the elder or capitalist to put up the initial seed or capital at the start of each productive cycle.

Implicit within the division of labour and distribution is a contradiction that those involved in production do not consume the fruits of their labour. The particular, limited interests of separate individuals, families or groups of families are set against 'the communal interest of all the individuals who have intercourse with one another' (Marx and Engels 1983:38). These particular interests in society take 'an independent form as the *State*, divorced from the real interests of individual and community' and 'an illusory communal life' according to the premises assigned to the differing distribution in society: family, lineage group, tribe, culture group, estate, caste, race, language and ethnicity, nationality and citizenship (1983:34–5). The 'communal interest . . . [exists] in reality, as the mutual interdependence of the individuals among whom labour is divided' (1983:34). The substance of the divisions of society, as constituted historically through production and intercourse, takes the form of classes, 'already determined by the division of labour, which in every such mass of men separate out', each with an objective form *in itself,* 'and of which one dominates the other' (1983:35).

As the productive forces arise in the course of production (production which is realizing or 'affirming' the original premise), the productive forces are simultaneously a new premise that increasingly contradicts the relations from which they arose. They bring forth new needs which can no longer be satisfied by the old relations, thus posing themselves as a negation of the relations determined by the previous premise, leading to the subsumption or diversion of the old social relations into new ones which are more compatible to the changing array of powers and interests in society.[21] New social classes with their corresponding forms of civil society, polity and ideas arise which are based on the changing premises offered by the currently existing productive forces. Opposing the old oppressive forces, they are able to present their own interests as representing those of the society at large, eventually spearheading the erosion and overthrow of the old social relations.[22] Inequalities, tensions and conflict inevitably arise between newly created groups and interests which are attempting to assert their growing presence over production and intercourse, and the old ones which are attempting to retain control over it. People are led to struggle not just symbolically (as sometimes presented in the anthropological analysis of ritual) or in terms of struggles of the state (as presented by history books); these 'are merely the illusory forms in which real struggles of the different classes are fought out among one another' (1983:35). The new combination of forces represents a negation of the old in which the new relations and their categories subordinate and made the old part of their movement and development, thereby imparting new roles and content to the old relations and categories and transforming them in the process. Marx dialectically conceived of this process in terms of Hegel's concept of 'subsumption'.

Here Marx argued that for a class to posit its interest as the general interest, it must capture political power, 'even when its domination, as is the case with the proletariat, postulates the abolition of the old form of society in its entirety and of domination of itself' (1983:35). In practice, this has been shallowly interpreted almost universally as capturing or entering the offices of the state, and usually by the self-assigned representatives (party 'leaders', intellectuals or 'vanguard') of the working class rather than members of the working class itself. But, as the state is merely the machinery of ruling class interests and the seemingly universal interest that it gives to itself, until the emergent class becomes preponderant throughout the material and mental life of the society, defined here in a broad sense given below of the full extent of human intercourse, such office-holding victories not only have been empty, they have tended to play into the hands of the current ruling class by diverting and dissipating the energy and focus of struggle. For capitalism, this was at least a thousand-year process that emerged out of the collapse of the Roman empire, with many diverse determinations; even the successive ascendancy one after another of particular elements of capital—mercantile, petty industry, large industry, finance capital, and monopoly capital—were each hundreds of years in the making. Hurrying the process along, as in the case of the Nepali peasantry, requires the hard work of developing a world historical conscious-ness and an action oriented by understanding rather than slogans.

What is this world historical consciousness? Since the productive forces of society are defined by relations that appear to be both *natural and social,* they consist of the full extent of human inter-course. From ancient times people all across Europe, Asian and Africa have been in close intercourse and intermixture. Certainly from the time that Europeans entered Asia, Africa and America— the entire period encompassed by modern social sciences—the productive forces available to humans and confronting them were not only global, but increasingly falling into the hands of a globally ascendant capitalist class and in recent millenniums increasingly subjected to commodity relations—a process with immense implications for people all over the world. Though the productive forces confront people differently in different parts of the world, depending upon the character of distribution, the same totality of productive forces have been shaping the lives of everyone in the world. As long as humans do not perceive themselves and act in terms of this totality of productive forces and the full extent of relations, they remain encumbered by a contingent 'false conscious-ness' which frames their being in terms of their alienated existence, subjected to a given division of labour and controlled and limited by their own products. This alienated existence is conceived in terms of a dichotomized world (developed–undeveloped, modern–traditional, Christian–Pagan, citizen–foreigner, untouchable–touchable, Black–White, theory–practice, etc.), because it fails to see all people as comprehended within one all-encompassing set of relations and thus unitedly confronting the productive forces as a common heritage of humankind. A truly scientific consciousness, which is also a 'revolutionary consciousness', seeks to identify the contingency which mediates human existence and eliminate it by changing the world. It is necessarily a 'world historical' consciousness in which people perceive themselves in terms of a universal world history and orient their actions (and thus research) accordingly. The prior separation of the world by social sciences into culture groups, societies or nations inhibits the development of such a transcendent consciousness.[23] Paraphrasing Marx, the end of science is not just to describe the world, but to change it. Modern science, though definitely having traumatically changed the world, has also for the most part remained under the aegis of scientific objectivity, within the limitations of old, worn-out premises.

Since the productive forces, as themselves products, provide the power for human labour, a scientific approach (which strives to remove contingency from understanding) 'must always be studied and treated in relation to the history of industry and exchange' (Marx and Engels 1983:31–2). Men's and women's consciousness of themselves, their relations, and their activity 'arises from the need, the necessity, of intercourse with other men. . . . Consciousness is, therefore, from the very beginning a social product, and it remains so as long as men exist at all' (Marx and Engels 1983:32). Consciousness as the medium of communication, language, is a 'practical consciousness'; it is also ideas, according to which people create their awareness of their relations. Although people's contingent, false consciousness is not that people produced the world they live in but that it was made by superhuman forces of some sort (gods, some spirit of the age, scientific laws, capital), this consciousness was nevertheless produced according to the needs that arose from production, that is, from life. In its various forms— visual imagery, ritual, theology, etc.—it is not reducible to material relations, yet it cannot be understood in an unmediated sense but must refer to them.

An illusory 'general interest', represented by the state but actually consisting of ruling class interests, is placed over and against the individual and competing class interests. Its hegemony is effected through institutions such as family, religion, schools, unions and parties, and the entertainment and information media (especially television). These institutions make it seem that this apparent 'general interest', which is actually alien and opposite to the interests of both the individual and the majority of the people, belongs to the individual and extends out of his or her own being. Furthermore, the real practical struggles taking place, such as between workers and employers and, ultimately, international finance, over wages, working hours, and control over the conditions and purposes of production 'makes *practical* intervention and control necessary through the illusory "general" interest in the form of the state' (Marx and Engels 1983:35). Since the ruling classes control the state, this intervention is generally to their own advantage. Furthermore, since the division of labour means that the interests of the ruling class are imposed onto the individual, the activity of the individual ends up serving the needs, wishes and purposes of the ruling class, so that his or her 'own deed becomes an alien power opposed to him, which enslaves him instead of being controlled by him' (1983:36).

NOTES

This chapter was developed from a series of lectures in the Marxist anthropology presented to the Anthropology graduate programme in the Kirtipur Campus of Tribhuvan University during the 1989–90 academic year.

1   'The premises from which we begin are not arbitrary ones, not dogmas, but real premises from which abstractions can only be made in the imagination. They are the real individuals, their activity and the material conditions under which they live, both those which they find already existing and those produced by their activity. These premises can thus be verified in a purely empirical way' (Marx and Engels 1971:19–20).

2   These same conditions allow the anthropologist to enter unhindered and uninvited into the 'field' and gain intimate access into people's lives and then to publicize it all on more or less the terms determined by the anthropological profession's norms and values

3   Quigley in a critique of Dumont makes the commonly repeated statement that 'genuine sociological explanation makes no *a priori* assumptions (nor "synthetic *a priori*" assumptions) about the precise mechanisms through which institutions actually are connected in particular societies at particular times. This is a matter of observation and record' (1993:44). This is a mistaken notion of science, which in contrast recognizes that all knowledge is based upon assumptions and that the scientific method consists in isolating and uncovering the manner in which the assumptions mediate understanding.

4   'The premises from which we begin are not arbitrary ones, but real premises from which abstractions can only be made in the imagination. They are the real individuals, their activity and the material conditions under which they live,

both those which they find already existing and those produced by their activity. These premises can thus be verified in a purely empirical way.

'The first premise of human history, is of course, the existence of living human individuals. Thus the first fact to be established is the physical organization of these individuals and their consequent relation to the rest of nature.... The writing of history must always set out from those natural bases and their modification in the course of history through the act of men.

'Men ... [t]hey themselves begin to distinguish themselves from animals as soon as they begin to produce their means of existence, a step which is conditioned by their physical organization. By producing their means of subsistence men are indirectly producing their material life.

'The way in which men produce their means of subsistence depends first of all on the nature of the actual means of subsistence they find in existence and have to reproduce' (Marx 1983:20–1).

This was described by Sweezy (1992:18) as Marx's key hypothesis: '... the first premise of all human existence and, therefore, of all history, is the premise, namely, that men must be in a position to live in order to be able to "make history" (Marx and Engels 1983:30)'.

5   'The first historical act is thus the production of the means to satisfy these needs, the production of material life itself. And indeed, this is a historical act, a fundamental condition of all history, which today, as thousands of years ago, must daily and hourly be fulfilled merely in order to sustain human life' (Marx and Engels 1983:30).

6   'The second point is that the satisfaction of the first need leads to new needs; and this production of new needs is the first historical act' (Marx and Engels 1983:30–1).

7   'The third circumstance which, from the very outset, enters into historical development, is that men, who daily remake their own life, begin to make other men, to propagate their kind: the relation between men and women, parents and children, the *family*' (Marx and Engels 1983:31).

8   'Subsumption' is a Hegelian concept used by Marx to analyse the dialectical supersedence of capitalism over other forms in his 'Results of the Immediate Process of Production', published in Ben Fowkes translation of *Capital*, vol. 1 (1977:944–1084).

9   'The family, which to begin with is the only social relationship, becomes later, when increased needs create new social relations and the increased population new needs, a subordinate one ... , and must then be treated and analysed according to the existing empirical data, not according to "the concept of the family", ...' (Marx and Engels 1983:31).

Godelier (1978b:63–4) says the same thing when he writes, 'One may note that the more complex the division of labour, the more does the kinship group or local community lose part of its economic function. A part of production develops outside the family or village framework, in different organizations that depend on wider social groupings (the tribe, the state, etc.). In new economic conditions, the kinship relations and the political and religious relations play a new role. It is the logic of the reciprocal modifications of the elements of social structure that forms the object of scientific study of societies....' The criticism here would be that Godelier sees life divided into categories of bourgeois society—economic, religious, kinship, etc.—which do not have real independent existence even in bourgeois society. This leads him to become bogged down in the following discussion around Polanyi. Continuing, 'Polanyi bases himself on this appearance in distinguishing societies in which economy is "embedded" in the social structure from those in which it is said not to be, in which it is "disembodied", as with commodity societies. This distinction seems to me to be a questionable one, since the term "disembodied" could suggest an absence of internal relations between the economic and the non-economic, whereas this relation exists in every society' (64). But this is where both Polanyi and Godelier miss the point, which is that in commodity dominated societies the family has been subordinated to the market, or more particularly, organization based upon the relation of capital to labour; and other kinds of relations, such as of kin, have been subordinated to commodity relations and made a part of their own movement.

Godelier calls this an 'autonomy' of the economy in relation to other structures, for example, 'the state, etc.' which leads to disappearance of control over the product by the direct producers and owners. But again, this is because the bourgeois class has taken control of the state and set it up to serve its purposes. The state is made into a trained cadre of bureaucrats; the capitalists themselves do not fill the positions and roles in it as their career. Thus the 'economic' seems autonomous as does the state, in which that cadre class develops its own interests.

I agree provisionally with Godelier's position that 'maximizing profit' is the social form 'characteristic of capitalist societies' (but I do not accept a reified society) and that as a social form it cannot be reduced to a particular economic significance, because it implies a particular way of functioning of the family and state. But where he says, 'In other societies, at other moments of history, economic rationality would have a quite different content', I disagree. There would be no such thing as an 'economic rationality', except perhaps of a merchant class—and in much less differentiated form, at that—as, without subordination of society to commodity relations, production of exchange values is not framed separate from the rest of society. The existence of an 'economic rationality' is contained within the premises of bourgeois society: of the special form of society, of control of human labour by exchange relations, of a particular kind of family producing and reproducing labour for the market and consuming from it.

Meillassoux (1978c:167) acknowledges the subsumption of kinship by class, but then he interprets such subsumption as the integration of people into relations of production of class through kin relations, whereas previously people were integrated into kin through relations of production. His mistake is that kin in both cases express a category of producer, not father in one and seigneur as father in the other. This category is the elder clansman, i.e. people holder, in the one and the estate holder in the other. One consists of control of people mediated through seniority and affinity, the other is control over people mediated through land, but relations to land defined in terms of senior 'patriarch'. In both cases, this means a relation in which the elder clansman's concrete existence comes through people's productive labour subordinated through him. For Meillassoux, in contrast, the immediate production within the kin group creates the patriarch as kinsman on the one hand; and ideological relations determine family existence on the other.

10   From *Capital*, pt. 3, Chap. 7, vol. 1, 'The Labour Process and the Valorization Process': 'If we look at the whole process from the point of view of its result, the product, it is plain that both the instruments and the object of labour are means of production . . .' (Marx 1997:287).

11   The objects of labour include (1) those things spontaneously provided by nature (virgin land, fish, virgin forests, ore in the ground) and (2) raw materials or those things filtered through the previous labour (extracted ore, prepared fibres, etc.) (Marx 1977:284–5).

12   The instruments of labour consisting of things the worker interposes between him or herself and the object of labour (1) The earth as supplier of the means to do things (e.g. stones for throwing, grinding, pressing, cutting, etc.) or 'itself as an instrument of labor' (as ploughed field for agriculture), (2) especially prepared instruments or tools: stones, wood, bone and shell which have been worked upon (3) domesticated animals, (4) holders of materials of labour (as versus mechanical): pipes, tubs, baskets, jars, electrical wires, etc. (Marx 1977:285–6).

      As an aside, 'man's bodily organs' are considered in association with gathering nature's ready-made fruits. But knowing that the brain, jaw, hand, limbs, feet, torso, etc. are themselves products selected over millions of years through application of the human body and mind in the labour process, they are also social products (compare with domesticated plants and animals similarly developed but over shorter periods by selection from already existing gene pools—until genetic engineering allowed direct intervention in biochemical processes). The use of a wider variety of means of production selected for particular bodily and mental traits, which in turn facilitated greater development of the means of production. In dealing with the productive forces, Marx emphasizes the development of the individual as the most important force available to humans, because humans are the subject of the labour process.

13   Instruments of labour appearing as the objective conditions of labour include 'Once again, the earth itself is a universal instrument of this kind, for it provides the worker with the ground beneath his feet and a "field of employment" for his own particular process. Instruments of this kind, which have already been mediated through past labour, include workshops, canals, roads, etc.' (1977:286–7).

      Note that Marx here saw land as both an object (note 11) and instrument of labour, even for primitive humans. Here Meillassoux (1978c:60) mistakenly writes '. . . the radical difference between a foraging-hunting economy and an agricultural economy is related to the fact that the first uses land as a "subject of labour" while the latter uses it as an "instrument of labour". The use of land as an instrument of labour means that the labourer has invested in the land with the expectation of a later return.' Meillassoux's definition of 'instrument' is actually a characteristic of the production cycle, that the product of land does not arise immediately but corresponds to seasonal periods.

14   'It follows from this that a certain mode of production, or industrial state, is always combined with a certain mode of co-operation, or social state . . .' (Marx and Engels 1983:31).

'In production, men not only act on nature but also on one another. They produce only by co-operating in a certain way and mutually exchanging their activities. In order to produce, they enter into definite connections and relations with one another and only within these social connections and relations does their action on nature, does production, take place. . . . These social relations into which the producers enter with one another, the conditions under which they exchange their activities and participate in the whole act of production, will naturally vary according to the character of the means of production. Thus the social relations within which individuals produced, the social relations of production, change, are transformed, with the change and development of the material means of production, the productive forces. The relations of production in their totality constitute what are called the social relations, society, and specifically, a society at a definite state of historical development, a society with a peculiar, distinctive production relations, each of which at the same time denotes a special state of development in the history of mankind' (Marx 1986:159–60).

15   'My view is that each particular mode of production, and the relations of production corresponding to it at each given moment, in short "the economic structure of society", is "the real foundation, on which arises a legal and political superstructure and to which correspond definite forms of social consciousness", and that "the mode of production of material life conditions the general process of social, political and intellectual life"' (Marx 1977:175, quoting from his preface to *A Contribution to the Critique of Political Economy*).

16   Common interpretations do not usually give the development of the individual as included among the productive forces, but Marx was explicit about this: '. . . the full development of the individual, which itself, as the greatest productive force, in turn reacts upon the productive power of labour. From the standpoint of the immediate production process, it can be considered as the production of *fixed capital*, this fixed capital BEING MAN HIMSELF' (Marx 1986:98).

17   Godelier defines forces of production as 'material and intellectual means . . . to work upon nature and to extract from it their [referring to members of society] means of existence' (Godelier 1978:763). Compare:

'The productive forces . . . are the products of human industry; natural material transformed into organs of man's will over Nature, or of man's activity in Nature. They are *organs of the human mind which are created by the human hand*, the objectified power of knowledge. The development of fixed capital shows the degree to which society's general science, KNOWLEDGE, has become an *immediate productive force*, and hence the degree to which the conditions of social life process itself have been brought under the control of the GENERAL INTELLECT and remoulded according to it. It shows the degree to which the social productive forces are produced merely in the form of knowledge but as immediate organs of social praxis, of the actual life process' (Marx 1977b:37–8; 1986:92).

18   'Because of this simple fact that every succeeding generation finds itself in possession of the productive forces acquired by the previous generation, and that they serve it as the raw material for new production, a coherence arises in human history, a history of humanity takes shape which becomes all the more a history of humanity the more the productive forces of men and therefore

their social relations develop. Hence it necessarily follows that the social history of men is always the history of their individual development, whether they are conscious of it or not. Their material relations are the basis of all their relations. These material relations are only the necessary forms in which their material and individual activity is realised' (Marx 1975:30–1).

19   From the standpoint of the individual, distribution appears as a social law which determines his place within production and enjoyment of its products, and therefore it seems to precede production. From the standpoint of society, distribution also seems to precede and determine production almost as a pre-economic fact in which certain forms of distribution are imposed through the course of migration, conquest, revolution, or legal, constitutional or sacred assignments, and so forth. However, though certain forms of distribution presuppose production, these, like the productive forces discussed above, are themselves products of production in preceding periods and therefore must be understood through analysis of this history.

20   'In its shallowest conception, distribution appears as the distribution of products, and hence further removed from and quasi-independent of production. But before distribution can be the distribution of products, it is: (1) the distribution of the instruments of production, and (2) which is a further specification of the same relation, the distribution of the members of society among the same kinds of production. (Subsumption of the individuals under specific relations of production.) The distribution of products is evidently only a result of this distribution, which is comprised within the process of production itself and determines the structure of production. To examine production while disregarding this internal distribution is obviously an empty abstraction; while conversely, the distribution of products follows by itself from this distribution which forms an original moment of production' (Marx 1973:96).

'The so-called distribution relations . . . correspond to and arise from historically determined specific social forms of the process of production and mutual relations entered into by men in the reproduction process of human life. The historical character of these distribution relations is the historical character of production relations, of which they express merely one aspect. Capitalist distribution differs from those forms of distribution which arise from other modes of production, and every form of distribution disappears with the specific form of production from which it is descended and to which it corresponds' (Marx 1959:883).

21   Writes Sweezy (1992:19): 'Marx retained . . . those elements of Hegel's thought which emphasized process and development through the conflict of opposed or contradictory forces. Unlike Hegel, however, he traced decisive historic conflicts to roots in the mode of production; that is, he discovered them to be what he called class conflicts. . . . It follows that the essential economic relations are those which underlie and express themselves in the form of class conflict.'

Presently, in the manner that the classical economists saw the conflict of capital versus landed property as the main conflict in Marx's time, in Nepal the conflict is seen as being between capital versus feudal forces by the Communist Parties and between the modern view versus the old regime—traditionalism or old landed property classes. Because capital is using the supposed 'traditional' relations to suppress the workers (for example, the monarchy continues to be supported and given respect) to ensure access to cheap labour and natural resources, 'This relation must form the center of investigation' (Sweezy 1992:20).

22   In his 28 December 1846 letter to Annenkov, Marx (1975:31) writes, '. . . men never relinquish what they have won, but this does not mean that they never relinquish the social form in which they have acquired certain productive forces. On the contrary, in order that they may not be deprived of the results attained and forfeit the fruits of civilization, they are obliged, when the mode of carrying on commerce no longer corresponds to the productive forces acquired, to change all their traditional social forms. . . . Thus the economical forms in which men produce, consume, and exchange, are *transitory and historical.* With the acquisition of new productive forces, men change their mode of production and with mode of production all the economic relations which are merely the relations appropriate to a particular mode of production.

In the *Grundrisse:* 'Beyond a certain point, the development of the productive forces becomes a barrier to capital, and consequently the relation of capital becomes a barrier to the development of the productive forces of labour. Once this point has been reached, capital, i.e. wage labour, enters into the same relations to the development of social wealth and the productive forces as the guild system, serfdom and slavery did, and is, as a fetter, necessarily caste off. . . .' (Marx 1973:133–4)

In *Capital,* vol. 3: '. . . each specific historical form of this [production] process further develops its material foundations and social forms. Whenever a certain stage of maturity has been reached, the specific historical form is discarded and makes way for a higher one. The moment of arrival of such a crisis is disclosed by the depth and breadth attained by the contradictions and antagonisms between the distribution relations, and thus the specific historical form of their corresponding production relations, on the one hand, and the productive forces, the production powers and the development of their agencies, on the other hand. A conflict then ensues between the material development of production and its social form' (Marx 1959:883).

23   H. G. Wells's (1951) *The Outline of History* is a good example of the attempt to develop a universal history of the world in which all human endeavour is dealt with as a common human project. He argues that the development of human ideas has been characterized by a growing consciousness of universal understanding, and that the human future depends upon the complete development of such consciousness, which no longer attempts to impose one world view as universal but sees other world views and experiences as an essential part of one's own.

CHAPTER 4

Unlocking Submerged Voices: African-American Scholarship and Nepali Social Science

> Here comes the penalty which a land pays when it stifles free speech and free discussion and turns itself over entirely to propaganda. It does not make any difference if at the time the things advocated are absolutely right, the nation, nevertheless, becomes morally emasculated and mentally hogtied, and cannot evolve that healthy difference of opinion which leads to the discovery of truth under changing conditions.
>
> —W.E.B. Du Bois

INTRODUCTION

WE NEED ONLY look at the various social science writings in Nepal to note that the development of sociology and anthropology here has been strongly influenced by Euro-American scholars and scholarship. Closer examination shows that this influence over the department and the social sciences in Nepal has furthermore been white, and moreover, mostly male. From the perspective of social scientists in Nepal, who are somewhat removed from the manner that the problems are represented and experienced in the West, this observation may seem to be meaningless. However, even when knowledge presents itself as objective and detached, it has never been a passive observer or a disinterested tool in the development of human society.[1] The cultural diffusion of the disciplines of anthropology and sociology from the United States and Western Europe according to the self-understandings of these disciplines as they are practised there also implies acceptance of their appraisal of the conditions which gave birth to them. For social scientists and the people they study, these conditions have been ones of colonialism, industrialization, imperialism, the development of monopoly capitalism and transnational corporations, embourgeoisement, unrestrained resource use, etc.—processes in Nepal which are represented and legitimized by the word 'development' or *bikas*. In the United States and parts of Europe, the representation of these global processes has been interrelated with categories and representations of race and gender. Furthermore, in the United States and Europe, the dominant viewpoint has been identified with white skin and male gender— the race and gender categories with which the dominant group identifies itself, even though many white males are not in the dominant class, and not all the dominant class is white or male.[2]

Within the United States, the categories of skin colour and gender have underlain and permeated the development of the social sciences from their inception in the nineteenth century, both in the manner that these categories have been addressed by social scientists and in the manner that the individuals signified by them have been permitted to participate in intellectual intercourse. Thus, in borrowing from the United States and Western Europe, entire traditions of sociological thought are easily excluded from the discourse of the social sciences in Nepal, for example those which have been developed by the oppressed populations of the United States—especially the progressive, critical and outspoken voices among them.[3] These include views of African-Americans, Native and Hispanic Americans and women of colour. The latter category includes women from all these other categories who, taken together as the most repressed group, have found that their own problems in large part are not being addressed, even within their own 'minority' traditions.

In the United States, these traditions are frequently prefixed with a minority status label, say 'black' sociology or 'women's' anthropology. This serves to denigrate the work and make it appear to be less worthy of consideration. In the words of Eldridge Cleaver (from his prison writings):

One device evolved by the whites was to tab whatever the blacks did with the prefix 'Negro'. We had *Negro* literature, *Negro* athletes, *Negro* politicians, *Negro* workers. The malignant ingeniousness of this device is that although it accurately described an objective biological fact—or at least, a sociological fact in America—it concealed the paramount psychological fact: that the white mind, prefixing anything with 'Negro' automatically consigned it to an inferior category. A well-known example of the white necessity to deny due credit to blacks is in the realm of music. White musicians were famous for going to Harlem and other Negro cultural centers literally to steal black man's music, carrying it back across the colour line in the Great White World and passing off the watered-down loot as their own original creations. Blacks, meanwhile, were ridiculed as *Negro* musicians playing inferior coon music. (Cleaver 1968:79–80)

If courses in the various 'minority' studies are at all available to students within sociology and anthropology departments, they are generally presented as electives—subjects that students are free to study but do not generally have to master or take to seriously. Furthermore, many students experience direct harassment. For example, women students and faculty report that the faculty in male-dominated departments sometimes pay more frequent comment on their dress than their work (which is minor compared to other problems). African-American professors often get so loaded down with committee assignments related to minority groups that their academic work and thus their careers suffer. When certain minority leaders have raised issues in their own terms rather than on those set by the dominant discourse and thereby have become too threatening, then the machines of the media and state are mobilized to silence them. I give a rather lengthy quote by Eldridge Cleaver both to illustrate my point and because the same methods are used by transnational corporate dominated interests to passivate people in the Third or deindustrialized World (as I call it) as well.

One tactic by which the rulers of America have kept the bemused millions of Negroes in optimum subjugation has been a conscious, systematic emasculation of Negro leadership. Through an elaborate system of sanctions, rewards, penalties, and persecutions—with, more often than not, members of the black bourgeoisie acting as hatchet men—any Negro who sought leadership over the black masses and refused to become a tool of the white power structure was either caste into prison, killed, hounded out of the country, or blasted into obscurity and isolation in his own land and among his own people. His isolation was assured by the publicity boycotts alternated with character assassination in the mass media, and by the fratricidal power plays of Uncle Toms[4] who control the Negro community on behalf of the white power structure. The classic illustrations of this quash-the-black militant policy are the careers of Marcus Garvey, W.E.B. DuBois [*sic*], and Paul Robeson.

Garvey who in the first quarter of this century sparked a black mass movement based in America but international in scope and potential, was caste into federal prison and then exiled to England. [The sociologist] W.E.B. DuBois, one of the intellectual giants of the modern world, was silenced and isolated in America as viciously and effectively as the racist regime in South Africa has silenced and isolated such leaders of the black masses as Chief Albert Luthuli, or as the British, in Kenya, once silenced and isolated Jomo Kenyatta. After attempts to caste him into prison on trumped-up charges had failed, DuBois went into exile in Ghana and later renounced the bitter citizenship of the land of his birth.

Paul Robeson was at the apex of an illustrious career as a singer and actor, earning over $200,000 a year, when he began speaking out passionately in behalf of his people, unable to balance the luxury of his own life with the squalor of the black masses from which he sprang and of which he was proud. The response of the black masses to his charisma alarmed both the Uncle Toms and the white power structure, and Paul Robeson was marked for destruction. Through a coordinated, sustained effort, Robeson became the object of economic boycott and character assassination. Broken financially, and heartbroken to see black Uncle Toms working assiduously to defeat him and keep their own people down, Robeson's spirit was crushed, his health subverted, and his career destroyed.

By crushing black leaders, while inflating the images of Uncle Toms and celebrities from the apolitical world of sport and play, the mass media were able to channel and control the aspirations and goals of the black masses. (Cleaver 1968:88)

In academia, a method by which these alternative voices have been silenced is that the 'minority' viewpoints are addressed from within their own separate disciplines, such as of African-American, Women's, Native American, or Hispanic Studies departments. While separate departments provide refuges from a white male-dominated world, it also means that it is even more difficult for the minority ideas to challenge, transform, and merge with the dominant ideas without being co-opted. Consequently, in regard to African-American Sociology in particular, most students pass through an entire course of study in sociology or anthropology without ever being introduced to the work of great names such as W.E.B. Du Bois, Franklin Frazier, Charles Johnson, St. Clair Drake or Oliver Cox.

They never come to know that in *The Philadelphia Negro*, for example, Du Bois (1899b) pioneered ethnographic participant observation and the survey method. They are never introduced to the rich, unanswered, one-sided dialogue in which these and subsequent scholars engaged with the mainstream white sociological tradition.

Although this dialogue—a dialogue in which one of the voices is suppressed—is called 'black' sociology, it is much more encompassing than the white male-dominated social sciences which present themselves as the *entire* disciplines of anthropology or sociology. Always for the African-American, Woman, Hispanic, and Native American in the United States, one aspect of scholarship has necessarily been the working out of their relationship to the society and scholarly discipline which they are a part, yet which does not recognize or accept them or their viewpoint as legitimate. For the mainstream white male on the other hand, his problem has been one of formulating and presenting his view of society according to scientific principles and terms, grudgingly and selectively allowing African-American and other minority voices to emerge only at times when pressures coursing through the society become too strong to resist. And even when these voices are allowed to emerge, they are generally tempered to make them acceptable to the corporation's viewpoint or co-opted to serve these ruling class interests (e.g. getting votes) against the very people who created them.

Regarding ethnography in particular, not only have minority voices been silenced in scholarship, minority positions within the societies studied are ignored or silenced. Ethnography generally presents generalized pictures of societies from the viewpoint of high class, high caste and high status males. The problems which have been framed as legitimate subjects of study further direct people away from the problems of the lower classes and the oppressed. For example, among foreign women doing work in Nepal, the scholarship oftentimes confuses the class interest of the researcher with a gender one, making it as regressive and patronizing towards lower class women, if not women generally, as men's scholarship. Regarding African-American or other minority anthropologists and sociologists, I know of none who are working in Nepal. This is in part because there are few of them, and in the past those individuals are forced to confront 'third-world' problems right at home, especially with the current retrenchment of capitalism.

Due to their disadvantaged position and low status within their professions and society, African-American sociologists were combining theory and practice long before the word 'praxis' became fashionable in mainstream social science. Simply in trying to do their scholarship and to make it in their profession, they were forced to confront their own personal and group conditions and status within society. This forced minorities from the outset to combine theory and practice, and objectivity and advocacy.

For the social sciences and humanities, the 'race problem' penetrates the very work itself, and there is no way out of the dilemma save to fuse into the work itself one's commitment to one's people and one's commitment to the 'objective truth' of scholarship and the 'objective standards' of enduring art.

Given the depth and pervasiveness of racism in the United States, if a man or a woman is a historian and black, a sociologist and black, then he or she is compelled to work out a distinctive role balance between scholarship and advocacy, between creativity and commitment. . . .

Whatever the gross unfairness of the racial pressures on the black playwright or essayist, the work itself must still come first and stand on its own; it is almost inevitably (though not necessarily) 'about race', yet it cannot be exclusively assessed 'according to race'. . . . 'When his work is recognized it is usually pointed to as the work of a Negro. He is a competent *Negro* sociologist, an able *Negro* economist, an outstanding *Negro* historian. Such recognition is as much the product of the racist mentality as the Negro restrooms in the Montgomery airport.'[5]

Judgement of the work itself—implied in such phrases as 'a competent sociologist', 'an able economist'—would constitute the essential standard if other things were equal, that is, if the society in general had been guaranteeing a rough equality of access to scholars and writers irrespective of skin colour. Since that has not been the case, and still is not, despite rapid changes in the direction of equality of opportunity, the racial designations are going to be applied by the dominant group in any case, whether from motives of discrimination, condescension, patronage, mechanical liberalism, or whatever. Therefore, the black social scientist owes it to himself and the black community to fashion his own sense of balance *inside the work itself*—objective, scholarly analysis of the racial situation, its history and its structure, *and* passionate advocacy of freedom, justice, and group identity. (Robbins 1974:57)

The consequence of the need to combine scholarship and advocacy is that African-American work from its inception pioneered in a personal way the same reflexive trend that the dominant sociological tradition is now discovering and developing as its own in a detached, academic sort of way (primarily through often watered down or highly selective reinterpretations of the works of Marx, Engels, Gramsci, and their epigones).[6] The consequence of having to combine theory and practice has meant that many African-American sociologists have left sociology and engaged in more direct and practical kinds of work, while at the same time publishing a rich corpus of material from their experience.

Typically, even now, only a few at the so-called 'radical' end of the spectrum of the social sciences are entering into dialogue with the African-American sociological tradition. Yet, African-American reflexivity has long had the mainstream in its purview. Thus whereas the mainstream social sciences offer just a partial view of the human experience in the United States and the world, African-American sociology must include both sides. African-American sociology has not meant just a study of race, it has meant a study of the society that creates race: the relationships of white and black, of oppressed and oppressor, of the various oppressed among themselves, of the peoples of the world to European and American corporate expansion, and of the conditions generally which have given rise to the relationships in which people are oppressed according to the colour assigned to their skins, or more correctly, to their lineage, and other social categories. Indeed, due to its partial viewpoint, mainstream sociology should be the one prefixed with 'white male' . . . or monopoly capital—the oppressor's representation of the world.

Better yet, however, is that the significant voices of African-Americans and other oppressed of the world assert themselves and be acknowledged in the theoretical discourse, on their own terms, allowing real alternatives to be brought to the fore in scholarship and society. For scholars in Nepal and South Asia, it is essential not to accept sociology and anthropology according to the dominant self-definitions as handed from Western countries and colonial traditions, especially since the most powerful voices most easily transfer themselves to Nepal, however inappropriate and formalized may be the grafts.[7] The experiences of African-Americans and other colonized peoples of the world (including women) have been suppressed or devalued. Yet these voices will provide a multidimensional understanding of sociology and the world which they take as their subject.

Generally, the minority Western scholars have much more in common with the great majority of the people of Nepal, since they are in an analogous position towards global power interests as the great mass of people in Nepal and the rest of the deindustrialized world. Their studies provide an alternative model from that of the mainstream *bikas* 'development' ideology which has had such disastrous consequences in the bankrupted continents of Asia, Africa, Latin America and Eastern Europe, as well as for the poor of the United States and Western Europe (and, needless to say, for the people of Nepal). And as Du Bois (1985b:241–2) points out, initiative for transformation in the world will come from those belonging 'to the disinherited of modern culture' and not 'from those who now so largely own and rule the world'.

W.E.B. DU BOIS

Of the most prominent early African-American sociologists, Dr. W.E.B. Du Bois stands out as one of the greatest sociologists who ever lived. Throughout his ninety-five years life, until he died in 1963 in Ghana, he analysed American society and world events in acute detail. Putting his practice into words, he continued to change his role and analytic perspective as the situation of the world changed around him and his own experience grew.

In the decade prior to 1895, he studied at Fisk, Harvard, and Berlin 'under the tutelage of an array of scholars whose combined distinction touched few, if any other young Americans' (Broderick 1974:3). In 1896, he engaged in his greater than one-year participant observation study of Philadelphia African-Americans.

Using a lengthy questionnaire, he did a house-to-house survey of all the black families in the ward. He compiled voluminous data on patterns of migration into and within the city, family structure, income, occupations, property holdings, social stratification, black community institutions, politics, pauperism. The data gave a dismal portrait of unemployment, job discrimination by both employers and trade unions, wretched housing, family breakdowns, substantial criminality, and widespread health and hygienic problems. On the other hand Du Bois's monograph was a brilliant description of the contours and functioning of the black community, its institutions, and its mechanism for racial survival and advancement. (Rudwick 1974·28)

Du Bois addressed the colour bar, by which African-Americans were prevented from entering mainstream occupations; even the quarter of the population engaged in business were being pushed out by white immigration and large-scale capital. He showed how the social problems, which characterized African-Americans, reflected economic problems. He directly tied together economic status and family structure. And he identified three factors responsible for the 'pressing series of social problems' of blacks in Philadelphia: the legacy of slavery, influx of new migrants from a changing rural economy in the Southern states, and '"the environment in which a Negro finds himself—the world of custom and thought in which he must live and work, the physical surroundings of house and home and ward, and the moral encouragements and discouragements which he encounters" (Du Bois 1899, p. 284)' (Rudwick 1974:31).

This latter statement was made more than a half century before the anthropologist Oscar Lewis coined the term 'culture of poverty'. Similarly, Du Bois's emphasis on 'the impact of discrimination on the personalities and aspirations of black men and women and their children' (Rudwick 1974:32) foreshadowed studies in culture and personality. And 'in stressing the importance of migration, Du Bois also prefigured a subject that would interest later sociologists studying black urban communities' (ibid.: 32)—an important topic in present-day Nepal as well. Unlike Oscar Lewis or the culture and personality school, Du Bois placed his analysis within a broad social, economical, political, ideological and historical context.

He approached his subject in terms of a class analysis which included four social 'grades' or classes: '"upper class" or "aristocracy"', 'respectable working class' (a half), 'the poor' (a third), and the group with criminal records (6 per cent). His identification of the extent of social variability knocked down the dominant racist stereotype of all African-Americans in terms of the last, smallest group. It also differed very much from the generalizing, normative tendency that characterizes much of cultural anthropology today. Compare the following statement to such characterizations of people described in terms of generalized Magar, Gurung, Newar, Nepali, or Japanese and American cultures typifying so many anthropological studies.

'"There is always a strong tendency . . . to consider the Negroes as composing one practically homogeneous mass. This view has of course a certain justification: the people of Negro descent in this land have had a common history, suffer today common disabilities, and contribute to one general set of social problems." Yet, if the numerous statistics supplied in the volume "have emphasized any one fact it is that wide variations in antecedents, wealth, intelligence, and general efficiency have already been differentiated within this group" (Du Bois 1899:309).' (Rudwick 1974:34)

In addition to writing 'a conscientious and perceptive sociological study', Du Bois, in his combination of theory and practice, took the role of social reformer. On the one hand, he called for 'a radical change in public opinion' from the whites. On the other, he saw that the greatest responsibility for change lay with the African-American and oppressed peoples themselves: in protest, in economic and social cooperation, and in the unity of all classes of African-Americans, and more broadly, of the working class as a whole.

From 1897 to 1914 he attempted to establish a major series of sociological studies of African-Americans within his position at Atlanta University. Despite extremely poor funding of less than $500 a year, he was able to produce a large series of monographs, providing a storehouse of information from the period and initiating for the first time serious sociological research into African-Americans. Again, his work combined an emphasis on social reform along with scholarly description. However, there was little interest in his work, and he saw that the pressing problems of the time demanded that he leave academia. Nevertheless, through the rest of his life he continued to publish a major book every five years, along with an immense number of articles addressing events and conditions in the world from a rich sociological perspective.

An example of the impressive depth and breadth of his analysis, with the African-American perspective expressed in all its breadth and intricacy, is Du Bois's 729-page *Black Reconstruction in America, 1860–1880* published in 1935. In his work he analyses the mostly unsuccessful struggle of the African-Americans to free themselves from slavery and gain full citizenship rights during and after the Civil War (1860–1865). He questions the myth of American history that President Abraham Lincoln freed the slaves, showing rather that the African-American slaves themselves went on a mass strike on the plantations during the Civil War, either refusing to work or fleeing to the initially unreceptive United States armies. Lincoln's proclamation of freedom for the slaves was merely a recognition of what the African-Americans had already taken into their own hands, and it was forced upon him by the need for 200,000 African-American Americans to man the US armies in the face of growing resistance of white workers to a fight what they increasingly saw to be a war benefiting only capitalists.

In the aftermath of the Civil War, the northern capitalists (still represented by the Republican party today) combined with the large southern landowners (represented by the Democratic party at that time) who they had just defeated, in order to destroy the labour movement in the United States by dividing white from African-American. The recently freed African-Americans in the southern United States were thrown back into a new kind of slavery based on share-cropping, insuring the renewed supply of cheap raw materials for northern United States factories. The great masses of white poor in the south, who again were unemployed because they could not compete against the African-American labourers, were recruited into the Klu Klux Clan quasi-religious terrorist organization to immobilize the African-Americans and suppress their freedom struggle. This of course isolated the white labourers and made their position all the worse vis-à-vis the large landholders and capitalists. In the western states of the United States, large capitalists destroyed the small free-holding peasant farmer in the industrial north, the large capitalists co-opted the labour movement, by making the white workers become obsessed with protecting their relatively high-paid jobs from African-Americans and women, rather than directing their combined demands at the capitalist. The result was to deeply affect not only the future development of the United States, but the trajectory of development throughout the world to this very day.

America thus stepped forward in the first blossoming of the modern age and added to the Art of Beauty, gift of the Renaissance, and to the Freedom of Belief, gift of Martin Luther and Leo X, a vision of democratic self-government: the domination of political life by the intelligent decision of free and self-sustaining men. What an idea and what an area for its realization—endless land of richest fertility, natural resources such as the Earth seldom exhibited before, a population infinite in variety, of universal gift, burned in the fires of poverty and caste, yearning toward the Unknown God; and self-reliant pioneers, unafraid of man or devil. It was the Supreme Adventure, in the last Great Battle of the West, for that human freedom which would release the human spirit from the lower lust for mere meat, and set it free to dream and sing.

And then some unjust god leaned, laughing, over the ramparts of heaven and dropped a black man in the midst.

It transformed the world. It turned democracy back to Roman Imperialism and Fascism; it restored caste and oligarchy; it replaced freedom with slavery and withdrew the name of humanity from the vast majority of human beings.

But not without a struggle. Not without writhing and rending of spirit and pitiable wail of lost souls. They said: Slavery was wrong; slavery must perish and not simply move; God made black men; God made slavery; the will of God be done; slavery to the glory of God and black men as his servants and ours; slavery as a way to freedom—the freedom of blacks, the freedom of whites; white freedom as the goal of the world and black slavery as the path thereto. Up with the white world, down with the black!

Then came this battle called Civil War, beginning in Kansas in 1854, and ending in the presidential election of 1876—twenty awful years. The slave went free; stood a brief moment in the sun; then moved back again toward slavery. The whole weight of America was thrown to colour caste. The coloured world went down before England, France, Germany Russia, Italy and America. A new slavery arose. The upward moving of white labor was betrayed into wars for profit based on colour caste. Democracy died save in the hearts of black folk.[8]

Indeed, the plight of the white working class throughout the world today is directly traceable to Negro slavery in America, on which modern commerce and industry was founded, and which persisted to threaten free labor until it was partially overthrown in 1863. The resulting colour caste founded and retained by capitalism was adopted, forwarded and approved by white labor, resulted in subordination of coloured labor to white profits the world over. Thus the majority of the world's laborers, by the insistence of white labor, became the basis of a system of industry which ruined democracy and showed its perfect fruit in World War and Depression. And this book seeks to tell that story. (Du Bois 1935:29–30)

Du Bois sees the solution to the great ills that have been brought onto the world as lying in bringing the broad participation of the great masses of people into governing the world. In this regard he has much to say to the present endeavour to establish democracy in Nepal.

When it comes to democracy, the placing of political power in the hands of the mass of intelligent people, there are many who regard this step as philanthropy and withal dangerous philanthropy. They think of the right to vote as a concession from the cultured elite to the inexperienced and irresponsible mass, with the threat of slowing up or even attacking civilization. Such retrogression has occurred and may occur in the progress of democracy; but the vaster possibility and the real promise of democracy is adding to human capacities and culture hitherto untapped sources of cultural variety and power. Democracy is tapping the great possibilities of mankind from unused and unsuspected reservoirs of human greatness. Instead of envying and seeking desperately outer and foreign sources of civilization, you may find in these magnificent mountains a genius and variety of human culture, which once released from poverty, ignorance and disease, will help guide the world. Once the human soul is thus freed, then and only then is peace possible. There will be no need to fight for food, for healthy homes, for free speech; for these will not depend on force; but increasingly on knowledge, reason and art. (Du Bois 1985a:242-3)

NOTES

This piece was originally presented to the First National Congress of Sociology/ Anthropology in Lalitpur-Patan, 4–6 Sept 1992. It was subsequently published by the Department of Sociology and Anthropology, Tribhuvan University, in *Contributions to Anthropology and Sociology, Vol.* 3. 1993.

1   See particularly articles by Bista (1987), Bhattachan (1987), Fisher (1987a, 1987b), Gurung (1991), and Bhandari (1991) on the development of the department and discipline of sociology and anthropology in Nepal in the first two issues of *Occasional Papers in Sociology and Anthropology,* published by the Department of Anthropology at Tribhuvan University.

2   This is comparable to the domination of Nepal society by Brahmanic ideas, which for the most part represent the interests of the economically dominant ruling class, although not all high caste individuals belong to the ruling class. Unlike race in Europe, caste categories (that is the two principles *varna* and *jati*) originally developed in combination with the ascendancy of the domination of landed property over society in its various stages. In India, caste has especially been taken up by the capitalists—both foreign and domestic—to secure the hold of large capitalist enterprises over the state and society, and thus continues with a somewhat different content.

    In contrast, the category of race developed with capitalism, entirely replacing the concept of 'estates', which had characterized the rule of landed property in Europe during the period of feudalism. Given historical trajectories of the development of landed property and the state in Western Europe and South Asia, neither the terms 'estate', 'guild', nor 'race' are interchangeable with caste, even if each shares certain common features with it.

    From a functional perspective (i.e. in terms of imposing the rule of a certain class, dividing the labour force, enforcing a certain division of labour according to descent controlling marriage, etc.) though not a developmental one, caste is more a subset of race than race being a manifestation of caste. The so-called 'caste school of race', which presented race in the United States as caste, attempted to give race an objective existence in the United States by equating it with caste. The flaw as that caste also lacks an objective existence—it is subjective, depending upon and arising historically out of human relations and activity and in society, and it can just as well be the object of the criticism that was directed at this theory by sociologists such as the African-American Oliver C. Cox (1942, 1944, 1945a, 1945b, 1948, 1987).

In *Mediterranean Citizenship and South Asian Caste* (chapter 16, this volume), I argue that caste and citizenship originally addressed the same problem of establishing the rule of a few over the vast majority by extension of kinship categories. Their differences are tied up with the particular historical conditions which framed the expansion of the city state from Mesopotamia into South Asia and the Mediterranean region respectively.

In this day and age, since capitalism used the metaphor of 'democracy' as the framework for its expansion throughout the world, it could not very well set off the exploited peoples of the world as non-citizens and slaves, as had been the case in the ancient world. So it conceived the category 'race', both to justify the disenfranchisement of the great masses of people domestically and internationally and to divide the working class internally. Within the Indian subcontinent, it hooked onto the categories *varna* and *jati* an already pre-existing form of relation of citizen versus non-citizen, which it set about to formalize constitutionally and turn to its own purposes. In the *Maluki Ain* of the Ranas, we can see this same process extended to Nepal as these pompous clients of colonialists and imperialists formalized caste to sustain, perpetuate and further expand the ghettoization and disenfranchisement of the masses of Nepali people within their own country while raising a relatively small class of grovelling landlord, bureaucratic, business and intelligentsia families, decorated and addressed with cheap ornaments of status, as dubious citizens within the global ruling class.

3   For example, the one African-American introduced to Nepali students in the course of study for their SLC examinations is Booker T. Washington. Yet he is widely criticized by certain African-Americans for compromising the movement for equal civil, economic and political rights to the big business interests which controlled the post-Civil War United States. One can see in the following quote from Du Bois that Washington's policy is basically the same as that applied to Third World countries generally, and thus it is no surprise that an American designed education system should eulogize Booker T. Washington in young people's text books, while remaining silent about more critical African-American viewpoints.

(After a humbling visit to the Tuskegee Institute while preparing this book for publication, I want to note that critique of Booker T. Washington should take consideration of the time and context of his work. Washington and his colleague George Washington Carver leave tremendous lessons in using local human and natural resources to learn and develop autonomously which should be opposed to the exploitative and destructive finance-driven, market-obsessed models of development which dominate the world today.)

4   'A black eager to win the approval of whites and willing to cooperate with them.'
5   Author's note: John Hope Franklin, 'The Dilemma of the Negro American Scholar', in Herbert Hill, ed., *Soon One Morning: New Writings by American Negroes* (New York: Alfred A. Knopf, 1966), p. 61.
6   This point was made in a panel on W.E.B. Du Bois at a meeting of the American Anthropology Association in New Orleans. Typically, few people attended this

panel, in which practice was presented in a simplicity and directness engendered by the more than hundred years of scholarship, while the mainstream panels discussing the 'newly discovered' academic praxis, which is generous with incomprehensible jargon and stingy in straightforward action. Next year, the membership of the American Anthropological Association will discover that practice is impracticable within the structures of power, status, and clientelism of the university and society, to say nothing of their life-styles, and rather than change these structures they will abandon last year's jargon—which will have lost its credibility—for a new one.

7   The white-male viewpoint dominates the major journals and books, reflecting both the dominance of these viewpoints over the discipline and the publishing houses. Furthermore, Nepali exchange students almost invariably go to departments dominated by white males, particularly those which are defined as prestigious. I know of no Nepali students who have studied in the great African-American colleges such as Howard, Fisk, or Atlanta. I know of one person studying at the Graduate Centre of the City University of New York, which has a much more ethnically mixed faculty and student body than more prestigious universities. A major reason, certainly, is that these universities have much lower operating budgets and may not be able to offer financing. Another reason, however, may be that these have been attributed lower status than white universities (by white scholars) and their lack of prominence. Finally, a large portion of the students of Nepal, like elsewhere, see education as establishing themselves in a privileged class position and prestigious occupations in Nepal and the global political economy. From this standpoint, schools built for the oppressed rather than the oppressor are much less desirable. I might add that I also passed through a series of white male dominated departments and think in retrospect that I would have been better prepared with a more varied experience.

8   Note that where mainstream US history frames the US Civil War in terms of the five years of actual military engagements beginning in 1860 and ending in 1865, Du Bois frames it within the period beginning with John Brown's insurgency in 1854 and ending with the full re-assertion of a second slavery in 1876. Observe furthermore in the following paragraph his assertion that slavery or oppression of one element of the labouring class ultimately means slavery for all elements, and the direct consequences of US slavery on the development of the division of labour worldwide.

PART II

The Democracy Movement and its Aftermath

CHAPTER 5

Social-History of the *Jaana Andalan*: A Critical Analysis

'Democracy' refers to a system of governance in which the elite elements based in the business community control the state by virtue of their dominance of the private society, while the population observes quietly. So understood, democracy is a system of elite decision and public ratification. Correspondingly, popular involvement in the formation of public policy is considered a serious threat. It is not a step towards democracy; rather, it constitutes a 'crisis of democracy' that must be overcome.

—Noam Chomsky, *On Power and Ideology* (1987)

STARTING WITH a mass meeting on 'Democracy Day', 7 Maagh 2047 BS (18 February 1991), and coming to a close on 10 April through an agreement between King Birendra and several of the party leaders, the *Jaana Andalan* or 'People's Movement' has been viewed as a benchmark in Nepal's history. The Congress Party of Nepal took credit for the movement, but it was a clandestine meeting of the Communist Party (Marxist-Leninist) in the forest near Nepal's southern border with Bihar, India, that brought it into being. As the members of the Communist Party were heavily warranted and operating underground, they decided that the Congress Party should provide the visible face for the movement while they undertook the organization and initiative; thus the movement was launched formally in the winter of 1990 by the Nepali Congress Party. Initially designated the 'Democracy Movement of 2047' and subsequently the 'People's Movement', this uprising led to the overthrow of the thirty year-old 'Panchayat system', a non-party, international-aid sponsored form of absolutist monarchical government in which political parties and all forms of party politics had been banned, and to the introduction of basic constitutional changes providing a multi-party, parliamentary monarchy. The laws of local government were also subsequently rewritten according to a rhetoric befitting the democratic pretensions of the new constitution, although, like the rest of the changes, it was more form than substance.[1] As of 15 April 1998, just eight years from the end of the movement, there have been seven governments, two parliamentary elections, three votes of no confidence, and twice the disbandment of parliament in the face of the threat of further no confidence motions. The last three (of five) governments consisted of coalitions combining one of the original partners of the democratic movement—first the Nepali Congress, then the Communists, and again the Nepali Congress—with one or the other faction of the old royalists against the other partner, leading to the sad irony of three governments under individuals who had first appeared as prime ministers under the despised Panchayat system. And even the governments under the previous opposition parties, both Congress and Communist, are said to be less and less discernible from the old regime overthrown in the first place. Understanding how this could have come about, and thereby facilitating development of strategies to counter it, requires studying the history of the emergence of the social forces bringing it about and how these forces manifest and interact on the historical stage.

Mainstream Nepali observers have come to frame recent political events and constitutional changes, taken in their own terms, as the primary problem and subject of the history of the period. The political movement of 1990 became the 'advent of democracy', and the various subsequent struggles and events are constantly being designated 'developments of', 'threats to' or 'conspiracies against' democracy, depending upon the prejudices and objectives of the observer with regard to the specific event. In contrast, my research and writing during this period have sought to understand these political events and constitutional changes in terms of the larger regional and global long-term economic, social, and cultural processes located both in civil society and bureaucratic administration and in urban quarters and villages. Although these processes lack the glamour and overt drama of historical events and personalities, I see them as providing the real substance of history and giving rise to the changing constitutional and legal forms of the state and its various personifications. Analysis of these processes requires adoption of a long view of history and a bringing together of disparate data using a critical synthesis (as opposed to the hodgepodge of eclecticism) of the theories and contexts which produced the data.

Characteristic of many insular national histories, Nepali historiography describes the present nation state as the product of the genius of a certain man, King Prithivi Narayan Shah (1720–75), who is presented as having given expression to a latent Nepali nationality within the many disparate feudal states and peoples of the region, a puzzle he summed as a 'Garden of many flowers'. Gardens, however, imply gardeners who cultivate and maintain an order. This leads one to inquire into the processes and conditions that gave rise to the project of state building and which led to the attribution of greatness to this and other men (and almost no women, despite their pervasive social role) in the dominant schoolbook history.

By the mid-eighteenth century the conditions giving rise to the Nepali state included a number of elements: the extension and development over the period of six centuries of the estate system and estate administration of north India in the form variously of Hindu caste (called the *chhabis* and *chaubis*—twenty-two and twenty-four—*rajyas*) over a large area now western and southern Nepal which provided the means to control sufficient men and women and their surpluses to allow a successful project of conquest and administrative consolidation; the gradual collapse of the Mughal Empire in the face of internal strife and European commercial and military onslaught and the consequent temporary lapse of Mughal (subsequently East India Company) suzerainty over the lowland kingdoms of what is now western Nepal, allowing their subjugation and incorporation by the conquering Gorkha armies; the introduction of European firearms and barracking of soldiers in a standing army, providing the kingdom of Gorkha with superior military power; and the existence of an exploited and desperate population which could be inspired or drafted into the project with promises of land and a sense of taking part in a transcendent project.

The creation of the Nepali state through military conquest was not the realization of some inherent national spirit and natural unity given it by historians, but part of a longer project of extension of the estates and administrative machinery of the conquerors of the region. The ideology that accompanied the estate system into the region had itself developed through the long history of state formation within the subcontinent. Thereby it represented the extension of already existing relations and forms of organization rather than a radical departure for something new. The subsequent recorded history of the Nepali state, although not expressed in these terms, has been the product of the consolidation and transformation of this estate system and the activities of these estate classes and other associated ruling classes, for example merchants, and their simultaneous gradual subsumption by global commercial, industrial, financial, and bureaucratic interests that were already well on their way to extending their sway over the region in the mid-eighteenth century.

From AD 1816—when Gorkha lost its war with the equally covetous and much more powerful East India Company, bringing an end to its territorial expansion—to the middle of the nineteenth century was a time of internecine conflict between the growing empire of the East India Company and the Nepali rulers for sovereignty over the region. Unable any longer to expand their territorial estates by external conquest due to the superior military power of the East India Company, the leading families of Nepal's ruling class fought among themselves for control of the government and intensified their exploitation of the direct producers on the land. As revealed by Stiller (1976), the toiling peoples of the country, who in the previous century had joined in the project of national conquest in anticipation of being set up as independent farmers on their own plots of land, found themselves thrown into worse penury, poverty, and suffering than ever before. Increasingly unable to make a living as farmers, they were driven in growing numbers into mercenary labour in the colonial Indian army. This history of mercenary labour, long presented by colonial ethnographers and military historians as expressing the essentially military character of Nepali culture and only recently subjected to revision (Mishra 1986, 1991; Mikesell 1986; DeChene 1990; Pahari 1991; Onto 1994), became increasingly amplified through time to encompass all kinds of migratory labour from agricultural and industrial labour to large-scale sex labour.

The year 1846 brought the bloody ascension to paramountcy over the state a group of Kunwar brothers, or 'Ranas', as the Kunwars and their descendants subsequently called themselves (befitting the aristocratic pretensions that tend to surround power), through a slaughter of the other competing families of the landed aristocratic ruling class in what became known as the Kot Massacre (Stiller 1981; Welpton 1991:158–64) and the capture of control of the prime ministry and the subordination of the monarchy to itself. Having wiped out their main competitors among the ruling classes, the members of the Rana family subsequently maintained their sovereignty over the Nepali state as prime ministers by giving recognition to the general suzerainty of the British imperial government, which had by then set itself up as the successor to the Moghals. The Ranas gave over control of their foreign diplomacy and conceded any ambitions for additional territory in exchange for recognition of their regime, non-interference in their internal affairs—including monopoly control over internal trade (a concession subsequently begrudged but never taken back) and many forms of exploitation of their indigenous peoples and resources— and collusion in suppressing all forms of dissent. The British did not go as far, however, as recognizing the Jang Bahadur's attempt to claim the Royal title, 'Sri Paanch'—five times honored—leaving him and his descendents to satisfy themselves with the lesser 'Sri Tin' and thereby preserving doubt in their claims to legitimacy.

The myth-making national history presents the state as a unified, autonomous entity and personalizes historical processes by focusing on the accomplishments and excesses of particular individuals and regimes. It does not willingly show that from this estate form of administration and domination, by which this Nepali conquest-state was consolidated and administered, there arose interests among portions of its subjects inherently divergent from those of the rulers in Kathmandu, itself an integral part of the development of the society and state. This initially bore itself out in terms of the gradual transformation of estates into private, heritable property, first *de facto* and eventually, in the early twentieth century, *de jure*. Eventually, this class development was presented in terms of the need to overthrow the illegitimate autocratic rule of the Rana family, without, however, bringing into question the regime of domination and exploitation that they represented and which was the real fount of illegitimacy in their rule. At most, the now hackneyed theme of land reform, which had been the real inspiration behind participation of the exploited classes in the original state building project of the second half of the eighteenth century, and which was made into law and given its own ministry in 1967, continues to be exhumed now and then for the purposes of legitimization, populist manipulations, or, when selectively implemented, pulling out the economic basis from certain elements of the ruling class which have, deservedly, lost their consent to govern (a consent always manufactured or disassembled by competing elements of the ruling classes, never from among the toiling direct producers).

The reason why the general regime of domination is never brought into question is that the apparent overthrow of old regime in each of the two so-called 'revolutions' or 'movements' of the last half of the twentieth century has actually resulted in the expansion of this regime to include newly emergent ruling classes from among those promoting the overthrow. From the time of the conquest of the Kathmandu valley, Nepal's merchant class began spreading out from the urban centres of the valley into the length and breadth of the country and, in the manner of the other 'up-country merchants' of the subcontinent described by Bayly (1983), was establishing its bazaar sovereignty over both the estates and rural toilers by the means of putting their shops and merchant communities at the disposal of burgeoning foreign industrialists and trading in the growing volume of factory-produced commodities coming out of the growing commercial and financial centres of the world. Simultaneously, many from among the estate-holder class, which had gradually expanded as an element of the expansion of the Rana family's administrative needs, were becoming increasingly disaffected with the Ranas' monopoly control over the state machinery. Suspected dissidents from among them were driven to India, where they formed an active exile community, while others were imprisoned or executed. The merchants, however, were establishing themselves through trading in commodities and extension of credit and thus for the most part did not come into direct competition with the old regime for estates or offices. They operated more quietly, if less courageously, by gradually usurping control over various property forms and asserting themselves over the productive, social and religious-intellectual life of the country. The toilers in the countryside strongly resented exploitation generally, but expressed their resentment more diffusely in the form of a desire for overthrow of their immediate exploiters, removal of debts, obtaining rights in their land, forests, pastures and other resources, and various forms of resistance. They lacked the education, national organization, international support and leadership enjoyed by the estate-holding and other property-owning classes, and could not exert themselves through any section of the government machinery (as did the estate holders and growing cadre of bureaucrats) or frame their demands in terms of any perceptible ideological pretexts that would lend them a universal character and enlist the support of large sections of the population (as did the merchants and bureaucrats). Nevertheless, now and then they made remarkably courageous attempts at resistance and rebellion, which were typically ruthlessly and cruelly obliterated, all of which is carefully excised from the sanitized schoolbook history by a current ruling class no less anxious to hide and forget these things than the old. The new ruling class has created its own heroes—particularly in its party leaders (preferably dead, comfortably senile or too enraptured with their own self importance to notice their transitory importance)—who serve their purposes better.

As the expanding property-owning classes of various kinds (especially the merchants and bureaucratic intelligentsia) asserted control over increasingly wider spheres of production and national life and developed a corresponding consciousness, particularly through education in India and experience in the anti-British struggle there in the 1930s and 1940s, they more and more saw the monopoly control of the Rana family over the state machinery, and thereby over large sections of economic life, as limiting their freedom to implement what they considered to be their new visions and to assert their own interests. Following Indian Independence, some of these individuals who had been involved in the Indian independence movement formed the Nepali Congress Party in 1947, from which the Nepali Communist Party soon split. Their chance to overthrow Rana rule came when the British patrons of the Ranas transferred colonial power to groups within the indigenous Indian ruling classes (Gosh 1985). In 1950 the new Indian government, sympathetic to anti-Rana sentiments to the extent that they could transform the pro-British sentiments of the Rana government into the pro-Indian ones of Nepali exiles in India in a new government, ceased its discouragement of the ex-patriot Nepali insurgency, allowing it to import and deploy Burmese-supplied arms and invade Nepal from within India's borders. But as the government armies gradually fell back before the insurgents and the countryside threatened to erupt into a wholesale rebellion against not just the Ranas but the general regime of class inequality and oppression in early 1951, Nehru and other Indian leaders stepped in to negotiate a compromise between the Ranas, the king (who had fled to India at the start of the struggle) and, side-stepping the socialist leader of the Congress party, B.P. Koirala, the more malleable and less principled lieutenants from among the insurgents in Delhi. This 'Delhi Compromise' established the palace as paramount over a basically unchanged state machinery and class regime and subordinated the Ranas to the palace within a cabinet consisting of a combination of the old rulers and the compliant leadership from among the insurgents (the insurgent leadership was nearly all from landholding families of the old regime as well). This became known as the 'Democracy Revolution of 1951', marked ironically by the day the Indian government returned the king from exile in Delhi, 7 Magh (18 February). In reality it was neither a revolution in the sense of a major rearrangement of the class organization and control of the society nor the creation of democracy, even in the limited sense of extending some sort of electoral franchise to any part of the population. It was primarily a shift of paramountcy over the state machinery from one family of the old regime to another and a begrudging and provisional opening of access to state machinery to a slightly wider group of the ruling class.

Lacking any real popular basis, the groups in power had to look outward for legitimacy and wealth, and the doors were opened for the first time to large-scale foreign aid. This began the creation of a whole class of commission agents and contractors who took their tithe of the foreign aid, part of which was distributed around to those in power and in the upper levels of the bureaucracy, magnifying the corruption and destroying any sort of popular accountability in the political apparatus. Indian advisors arrived to expand India's corrupt and unwieldy colonial bureaucracy to Nepal, which set about in turn to extending its control over local communities to undermine their autonomy, dispossess them of their natural and biological resources, and generally destroy their social and ecological viability and productive base. United States Aid for International Development (USAID) assisted in the development of a public school system formally modelled on the theories of American colleges of education and agricultural extension, with little relevance to the experience and needs of the people. It devalued local knowledge and culture and taught young people, most of them farmers, to despise farming and rural life. It also engaged in a massive project of defoliation of Nepal's lush lowland forests through chemical suppression of malaria and construction of the largest sawmill in Asia at the time, which brought the enthralment of the plainsmen by upland bazaar merchants and the transformation of the complex subtropical ecosystems into commercially oriented agricultural lands. The US, Indian and Chinese governments all engaged in road building with the prime objective of connecting Nepal's urban centres and the fertile lowlands to their own commercial and industrial centres, since they saw the font of wealth and creative change as lying in these areas and the Nepali people as a merely supine, passive populace requiring outside stimulus and input. This understanding necessarily followed from the alliance of these countries to the local ruling classes, which had no interest in changes that would affect their own privileged situation, that is, to bring meaningful, creative change.

A constituent assembly promised by King Tribhuvan on his return to Nepal to conciliate popular demands for overthrow of the old regime and bringing real change never materialized. During the 1950s the palace created a series of ministries and shuffled cabinets among the self-appointed 'leadership' of the various political parties, allowing first one group and then another to dip momentarily into the foreign-aid gravy train to overcome their ideological pretensions and undermine any illusion of claims of legitimacy they may have been able to make on the population. In the face of growing popular discontent, the palace finally drafted a constitution in 1957, and elections for parliament took place in 1959. Riding on the popularity of its leader B.P. Koirala, and the memory of the party's role in the anti-Rana insurgency, the Nepali Congress Party won an over-whelming victory against the other parties, which, except for the landlords and merchants of the old regime, lacked both organiza-tion and any sort of constituency. In the face of in-fighting among the leadership of the ruling party, which was devoid of any sort of ideological coherence beyond the socialist ideals of its leader and its loyalties to its propertied class origins, and with anticipated land reforms causing mounting pressure from the old regime of landlords (the support base of the palace and still strongly influential in the countryside), the king in a night-time palace *coup d'état* dissolved the parliament, arrested its members, and took over the government. Blaming the parties for introducing divisions in the country which actually stemmed from divisions among the various elements of ruling class fighting for political spoils on the one hand, and the real socio-economic divisions and inequities fracturing the society on the other, the king outlawed all parties and began absolutist rule through the bureaucracy.

To provide an illusion of legitimacy, to quell the clamour of the masses for social and economic justice, and to confuse and divide the opposition, a 'democratic' constitution was framed by an intellectual from the landed classes (subsequently sponsored for further study by the University of California, Berkeley, political science department) and promulgated in 1962. This constitution established a series of representative assemblies, called panchayats, at the local, district, regional and national levels. These assemblies were partly elective and partly selected, but subordinate to the ministries and palace. Various class organizations of peasants, workers, women and intellectuals received representation in the National Panchayat, but these also were created with the intention of subordinating all kinds organization and initiatives within the civil society, as well as the state, to the palace and its bureaucracy. The ministries, formed and dissolved at the whim of the king from among the national assembly members, were used to divide the opposition and take the blame for the widespread corruption and abuse of authority associated with the regime. Lucrative participation in the panchayat assemblies, as well as access to government jobs, contracts and commissions, required swearing absolute obedience to the king and completely repudiating any sort of loyalty to political parties. Party activity or opposition to the regime was ruthlessly suppressed with black listing against serving in government jobs, long terms of imprisonment, extrajudicial torture, executions, widespread general persecution, and the creation of an environment of and surrealistic double-speak and stultifying fear. Even possession of a piece of party literature or a careless word could mean prison, torture and disappearance. The virtual carte blanche extended to retainers of the palace, panchas (elected representatives at all levels), and bureaucrats, and the lack of accountability of the government to communities, led to a growing discontent expressed outwardly in a pervasive cynicism and guarded black humour among the intelligentsia, bureaucrats and businessmen, increasingly bold speaking out and actions from among the students, and determined organizing among working class groups, particularly the small industrial proletariat in the towns along the Indian border.

Land reforms placing ceilings on various categories of individual property were again legislated in 1967. But property in Nepal is, or was, de facto (as well as de jure) paternally controlled family property, and various men of families holding land over the ceilings effectively undermined the reform by parcelling family plots in the names brothers, sons, household servants, retainers, and even dogs to make it seem that no one individual owned all the land—that along with bribes paid to the land reform office and the courts. Thus there was and continues to be no significant land reform or reorganization of the extremely exploitative and cruel conditions of rural society or extension of any other relief to the rural cultivators. Whereas the extension of bureaucracy and corrupt, bureaucratically controlled local councils, like in India called Panchayats, led to the emergence of a new class of local and national exploiters, the palace being just the biggest among many, who have devastatingly dismantled village society and production and appropriated communally controlled and husbanded resources in the name of 'development'.

Nearly all foreign governments, international agencies, international Non-Government Organizations (NGOs), and benevolent organizations, secular and religious and from both the so-called capitalist and Communist blocks, intentionally and unintentionally funded and underwrote this whole process and its associated corruption. A system of sinecures that had once provided control over village labour and various other sources of income to administrators through the distribution of estates and government offices among the various ruling class families of the old regime was extended to access a torrent of foreign-aid funded sources of income through distribution of offices and positions in the government and government-owned or sponsored corporations and institutions. This led to the burgeoning growth of a bureaucratic ruling class which used its new wealth to purchase properties and build houses in the urban areas, especially the capital city, and furnish itself with all the associated appliances of convenience and accoutrements of status from automobiles to refrigerators to Johnny Walker whiskey (proudly displayed next to Barby dolls in the glass cabinets of middle class homes). The construction of a national television station with Japanese aid in the mid-1980s saw the eruption of a forest of rooftop television antennae at the end of the decade. That was followed by the bloom of satellite dishes following the introduction of satellite channels by international broadcasting corporations in the 1990s after the 'parking' of satellites over the subcontinent by the space shuttle. The new urban class furthermore used its new-found foreign-aid wealth to speculate in rural properties and extend its control over or evict the rural direct producers, leading to unprecedented devastation of the village communities and environment. This completed the destruction of the viability of small-hold rural life which had started with the introduction of industrial commodities through the rural bazaars in the nineteenth century.

The real problem of exploitation and inequality has not yet been addressed; rather, it has been built upon as one of the premises of everything that is taking place. The consequence has been a burgeoning migration out of the rural communities by the young and capable labour, lured by illusions and delusions of wealth and facilitated by blood-sucking commission agents and labour traffickers of all kinds. This includes an unconscionable flesh trade in more than 200,000 miserable and shattered Nepali women, potentially the vibrant life blood of the country, to brothels in Mumbai, Calcutta and other destinations in Asia, the Middle East and now even Europe and the United States.

As the flow of foreign aid increased to more than seventy per cent of the national budget, the regime had to construct an appearance of accountability and legitimacy for presentation to the foreign officials. These latter emissaries and brokers of commercialization and globalization (euphemistically called 'development experts') have been only too happy to comply in the process of self deception, because they have had their own quotas to fulfil, contracts to distribute, careers to advance, children to educate, and personal investment portfolios to build. Every office from UNICEF to the village panchayat had its charts on the walls graphing out projected versus successfully fulfilled quotas and colourful photos of well-dressed office chiefs standing among shabby peasants. The ubiquitous graphs, made proportionately large to amplify the insignificant absolute difference between before and after, and the busy pictures always looked impressive, but the numbers they presented were hardly so, even if there had been any truth to them, and the peasants in the pictures tended to look a bit incredulous. Most telling was the difference in dress and outlook represented by the pictures. Proposal and report writing were developed to such a fine art that foreign representatives could expect to receive exactly what they wanted to see and hear, even in their own rubric of the moment, be it 'centralization' or 'decentralization', 'infrastructure development' or 'sustainable development', 'international help' or 'self help'—just so the money could keep flowing. Nepali officials were generous with flattery, which, if they had any integrity, lowered the international representatives' guards and made them compliant. The foreigners in their turn generously served alcohol and distributed grants, automobiles, computers, overseas 'training', and organizational posts, which made the officials compliant. And the colonial legacy of the foreign missions and agencies to rotate their staff among different international posts on a regular basis, just as the Nepali government does with its domestic bureaucratic appointments, prevented them from developing any sort of effective knowledge of the country, understanding of the manipulations of the experienced bureaucrats and officials, or sense of the terrible system of exploitation, domestic and international, in which they were participating. The whole process of foreign aid and development became a massive process of mutual deception and generalized waste, especially of human beings and the environment, aimed basically at building a compliant ruling class lacking any sort of personal or official integrity, legitimacy, or accountability to its own population. Its orientation is towards the global corporate and agency bureaucratic class with which it shares values, consumption patterns, association, and commitments; and its loyalties are towards its own class in the individualized sense of its imported ideology.

By the early 1970s these developments were providing the oppressive conditions conducive to the growth of an underground Communist insurgency, inspired by the Naxalite movement of India, in Jhapa, the easternmost Nepali district adjoining Naxalbari, India.[2] Founded by young energetic cadres and splitting off from the moribund Nepali Communist Party in the beginning of the 1970s, it initially called itself the Jhapali Khand (the Jhapa incident) and sought to 'annihilate landlords' in a vanguard-led guerrilla 'people's war'. But with high attrition due to imprisonment and death of its cadres, it changed its name to the Communist Party Marxist-Leninist, taking the Nepali acronym 'Ma-Le', and abandoned the people's war for underground educating and organizing in village, town, school and campus in order to build a mass movement. This marked the first emergence in Nepal of a large, cadre-based and ideologically coherent party with a strong organizational base among the masses. Although the Ma-Le continued to draw its leadership almost completely from the same national propertied classes that had been vying for state power, the party represented itself in terms of a radical programme along the ideological lines of the Chinese cultural revolution, and for the first time Nepali Communist Party members lived and worked among the rural and urban working classes on a relatively large scale (consisting of about 800 cadres just prior to the 1990 Democracy Movement). The Ma-Le launched a student movement in 1979 which was stopped short when the Congress Party leader B.P. Koirala, typically under-estimating the lack of government good faith in hope assuming power without any kind of credible organization, agreed in India to settle the issue with a referendum on the continued existence of the panchayat constitution. The walls of the cities became a riot of hopeful election posters, banners and propaganda. But military and bureaucratic control of the ballot boxes along with violent intimidation of the voters under the then Prime Minister Suraya Bahadur Thapa allowed the pro-panchayat forces to swing the election by adding far more ballots than there were registered voters to quash the referendum—a continuing characteristic of the 'democratic' elections today (ironically, two decades later, except for judicial intervention, Nepal nearly had yet another election under the same prime minister). Another student movement in 1985 which had been fuelled by police firing on unarmed students in the classrooms of Kathmandu's Durbar School was ended by bombings in 1985 that are thought to have been contrived by a palace with its back against the wall to create a 'national emergency' that could be used to disrupt the upsurge of opposition.

Finally in 1989, with the collapse of autocratic governments in many parts of the world and a maturing of their own organization, the Ma-Le leadership thought the time ripe to launch another move-ment, leading them to call the Fourth Convention of the Communist Party Ma-Le. Under extremely tight security—twice the meeting was called off and the venue changed due to slight lapses; and even today the meeting is not common knowledge—ninety delegates from all the regional committees of the country, nearly the entire top-level leadership of the party, met from 9 to 13 Bhadra 2047 BS (August 1989) in the forest of Chitawan near Siraha. As discovery would have meant the obliteration of the party's entire underground political organization, which at that time was very compact and consisted of just 800 cadres, cadre sentries encircled the meeting for five miles. The party leadership decided to call upon all the eleven Communist factions and the Congress party to unite to bring an end to the panchayat system. Seven Communist factions united into a United Left Front (except for the two Masal groups and the Revolutionary Workers Party, which continued to maintain the 'people's war line' and united into their own front to support but not formally participate in the movement). In December 1989 the United Left Front got the Nepali Congress Party to join them according to a minimal, 'one-point' agreement of ending a ban against parties— as the Nepali Congress, like the Indian Congress Party with regard to the British, was interested primarily in inheriting state power and not extending social and economic justice to the toilers.

As the Communist leadership and cadres had all been under warrant and were working underground, the Nepali Congress Party received the role of officially announcing the movement at a crowded and exuberant *samelan* or 'mass gathering' of party functionaries, sympathizers, Indian politicians, various foreign embassy representatives, young people on tree branches and roof-tops, and seriously countenanced, photo snapping undercover police in the Thamel, Kathmandu, compound of the party's Supreme Leader, Ganesh Man Singh, on 18 February 1990. The Nepali Congress party leadership, accompanied by Indian Congress and Janata Dal leaders who had flown in for the occasion, sat above the crowd on a festooned dais, leaving no doubt as to who was to be seen as the active subject of the movement and to receive credit for its eventual success. Thus even though it was the Communists who initiated and organized the movement, it was the Congress leadership who took to calling themselves the 'Fathers of Democracy' and their party the 'Democratic Party'.

Following the *samelan* and the departure of the Indian leaders, the government immediately began posturing threateningly and making arrests. It trucked in crowds of morose villagers to fill large counter-demonstrations in urban centres to lend an illusion of mass support for the government. The panchas emptied the government coffers and national bank reserves at every level of tens of millions of rupees to pay the villagers to make them come to the demonstrations, with the bulk of the money falling into the hands of commission agents, contractors, and the panchas themselves. The villagers complained that they were left stranded without any transportation to return home after the demonstrations and little of the promised money. Squads of police swept through the villages picking up young men and packed them together into police posts where they were forced to sit without food and water or access to toilet facilities, sometimes for days at a time. Policemen beat them with cane sticks, burnt the soles of their feet, and dunked them in water to force them to sign confessions.

Despite this big show of force and masquerade of mass support, once the movement started the government collapsed in a surprisingly short seven weeks. The movement culminated on 6 April 1990 with a massive demonstration initiated by ten thousand Jyapu peasant women armed with scythes and other farm tools streaming out of Patan towards Kathmandu and incredulous police being told by radio to fall back as more and more columns of people joined them. As this great, colorful mass of people orderly serpentined through the streets and back alleys of Kathmandu, their swelling roar of voices was greeted by the swish, swish of sparking, cooling water thrown from upstairs windows filled with exuberant, smiling faces. They turned back at barbed wire barricades set a block from the palace to gather with their red banners and flags in the centre of the city, and then as they surged jubilantly into the two boulevards leading toward the palace, the lines of soldiers blocking the two roads suddenly opened fire with automatic weapons. The crowd dissipated in terror into side streets, leaving the bodies of some fifteen-hundred dead to be carted away by the truckload and buried or incinerated in the forest and erased from official memory.

Three days of tense stand-off followed, between a military nervously standing behind wire barricades on empty streets, shooting dead among others a mother hurrying a sick child to the hospital and a woman fetching water, and a euphoric urban population waiting it out in their houses. The above-ground representatives of the Left Front–Nepali Congress alliance, and thus not the underground Ma-Le leadership—the real initiators and organizers of the movement—eventually signed a compromise with the king on 9 April. Previously worked out by the Nepali Congress leadership and the king, it changed nothing beyond a suspension of the article in the constitution banning parties. A multi-party interim government was formed consisting of two representatives from each of the groups involved in the movement (Nepali Congress, Left Front, and Palace) plus two independents (one with

Left orientation, the other with a Congress one). As the palace and Nepali Congress interests now converged, being that the Nepali Congress had finally gotten access to state power but neither king nor Congress wanting to democratically turn initiative and control over to the rural masses, the Left Front found itself in a distinct minority and thus its demands for the constitutional assembly originally promised in 1951 were avoided. In compensation and to belie the reality, the name of the movement was changed to the *Jaana Andalan* 'People's Movement'. A drafting committee framed a new multi-party constitution based on a Westminster-type parliamentary model. Upon being confronted by mass demonstrations after attempting to undermine the process by introducing his own constitution and after his final review and changes, the king promulgated the constitution on 9 November 1990. For this first election the Nepali Congress inherited the political and bureaucratic machinery which had been developed over the past three decades (by the next election it had reconsolidated into its own political party) and won a 110 seat majority in the 205 seat lower house in the elections of May 1991.

The parliament subsequently drew up the local law and passed it in May 1992, giving few significant new powers to local bodies, despite prominently framed slogans of 'autonomy' and 'participation'.[3] The Nepali Congress won the local elections that summer, as one Congress member of parliament gleefully told me, by putting up as its candidates individuals recruited from the old regime, the 'Chait Congress' (the Panchas who had come over to the Nepali Congress following the victory of the movement in the Nepali month of Chait), who used the patronage relations they had built up in the countryside over the past thirty years to win a majority of the local councils. A split within the ruling party in the face of the threat of an inquiry into the prime minister Girija Koirala's role in the allocation of the European dealership for the national airline to his German son-in-law and his forcing the decision of a supposedly independent committee in its choice of the company for renting an additional plane for the fleet, his extra-constitutional give-away of Nepali land to India at the Tanakpur dam, and his generally imperious control of his own party machinery led to the rebellion of thirty-seven of his own party's members of parliament and failure to win a vote of support for his speech opening the seventh session of parliament. To prevent the dissolution of his ministry in a no-confidence vote, Prime Minister Girija Koirala pre-emptively dissolved the parliament and called new elections in the spring of 1994. He had expected to reassume the prime ministership with a parliament dominated by his personal supporters, but much to his surprise the Communist Party (UML) won eighty-eight seats due to the bitter divisions within his own party and formed a minority government under Man Mohan Adhikari, the figurehead leader of the Left Front and now of the UML.[4]

Despite a promise by the UML to rule its entire five years ('a hundred years' in the words of MP Rajendra Shrestha), Adhikari himself dissolved parliament under the threat of a no-confidence motion in June 1995 and called new elections for 23 November. The leadership of the opposition Nepali Congress, Rastraya Prajatantra (the reconstituted Panchas) and Sabhavana (Hindu nationalist) parties challenged this dissolution of parliament in the Supreme Court, which on 29 August reversed the prime minister's act in what many thought to be a decision tainted by a legislative character and ill-considered partisan comments of the chief justice, who compared Nepal's constitutional situation to that of the Weimar constitution prior to the ascension of the Nazis to power in Germany. This opinion meant to imply an analogy between the German Nazi Party and Nepal's Communists, despite the former's close links with German industrialists and military and strongly anti-Communist suppression of organized labour, and despite Hitler's rise to power through concession of the chancellorship to him in total contradiction to the former chancellor's election promises, and not by elections or the constitution. The Nepali parliament reconvened on 5 September and returned a vote of no confidence to Adhikari's ministry on 9 September, bringing Sher Bahadur Deuba, the Home Minister in the previous Nepali Congress government and a good personal friend of the US ambassador under the Reagan administration (subsequently on the board of directors of the Bank of America, the bastion of US post–world war imperialist expansion) back as prime minister over the first of a series of coalition governments. That his twenty-two member ministry incorporated no one from the Nepali Congress dissident group which had helped tumble the Girija Koirala ministry from power a year and a half before indicated a lack of consensus from the start.

Continued divisions within the Nepali Congress, the government's minority status in the parliament, and corruption and mounting costs incurred by this large ministry of opportunity increasingly weakened Prime Minister Deuba's government. Deuba added more and more parliamentarians to his cabinet from among both his own party and the royalist RPP so as to head off a vote of no confidence. Finally bloated to 57 ministers, assistant ministers and deputy ministers, many without portfolios (though all had automobiles), the government became butt of snide jokes and irreverent newspaper columns.[5] It came under close threat of collapse when many of the RPP ministers threatened to join the opposition in a vote of no confidence, but survived when they did not show up to vote. However, when Deuba took back these same ministers into his cabinet, the members of his own party revolted against him with a no-confidence motion on 6 March 1997.

A coalition of the CP-UML and ten dissident members of the RPP then took over the ministry. Although the CP-UML was the largest party in parliament, it allowed the leader of the RPP dissidents, Lokendra Bahadur Chand, to become prime minister in order to gain a majority in parliament through his and his break-away RPP parliamentarians' support. The UML's general secretary, Madhav Nepal, was deputy prime minister and foreign secretary, and Bam Dev Gautam, the head of the UML's minority faction was given the important post of Home Minister. Ironically, though Chand was the last of the pancha prime ministers and the one who had sat over the 6 April 1990 massacre at the end of the Democracy Movement, he was now back as prime minister under a new democratic constitution which had supposedly done away with the Panchayat system that he had represented. Many condemned Madhav Nepal for having sold out the party's principles to get into power, but through the party's control over the Home Ministry portfolio during the local elections, the UML was able to keep the Congress-RPP alliance from dominating the polling booths as they had done in the first local government elections five years before (under the Congress banner), allowing the UML to win control over a majority of the local governments. Whether this counter-balances the corruption that the UML became party to by joining the government with the RPP is another question.

This problematic Communist alliance with the old regime followed from the UML leadership's choice of the parliamentary road, which the previous late UML general secretary Madan Bhandari called *bahudaliya jaanabad* 'Multi-party People's

Democracy'. He proposed this theory of obtaining power through parliament as means to socialism as a radically new alternative to the old Communist strategy of armed revolution, but the parliamentary approach has appeared in countless other countries where it always resulted in the co-optation of the Communist leadership, supposedly the vanguard of the working class, by ruling forces and a general discrediting of the Communist movement. The parliament can be used imaginatively without subordinating the party to parliamentarianism, but in Nepal the UML leadership turned the entire party machinery over to parliamentary politics and ended up appropriating it for nominating themselves to parliamentary seats. If they had had any inclination towards the 'Communism' they profess, which, by definition, should be democracy par excellence, they needed to build organizations within their constituencies which could nominate their own parliamentary representatives and exert control, through recall, over these representatives. The party should have facilitated this process, not replaced it. If not this, at least they needed to place carefully groomed lower-level cadres in parliament, obedient only to the party and thereby keeping the Communist party from being reduced to parliament's own level in what Rosa Luxemburg called its 'hen house' squabbles and its corrupting influence, while working class power in society meanwhile is being exercised and concentrated through other venues, mechanisms, and institutions—as the commercial and financial interest have long been doing.

The UML-RPP coalition predictably fell to a no confidence vote in its turn and was replaced by a ministry made up from a coalition of Nepali Congress, RPP and Sabhavana parties, this time under the prime ministership of the leader of the other faction of the RPP, Surya Bahadur Thapa. Like Chand, Thapa had also been prime minister during the panchayat period, at which time he presided over the 1980 referendum for choosing between a reformed Panchayat and multi-party constitution. He is remembered for the rigging and widespread intimidatory violence and killings that occurred in that polling.

In February 1998, Prime Minister Thapa recommend to the king to disband parliament in the face of a yet another no confidence motion. Opposition legislators responded by filing their own petition to convene a special session of parliament. In the previous two instances, when prime ministers Koirala and Adhikari recommended dissolution of parliament, the king simply acted upon the prime minister's recommendation, leading to high-profile cases in the supreme court which upheld and overturned his action respectively. This time the king delayed his decision until he had consulted with the supreme court justices, who advised him to ignore the prime minister's recommendation and reconvene the parliament instead. The prime minister's supporters and the pro-government newspapers reacted with outrage at what they saw as the king's active interference, whereas the opposition and its supporters applauded the action. As it turned out, the prime minister avoided being deposed by three votes, as potentially dissident Nepali Congress MPs were brought over on the promise that Thapa would transfer the prime ministership to Girija Koirala once he had survived the no confidence motion. The two Nepal Farm Labour Party MPs, led by their general secretary, Narayan Man Bijukchhe (Comrade Rohit), also sided with the Thapa government, with Bijukchhe expecting to get a ministry out of it when Koirala comes to power. Thapa resisted resigning the post, at first saying that he no longer saw need for interim elections or resignation, as he had showed a parliamentary majority. But dissidence among the Nepali Congress MPs grew increasingly strident as he held out from turning over the prime ministership to Koirala as promised. Bijukchhe also threatened to withhold his support of the Thapa ministry in a future no confidence vote. Thapa finally resigned on 10 April 1998, saying he was doing so according to the agreement the RPP had with the Nepali Congress. Although the Nepali Congress could not find a suitable partner, the UML promised to give its support to a minority government under the Nepali Congress.

The reason for the supreme court's involvement in nearly every vote of no confidence is that the constitution contains two conflicting Articles 53 (3) and (4). 'Of the provisions, Art 53 (3) provides for summoning of a special session of the House, as demanded by the opposition, while Art 53 (4) provides for dissolution of the House as asked by the Prime Minister.'[6] Following the ratification of the constitution in June 1991 all prime ministers except Deuba have preemptively dissolved parliament and called new elections when threatened with a vote of no confidence. As the king then asks the prime minister to remain in office until a new government is elected, calling new elections favorably positions the standing prime minister and his followers to shape the outcome of the elections. This is because electoral success depends largely upon controlling the election machinery and the Home Ministry, which enforces the election laws and maintains peace during the elections. The one time that the supreme court allowed the strategy of dissolving parliament to actually be carried through was under Girija Koirala in 1992. Koirala had expected that his position as interim minister would allow his party to regain a parliamentary majority in which dissidents from within his own party would be removed and his own men able dominate. The strategy backfired because Koirala had so badly alienated sections of his own Congress party, a dissident group of thirty-six MPs (referred to as the 'Group of Thirty-Six'), that he could not garner support from his party for his candidates, allowing the UML to capture 88 seats in parliament, more than any other party though not the absolute majority of 103. Subsequently, starting with its intervention in the UML's Adhikari's attempt to dissolve parliament, the supreme court has more and more restricted the prime minister's ability to preemptively disband parliament under the threat of a no confidence motion.

As related above, although the UML has been the largest party in parliament, its plurality was insufficient for it to hold power for long. Furthermore, it has experienced in-fighting of its own ever since it emerged from underground following the democracy movement. Initially it experienced a split between its General Secretary and the leader of its majority faction in its central committee, Madhan Bhandari, and C.P. Maineli as the leader of its minority faction. Following the deaths of Bhandari and Ashrit in 1993 in a controversial automobile accident at Dhasdunga, on the Narayani River between Muglin and Narayanghat, the split has continued between Bhandari's successor, Madhav Nepal, and Bom Dev Gautam, the Home Minister in the recent UML-RPP government.

Initially this split of the party's central committee between a majority faction under first Bhandari and then Nepal and a minority faction under Mainali and Gautam has formed into a struggle over the ideological orientation of the party between a 'Multi-party People's Democracy' versus 'New Democracy' respective. Ideologically, this struggle has seemed to be over the question of whether the party should follow a parliamentary road in which power would be captured through parliamentary elections, allowing Communism to then be legislated, or a cadre-based orientation in which people elect representatives through their own local organizations (according to Chairman Mao's writings on New Democracy, although what actually is meant by these terms in Nepal is not clearly said). Bhandari's position won out due in part to the Bhandari's own charisma and ability to communicate with the masses. His followers' used their majority position to capture control of the politburo and dominate the party bureaucracy while undermining the autonomy and initiative of the cadre base. According to the party constitution, the politburo is an executive body for implementing policy and decisions determined in the larger central committee. This use of the politburo by one section of the party to force its position on the central committee led to growing dissatisfaction among the central committee members, and in 1996 the politburo was turned into a 'Standing Committee', supposedly with restricted powers.

In the Sixth National Congress of the CPN (UML) in January 1998, this struggle finally came to a head with the minority Gautam faction demanding that it receive the same sixteen seats it previously held in the central committee and that the party declare the United States to be an 'imperialist power' and India a 'regional hegemonist power'. When the majority only offered nine seats and made no such statement, the minority refused to join the central committee at all. Appraising his majority's total domination of the power following the congress, Nepal claimed that the divisions within the party were solved. However, on 6 February, within a half hour of Nepal taking action to expel Gautam and his supporters from the party, and thereby from parliament, Gautam and 45 other UML members of parliament registered a new party, the Communist Party of Nepal (Marxist Leninist). Since then large portions of the UML and its organizations have been peeling away into the new party, possibly as a sign of dissatisfaction against the centralizing tendencies of Nepal and his predecessor, Bhandari. It may also be significant that most of the Newar and non-high caste MPs have followed along with Gautam.

The practical significance of the split between Multi-party People's Democracy and New Democracy is poorly enunciated. The former definitely seems to be the usual attempt of leadership attempting to concentrate power in the Communist party bureaucracy by shifting initiative from the cadres and constituencies to parliamentary elections. Communism is held out as something that will follow from parliamentary victory (just as previously it was to follow from a military one), but exactly how this will come about has neither been thought out nor prepared for, and probably its practitioners do not believe in its imminence any more than most other priests believe in the immediacy of a religious salvation. However, New Democracy, which has received little more elaboration, seems to be a slogan for intra-party power struggles. Nobody that I have talked to seems to understand Mao's theory of it, which had to do with shifting power to autonomous workers' organizations, and even for Mao practice diverged radically from theory. The ML leadership is calling for simple living and high ideals but has offered no drastically altered strategy. Few seem to understand that Communism, and the socioeconomic democracy it implies, will not come simply by capturing state power. It must receive form in the process of the struggle itself. Anything else is millenarianism and usually carries a ruling class, not revolutionary, agenda along with it.

The practical significance for parliamentary politics is that this split put the Nepali Congress into power as a minority government. The UML's support for the Nepali Congress arose from the desire to keep the break-way ML from joining in a coalition government with the Nepali Congress. Evidently the ML's split from the UML is introducing a new factor into the political equation, as the choice no longer is simply between a coalition either of the Nepali Congress or the Communists with the RPP. The parliamentary road does not present itself as the viable option to the Communists that it seemed to be when the CP-UML formed one large block. If the two parties go at each other over gaining seats in parliament, they will gradually wear themselves down in a war of attrition and become irrelevant to the Nepal political scene. The one positive possibility is that the two parties might focus on divergent strategies which in the long-run could complement each other—e.g. one continuing to involve in parliamentary politics, the other in grass roots organizing, or developing an urban insurrection, or taking some other initiative. This would be likely if the parties have fissured along the lines of substantial social groups or class orientations which might have had a contradictory co-existence within the party. This could lead to two very different sets of interests in the two daughter parties according to the social position and capabilities of their respective constituencies. But if the split is just a leadership struggle for control of the party machinery and control over the nomination of the parliamentary candidates, as it seems to be, then the possibility of a fresh strategy coming out of the split would be unlikely. In fact, what seems to be happening is that the two factions' cadres are engaging in violence against each other and their respective leadership. As a consequence I am told that the situation is becoming much more dangerous for the rural and working class populations. My feeling is that the problem results from the manner that it is ruling elites who make up the leadership even in the Communist party, and it is easy for these people to confuse class struggle with power struggle.

Another quite different Communist initiative has also come up. During Sher Bahadur Deuba's Congress-RPP ministry's tenure on 12 February 1996 the Nepali Communist Party (NCP) Maoist launched its People's War to 'smash the state' and establish a workers' paradise. Armed young people descended upon police posts and the houses of local party functionaries, government representatives and landowners. Although the Home Ministry and its police launched severe counter measures, the movement's momentum has continued to grow since then. Prime Minister Deuba's Congress-RPP coalition reacted with heavy police action but failed to repress the insurgency. The opposition parties in the parliament and Chand-led minority group within the RPP presented this failure as one reason for its no-confidence vote against the government, but they in turn also failed to stop it despite continued police action.

The problem is that this self-described People's War feeds on real, pervasive dissatisfaction and suffering in the countryside and, especially among the youth, frustration and anger. The recent democratic constitutional transformation has aggravated and deepened the exploitation and inequality always at the basis of the state. Consequently, repression of the Maoists, whomever or whatever they are, must take the form of a war against the countryside which by necessity would escalate to the scale of Suharto's massacre of one-half to a million of Indonesia's populace in 1964. Although many of Nepal's leaders might have it in them to do this, as evidenced by the willingness of various ministries to shoot on their citizens, the conditions are not ready for such a 'solution'. Nepal is not yet so fully dominated by multinational corporations and plantation owners as Indonesia at that time; wealth, power and property are not as concentrated; and the effective ruling class is much more fragmented. No government could dare mount a full-scale war and survive until the position of a wide array of the ruling class becomes desperate. Urban elites and opposition parliamentarians instead constantly call for a 'political solution', but it is difficult to tell what is meant by such a call. It seems to be aimed more at bringing into question the ability of whomever is in government to govern than any sort of desire for effective political action. Such action after all would require getting to the heart of the problem, which is to transform the unequal and unjust order in the countryside. This would mean overthrowing the general regime of exploitation by the landlord and business classes and by the city over the countryside which makes up the political equation of the state, something that would undermine the socio-economic position of just the groups making the call for a political solution.

The drastic transformation that would be required of a real political solution of course is what the Maoists say they are aiming for, and whether such a vanguardist party eventually effects it or other kinds of initiatives emerge, such a social transformation is going to be extremely threatening not just to the leadership of all the current parties, but to rural landlords and moneylenders, town and urban businessmen, multinational corporations, privileged intellectuals, bureaucrats, and all the others whom the journalist Sainath calls the 'beautiful people'. Thus, in most cases, calls for a 'political solution' cannot be taken seriously and must be analysed in terms of hiding other agendas. In fact, at the time of this writing in 1998, the parliament is considering Draconian anti-terrorist legislation. It was unable to muster the necessary political support under Surya Bahadur Thapa's weak ministry, though it might pass under the historically hard-line Girija Koirala, who announced a 'priority (to) end Maoist insurgency' in his swearing in as prime minister on 15 April.

Despite the great promises that have been held out for multi-party democracy for the last thirty years since the king's dissolution of parliament in 1961, multi-party democracy has not allowed the common people to actually propose their own representatives or start to govern themselves. Indeed, most of the abuses of the Panchayat Regime continue today, and in many ways conditions are worsening. This has led many of the urban classes and other 'beautiful people' to look back nostalgically to that time and even consider absolutism as a viable alternative. The groups and interests which had been dominant in that time play on this nostalgia as a means to reassert their authority and suppress challenges to their power and position, and foreign corporations such as international banks and large hydroelectric contractors, along with their government embassies, are amenable to absolutism as a means to suppress all forms of dissent and opposition against their incursion— in the name of suppressing anti-market anarchy, of course. The villagers—90 per cent of the population—are ambivalent because they have seen no change except that life continues to grow precipitously more difficult: agricultural development schemes leave them more in debt than ever, urban speculators take their lands, the commons continue to be encroached upon, their daughters are abducted to foreign brothels, and the list goes on. The individuals who mobilize them with their slogans and promises disappear when they get into parliament or when the crisis of the moment passes.

In the manner pointed out by Max Weber nearly a century ago, the selection of candidates in elections remains under the control of party bosses and bureaucrats, so elections just mean voting between different 'chosen rulers' selected by the people controlling the various parties. As mentioned above, the leadership of the parties consists almost entirely of the members of the propertied classes, for the most part high castes, and the local landlords and small businessmen dominate among the local cadres in the villages for all the parties—Right, Left and Far Left—as they are the one's able to educate their children, engage in organizing, and participate in the dominant discourse. Many villagers are more capable due to their direct engagement in productive activities and involvement in rural communities, but the structures of legitimation such as caste, family connections, educational certification and mastery of Marxist texts—however facile—contribute to disqualifying farmers, women, Dalits and other labouring class individuals. Except for the Communist parties, to the extent that their officers and committees are elected (although still dominated over the years by the same leadership), there is no internal democracy within the parties and no mechanism among *any* of the parties to enable constituencies to assert themselves against the party machinery or make the elected representatives accountable to these constituencies. The selection of candidates generally is a product of power struggles among the elite within the parties.

Even in the unlikely event of the toiling peoples receiving candidates who actually represent their interests, the party in power and its domestic and international sponsors can determine the outcome of the elections to a large extent, since the party in power controls the bureaucrats who register the voters and administer the elections, directs the police and military charged with protecting the ballot boxes, and holds sway over the election commission and the media. A party's ability to determine the outcome of an election depends heavily upon the strength of its party organization in the various constituencies, enabling it to capture ballot boxes or prevent others from doing so and to intimidate potentially hostile constituencies, particularly the poor—a precedent in all cases set by the panchayat elections and the more experienced democracy to the south of the border.

This 'booth capturing' and intimidation continues to be undertaken to the largest extent by the same groups which dominated the Panchayat Regime prior to the democracy movement, since, as Panchas, their control over the government machinery and foreign aid spigot enabled them to build a strong patronage-based organization in constituencies all over the country during the course of the panchayat system's thirty years of existence. In the districts along the southern border with India, large numbers of Indians are systematically trucked in, some as far as the Kathmandu valley, to vote or forcibly capture the ballot boxes and bring Bihar democracy to Nepal. These practices generally favour the Nepali Congress party due to its strong ties and shared agenda with the powerful Indian Congress Party and the strongly shared common interests of landlords, bazaar merchants and contractors on either side of the border.

Routine irregularities aside, it is difficult for the toilers to formulate their shared interests and exert themselves collectively, since they generally lack strong organization in their villages and they are poorly 'schooled', as opposed to the strong organization among the propertied classes and their consciousness of a shared, common interest. The toilers are swayed and coerced to-and-fro by slogans, promises, propaganda and pandering of the different parties. The Left has been able to mobilize these constituencies with slogans, but slogans work on people's emotions and prejudices rather than by building understanding. They thus provide a poor basis for organization over the long term, as they lend no sense of the extent of the struggle that people are involved in, in reference either to time or space, nor do they provide a sense of commonality of interests with others in the same situation as themselves. Confronted with adversity, people mobilized through the use of one set of slogans yesterday are just as apt to be easily manipulated by the opposite one tomorrow, since their understanding arises only in reference to their immediate perception of their situation, while a larger, more comprehensive understanding remains confused, and intentionally so.

Enter into this the cacophonous but alluring and purposeful facade of glitter and non-stop music of M-, Zee-, Star and all the other TV's which have fallen like manna from the corporate-owned satellite heaven into the popular conscious to remake and mould a mass of individual unconscious in millions of households of entranced, grateful viewers. Viewers furthermore who are consumers, reproducing through their own labour the means of this one-way communication in every household with the purchase of individually 'owned' television sets; sets which in turn actually own the purchaser by remaking them into universal consumers. Gone is the almost constant discussion, the attention given to children that I observed up until the mid-eighties, and in its place the entrancing clichés hiding the reality that people are less and less setting their agenda, determining the issues, or acting according to local needs and requirements.

NOTES

1 The divergence of rhetoric from the effect of law is elaborated in 'The Local Government Law and Participatory Democracy' (chapter 8, this volume).

2 Most of the material on the Communist party and the associated movements is drawn from Pande and Mikesell n.d., and based on Surendra Pande's notes and interviews.

3 See chapter 8, this volume.

4 There was an interesting rumor that the US embassy had sanctioned the Nepali Congress allowing the Communists to form a minority government on the advice that the UML, which had been growing increasingly popular in the opposition, would quickly discredit itself allowing the Congress Party to recapture its majority in another election a year later. Although the role attributed to the US embassy is probably apocryphal, it did anticipate the fate of the Communists.

5 The following satirical piece entitled 'My Friend, the Minister of Street Dogs' (Mikesell 1996) was my contribution.

'It is a *consensus* ministry, don't you understand?' said my friend who had just become the 103rd minister. Brushing away vermilion and flowers from his forehead, he explained, 'It is a new milestone in democracy in the country . . . in the world even! Think of it, parliament becomes unnecessary.'

Astounded, I said, 'But isn't that undemocratic? And you being a democrat.'

'Oh pooh! How can something that keeps us democrats in power be undemocratic?'

'That is a way of putting it. I had not thought of it that way.'

'Think of all the undemocratic controversy that will be saved: no useless arguing over bills, no votes of no confidence. A real *democrats'*democracy!'

He paused to accept another *malla* [garland] of flowers around his neck from the big line of relatives and friends, many of whom I'd never seen before, coming to congratulate him for his promotion.

'But it is a really strange portfolio they have given you. Don't you think that being the Minister of Street Dogs is kind of scratching the bottom of the barrel? Really, my friend, I never thought that you would stoop so low.'

Bowing his head for another *malla*, he said, 'But street dogs are one of the major problems of the country. Didn't you read yesterday's paper? Some cities of the Terai have over 30,000 dogs. Their barking all night long keeping people up really lowers the country's productivity. Furthermore, it disturbs democrats.'

'They are probably just barking to get into the House because they've been locked out.'

'Into the house, indeed! To *disturb* the house. They must be caught, repressed, shot, if they don't quit their yapping.'

'Don't get carried away, you aren't the Home Minister, after all. . . . Well, anyway, I guess you should be satisfied that you got *some* portfolio. There are some ministers who have none at all, I hear.'

'Not only a portfolio,' he exclaimed, proudly, 'I'll get my own automobile and flag. Imagine me driving around with a flag!'

'The way you drive, I hope you don't hit something more than dogs.'

'Don't worry, I have a driver too, ha, ha!' he chortled. 'You can't say I'm a nobody anymore.'

'And does the Honorable Minister of Street Dogs require the army to guard his house?' I asked, noting the soldiers setting up the usual command post in the lawn below.

'Why of course! It is one of the most dangerous ministries. Did you see how angry people get when our dog catchers try to catch the street dogs? And think of all those prowling beasts waiting to attack me.'

'After your position, no doubt', I observed. [Mikesell 1996]

6   *The Kathmandu Post*, 13 January 1998.

CHAPTER 6

Health Workers and the Movement

DOCTORS AS INTELLECTUALS

INTELLECTUALS have played key roles in the revolutionary movements of the last two centuries, but excluding lawyers, it is unusual that any single professional group has taken such a central and powerful role as the doctors in the recent movement in Nepal. Usually, it is those intellectuals who deal with the ends and purposes of society who are at the forefront of revolution and upheaval, such as poets, teachers and social philosophers, and not the more technical intellectuals who are concerned with the means by which these ends will be obtained. No one is surprised when a teacher is sent to jail. Teachers are poorly paid, have low status, and are trying to introduce new ideas into a society riddled by entrenched private interests. Doctors on the other hand, enjoy high status and prestige. They can earn extra money in their private practice, and their concern is the human body. Why then should the doctors of Nepal also treat the body politic? And why were the rulers powerless to contravene the doctor's prescription? Their condemnations, arrests and beatings of doctors and other health professionals were like the festering of a long submerged infection which helps it to heal; they strengthened the doctors' role in the movement and weakened the position of their detractors.

Doctors were placed in a potentially revolutionary position by the phenomenon that is called development. Development, in the limited sense that it is being used, meant the introduction of capital, in other words accumulated human labour in the form of technology, to make less labour more productive and more labour redundant. Introduction of this new technology and relations required the body of complex, specialized knowledge that had arisen in accompaniment with its development. The old forms of accumulated technical wisdom of farmers and craftsmen, however appropriate they might be, were no longer seen as sufficient to produce crops and manufactures, and the old knowledge of priests and shamans could no longer alone provide a purpose for a society undergoing vast changes. A new specialized, secular intelligentsia class was created in order to direct and facilitate the introduction of entirely new forms of relations and technology. The self conscious purpose of this intelligentsia was to implement these changes in society, without which they could no more exist as intellectuals than a farmer could be a farmer without crops to harvest.

This 'development' was being mediated by the monopolistic control of a ruling class represented in the Panchayat system, whose interest in the transformation of society was only incidental to preserving and extending their position of privilege and wealth. Thus the purpose of the classes that controlled development both went against the people whose lives development purported to be changing and controverted the purpose and role of the intelligentsia. In order to make this bitter pill more palatable to the population at large, it was wrapped in the sugar coated promises of future prosperity, higher levels of consumption, more leisure, and better health. Albeit it was a very thin sugar coating of merely the provision of 'minimum needs' by the end of the millennium, while the real fruits of development fell into the hands of a few in the form of royal gratuities, fraud, partially fulfilled contracts, graft, bribery, monopolistic profits and other forms of veiled and unveiled theft.

The regime gave medicine a showcase position of demonstrating its commitment to the development of the well-being of the people. The queen, the health minister, and the king's aunt frequently starred in the role of the benefactors and source of all new medical benefits being given to the people (large gratuities for their performance aside), receiving international acclaim in the process. Medical professionals had to work within diverted budgets and under people totally unconcerned with the needs and goals of medicine. They found that the same regime that used medicine to legitimize itself was making a mockery of their efforts to practice as professionals.

While this was much the same problem faced by most of the

intelligentsia according to their own professions, more than any other group of intellectuals the medical professionals had to rectify the effects of the economic violence of the regime. They had to heal in the body the effect of the injustice and exploitation in society: inadequate nutrition, contaminated water supplies, poor sanitation, overwork, ignorance, smoky hearths and inadequate ventilation. Inadequate facilities and supplies forced a negligence onto the health professionals which was not their own doing. The daily experience of watching children die from simple diseases due to poverty and inadequate medical supplies, of sharing the bereavement of their families, produced a much more intense effect on their consciousness than on other professionals. What for engineers or economists are merely logistical problems, such as how to uproot communities to make way for roads or dams, are for a doctor an intensely personal one.

The physicians in Nepal are also strongly influenced by a changing self-consciousness of the medical profession globally, that bodily and mental health are rooted in the socio-political and environmental health of the world. Medical professionals have been influenced by books such as Ivan Illich's *Limits to Medicine, Medical Nemesis: the Expropriation of Health,* in the manner that teachers were influenced by the same author's *Deschooling Society* and Paulo Freire's *The Pedagogy of the Oppressed.*

They have become aware of the manner that medicine has fallen under the control of governments and large corporations to such an extent that the unreflective practice of medicine may itself contribute to the social causes of ill health. A consensus is growing that doctors cannot successfully treat people if they leave the society undiagnosed and untreated. This has been reflected in the growth of such organizations as Physicians for Social Responsibility and within Nepal, the Forum for Protection of Human Rights.

Thus the doctors realized that their technical knowledge and practice as physicians is inseparable from a practical concern for the ends and purposes of society. This experience and consciousness of the health professionals meant that the regime had set up as the basis of its legitimacy a profession which, by the nature of its job, was forced to stand in direct opposition to it. Professionals can no longer simply cure people, educate children, or build dams without asking the question, 'for what purpose?' 'what effect will it have?' and 'whose interest am I serving?'

DOCTORS AND THE MOVEMENT

From the moment that the first person was injured, the movement threw the doctors directly into the struggle. Whereas the doctors' class and professional position attached latent political implications to the medical profession even in times of relative peace, during the movement a straightforward attempt to offer treatment to victims became overtly political. Anticipating this, Professor Mathura Shrestha, chair of the Department of Community Medicine in the Institution of Medicine, made the following order to emergency rooms from his hideout in central Kathmandu on the morning of 18 February, the first day of the movement: 'Treat all patients according to medical ethics. Treat all the injured, both civilians and police, in order of the seriousness of their injuries. Do not let the police force you to treat their people first.'

While this straightforward question of priority of treatment does not seem to have arisen, the attempts by the regime to suppress the movement forced much more serious problems onto the medical professionals which necessitated more militant responses. If they had not responded, in addition to the moral questions involved, they could have been accused of suppressing evidence and aiding and abetting crimes. In the manner that some of the doctors and health care professionals had already become activists in the less obvious political implications described above, the overt and violent suppression of the movement taken by the regime forced the entire profession to come out as activists. This eventually included even some of the more conservative doctors.

Some questions had to do with the prerogative and duty of doctors to treat patients. The police were ordered to withhold treatment of civilian injuries, often resulting in death. Many civilian patients were taken to police or military hospitals to insure their eventual arrest, even when they could not get sufficient care at these hospitals. The bodies of the dead were confiscated or withheld from the hospitals, families or both. The police interfered or prevented ambulances from reaching the wounded, and sometimes verbally or physically abused ambulance crew members.

Other questions did not have to do so much with treatment, but in the course of treatment health professionals could not help but become witnesses of activities of criminal character. They treated numerous cases of tortured people. They not only were treating or doing autopsies on unarmed civilians suffering bullet wounds, they discovered that the bullets were soft-tipped ones that had been outlawed in international conventions.

One consequence is that the hospital emergency rooms became communication and information centres. They not only were sending out and passing on information about atrocities of the government to other doctors, intellectuals and the population at large within Nepal, but they were passing information to the international press. Since the entire existence of the regime was being sustained and perpetuated by foreign aid, this had grave consequences. Unlike the Chinese government, the regime could not go and shoot its population and then thumb its nose at the world.

The medical professionals responded with 'black day' demonstrations in which they wore black arm bands, engaged in strikes in all but emergency care, and issued statements condemning not only the activities of the regime, but its entire existence. During the first 'black day' demonstration, on 23 February at the government-run Teaching Hospital, although the police were unable to interfere in the strike due to the focus of the press, they sent eight policemen to arrest the person they identified as the instigator, Professor Mathura Shrestha, from his house at 10:30 P.M. The combination of a subsequent strike by the doctors and international condemnation from all over the world, including some 5,000 faxes of protest, forced the regime to release him twenty-four hours later.

Following the next 'black day' demonstration at the Teaching and Bir hospitals on 25 February, the government issued reprimands to all participants, requesting explanation of their participation in the demonstration. The health care professionals not only refused to receive the letters, a statement issued by the Nepal Medical Association forced the government to retract them.

Later, when Dr. Mathura Shrestha was again arrested when he lectured to a meeting sponsored by the Tribhuvan University Teachers' Association, the threat of a doctors' strike won his release.

The violently repressed demonstrations of the health and other professionals against the police attack on the Amrit Science College and Shanti Bidhya Griha in Thamel in which the police threw two students from the roof of the hostel started a series of increasingly large demonstrations which brought down the government eleven days later. During the week, the Teaching Hospital was surrounded by the police much of the time to capture wounded and to confiscate bodies. A strike by all the hospitals from 31 March expanded into a nationwide hospital strike, and the Nepal Medical Association met and issued a statement condemning the government.

The regime was immobilized in the face of the health professionals' actions. It had bound its legitimacy and prestige to the provision of health care to the people. When the health professionals found that the regime's interests and actions contradicted their own roles, to say nothing of their moral integrity, they refused anymore to cooperate with the government. The government responded by attacking and arresting the health professionals and other intellectuals. But this only served to show that their real interest was in the preservation of their power and not in health care or other kinds of development, on which they had constantly been harping. All that was anymore associated with the regime were the coercive and oppressive aspects of government, not the service ones. Consequently, they knocked out the last tenuous pretensions of legitimacy.

Although for similar reasons, attacks on students and intellectuals proved the illegitimacy of the government, its attacks on the health professions most directly affected the people in the country. Medical treatment is a matter of life and death for the people, and suspension of it affects all people immediately in need, regardless of class. Furthermore, people identified with the medical workers and not with the government.

A NOTE IN RETROSPECT

Five years later the glowing affirmation of the role of the health professionals expressed in this article seems a bit naíve. Having done some research on the system of health delivery to poor people, I found that their sensitivity and commitment to the poor leaves much to be desired. The medical professionals' were certainly involved because they were thrown into the movement and forced to confront the oppressive forces of the government by its own doing. However, I would argue that they are not interested in radical change so much as acceptable working conditions, control over their working place, and no interference from the government or police in their work. Many doctors are highly motivated, but far greater numbers are more interested in advancing their class position and providing service to the powerful pharmaceutical industry which such advancement involves. Few are interested in serving the poor or changing the society which exists to impoverish its population and destroy its social and natural environments.

NOTE

This piece was originally published as 'First Aid for the Nation: Health Professionals and the Movement', in *Media Nepal*, Vol. 5, No. 3, 1990, pp. 42–4.

CHAPTER 7

The Interim Constitution and Transition to Democracy in Nepal

> Most revolutions are precipitated . . . by the excesses of the ruler, and by the attempts at strength and firmness beyond the compass of the law; and most revolutions swing by a kind of necessity towards an extremer conclusion than is warranted by the original quarrel.
>
> —H.G. Wells (1951:807)

THE SIGNIFICANT feature about the interim constitution and the constitutional assembly in Nepal is that neither came into existence. The decision not to promulgate an interim constitution or form a constitutional assembly led to tensions, though no actual rift, between the coalition of opposition parties which had come together in the People's Movement (18 February to 9 April 1990). Members of the various Communist party factions, from both the Left Front,[1] which is in alliance with the Nepali Congress Party and sits in the interim government, and from the opposition United National People's Front,[2] demanded the promulgation of an interim constitution and the formation of a constituent assembly. The main leaders of the Nepali Congress Party had opposed both demands, against the opposition of not only the two Communist groups but many young members within the Congress Party. In the end, the position of the older leaders of the Congress Party superseded that of the others. Consequently, the constitution was written by a constitution drafting committee. Then it passed through revisions, first by the Prime Minister and later the Council of Ministers. Some lawyers felt that with succeeding revisions the original draft constitution became worse, since the ministers failed to understand the significance of aspects of the first draft. In some aspects, such as the citizenship status of women, the draft constitution is actually more backward than the Panchayat constitution, since now only a child of a Nepali man becomes a citizen when previously the child could be from either gender.

According to the president of the Constitution Commission (Upadhyaya 1990), the original constitution insured that all the main political powers—king, Congress Party, and Communist Party—were represented in the Council of Ministers, whichever government held the majority in the parliament. This was to insure that no party was to hold monopoly control over the state merely by control of an electoral majority. The Council of Ministers, however, in what Upadhyaya perceived as chasing after the limited interests of their parties, changed this feature to give total control over the council of ministers to whichever party held a parliamentary majority.

Except for motions of travelling through all the districts and talking to the people for their suggestions, there was no attempt to involve the people in the constitution writing process. The drafts were not made public. Half the population, the women, did not even have one representative on the committee, which was made up of urban, high-caste Brahman males. Thus just by its content, the committee had real problems of transcending age-old divisions in society: gender, mental versus physical labour, city versus countryside, ethnicity, and religion. The constitution called for the equality of women, yet it still provided for outright inferior status in regard to marriage, maternity, and inheritance.[3] Within the new constitution, this was reflected in the lack of imagination either in addressing these divisions or in addressing the changing character of the state in the world. More immediately, by failing to involve the people as the main force, the independence of the draft committee and ministers vis-à-vis the palace was weakened, as the real power in the movement had been the people, thus placing the constitutional process in great danger of co-optation by the palace.

This led to a shock when King Birendra introduced his own reactionary and regressive draft constitution on 24 October 1990. The situation in Kathmandu became extremely tense. The Communist Party subsequently organized demonstrations of tens of thousands of people all across Nepal, the Congress leaders made verbal warnings that they would call the people back into the streets. The Left leadership resolved to bring out demonstrations daily until the new constitution was implemented according to the wishes of the people.

With the king's draft constitution, many people were expressing regret that an interim constitution had never been formulated. However, the palace seems to have given in with relatively small compromises. And worries and rumours that the palace or a faction of the military would attempt a coup were never realized. The Council of Ministers met on 25 October and promised not to give way on major issues. The next day, the Congress members of the ministry met the king, who is said to have finally agreed that the constitution was to be promulgated on 9 November. The Congress leaders explained that the king's draft was not a draft but merely 'suggestions', which were his right to give. Misgivings continued in regard to the two-week delay in the date of the promulgation, which the king said was necessary for astrological reasons.

Since without an interim constitution no interim representative assembly was elected, the one section of the populace that was unable to study the draft was the people or their elected representatives, even though the constitution was written in their name. Rather than having a parliament vote on accepting or not accepting the draft or its parts, the constitution was promulgated on an arrangement between the king and party leaders, who are in power merely due to their positions in the group of parties that had initiated the movement. They neither represent all parties nor present any leader who has risen from the masses.

Thus the constitutional process has not been democratic, even though it is supposed to be creating a democratic state. Especially after the king suggested his own constitution, these misgivings were expressed in daily demonstrations of many tens of thousands brought out by various factions and fronts of the Communist Party in Kathmandu and elsewhere in the country. People were so certain that the process would collapse that they had even begun donating their blood for renewed struggle. Evidently all sides engaged in a certain degree of dramatics to force the issues one way or another.

THE UNDEMOCRATIC PROCESS OF DEMOCRACY

The misgivings of the opposition were not unfounded, because the leaders in power in the interim government did not show particular confidence in the people, while at the same time they seem to have taken the people's support for granted. At first the people were asked to participate in the movement. Once this participation gained momentum, became spontaneous, and finally brought down the government, thereafter the people were asked to demobilize and not participate, but put their faith in their leaders who in the name of the people, the 'martyrs', and the People's Movement legitimized their decisions and actions.

During the last three days of the movement,[4] with the old Panchayat regime totally besieged, the government was desperately extending a military curfew over a growing number of inflamed cities across the country, and the palace was desperately looking for someone with whom to negotiate. Ganesh Man Singh, the leader of the Congress Party, who had just seen masses of people gunned down in front of his hospital window, refused the palace's advances in no uncertain terms. Krishna Prasad Bhattarai, the second in command in the Congress Party, however, unilaterally accepted the offer of a minimum concession (suspending the word 'partyless' from the constitution). The Left Front was brought into the discussion after everything had already been arranged. Bhattarai accepted the offer to become prime minister and form a cabinet from conciliatory members of the opposition (3 Congress, 2 Communist, 2 Independents) and 2 appointees of the king, popularly termed the '007s' or spies planted by the Palace to protect its interests (strategically the king selected one ex-Congress and one ex-Communist who had switched over to the Panchayat side).

While there was relief that the military curfew had been lifted and the movement ended, the general sentiment seemed to have been one of surprise. People were surprised that the leaders of both parties had not held out a few more days and forced much larger concessions from the palace prior to entering negotiations—after all, the crowds had been calling for the removal of the monarchy not many days before. There was surprise that people of reputed integrity would agree to sit in a government formed on the basis of such a blatant compromise. Although the king had just ordered the firing of automatic weapons on his own population and Ganesh Man Singh had reported seeing bodies carted away by the truckload from in front of Bir Hospital, the king had suddenly become, in Bhattarai's own words, a 'gentleman' who could be taken at his word.

The small concession won by the People's Movement was enough to allow the leaders to assert that democracy had been won. However, their next move was to demobilize the people and domesticate the movement. After nearly two months of struggle and sacrifice, the people were asked not to make demands, to be patient, and to let their leaders take care of things in order to 'preserve' democracy, as if a minimal concession by the palace had created democracy. Yet the movement had only started to become successful once it had gained its own spontaneity and the initiative had passed out of the hands of the leaders. In the subsequent process of negotiating agreements, drafting a new constitution, and formulating laws, attempts were made to insure that there was no popular involvement in the process, although at every stage it was done in the name of a nebulous 'people'.

Once the leaders had demobilized the masses prior to any substantial constitutional changes and no longer had the initiative of the masses pushing events, they were forced to rely on the supposed 'generosity' of the palace for concessions. The problem then became a matter of not making the palace 'suspicious', of not 'threatening' it, or again in Bhattarai's words, of 'not hurting the king's feelings'. Since the elderly leaders had thrown in their lot with the palace, they found themselves in the position of defenders of the constitutional monarchy and, as such, defenders of the prerogatives of the rulers in the name of the people and democracy.

Strategically, the effect of demobilizing the people prior to negotiating an agreement was that the leaders were in no position to demand an interim constitution. Nor did the leaders seem to trust the masses sufficiently to allow themselves to demand one. What this meant was that the interim government was trying to function and create a constitution while it remained under the Panchayat constitution.[5]

An extreme example of the consequences of this compromise of the movement is that during Teej, the festival of the lights, when in October the women go to worship at the temple Pashupatinath on the Bagmati river, the queen's automobile was attacked by a group of men who turned out later to be in the pay of the palace. The ministers of the interim government and representatives of the Congress Party, without considering the circumstances of the attack, immediately scrambled over each other to condemn it as a 'heinous' crime against democracy. They demanded that the perpetrators be prosecuted. As it became increasingly clear that the attack had been engineered from within the palace itself, they became strangely quiet. A special court under the palace, which still existed under the old constitution, charged individuals who had been most outspoken with throwing the stones, as supposedly observed by the police who had signed the warrants, under a law punishable by the death penalty. A number of people were arrested and some tortured, according to the usual practice of the Nepali police. Yet most of the people charged had not even been at Pashupatinath at the time, some were even outside of Kathmandu. One was meeting with the Health Minister at the time. Most of the people charged were those who had been most outspoken against the regime and who had turned the Teej songs traditionally sung by women against patriarchy to condemn the queen, who had acquired the epithet Pampha Devi (Smuggler Goddess) in the course of the movement. Apparently the entire incident had been concocted to silence those people and recreate sympathy for the rulers, particularly the queen, who had been extremely discredited.[6]

A bigger question is how an attack on a monarchy, even if authentic, is an attack on democracy—especially since just several months before, the democratic movement had been calling for the removal of the monarchy. Evidently, by this time the leaders had so much aligned themselves with the idea and interests of a constitutional monarchy that they misinterpreted an attack on the monarchy as constituting an attack on democracy. Indeed, as a consequence of their denunciations of the supposed perpetrators, they helped suppress the most vocal opposition to the palace and to confuse the populace with their sudden alignment with the discredited palace. Furthermore, considering that the people charged had been associated with a radical viewpoint generally, and because they were for the most part women who made a nuisance of themselves by loudly speaking out uncomfortable positions, the ministers did not seem to feel it of any great importance to rectify their mistakes when found out. Rather, they promised that the changes in the constitution would take care of the problem, including elimination of the special court and the death penalty, which according to lawyers the king had opposed in his own draft, purely for the purpose of being able to eliminate persons opposed to the regime.

Because the interim government feared the spontaneity of the masses, a constitutional convention seemed undesirable. There was a great fear that the events would get out of their control and the current leadership would be sidelined. Excuses were given that the revolutionary elements of the population were limited to certain areas, and that reactionaries could assert themselves in any constitutional assembly. They said that a democratic constitution could still be created by a constitutional committee, and that a convention was unnecessary. The Communist opposition's argument was that democracy only in form was meaningless, and that a democratic constitution required a democratic process of creation.

While this discussion was going on, the king attempted to pre-empt the process. He initially formed his own constitutional committee when the interim government continued to delay the formation of its own. This was immediately confronted by massive demonstrations, and the king quickly backed down, saying, in retrospect, that he wished to follow the will of the people. The palace, Nepali Congress, and Left Front then together created another committee, which was widely perceived actually to be more conservative than the one originally created by the king. Furthermore, despite the widespread and instrumental participation of women in the movement, not one woman was put on this committee, although there had been a women on that of the king's. Later when the king tried to introduce his own draft constitution in late October 1990 when the process again seemed to be stalled due to argument over the committee's draft, people again came out onto the streets to force him to withdraw. This threat of even an more reactionary alternative succeeded in quieting opposition to the committee's draft and bringing about its final promulgation on 9 November 1990.

CRITIQUE

The manner in which movement had been brought to an end was anything but democratic. One person or a small group of elites should never have been allowed to make unilateral decisions. The Left Front had been so cautious in entering into alliance with the Nepali Congress that its leadership thought it sufficient just to unify around one point without laying out strategy that should have been followed once this had been won. The Panchayat Regime seemed so formidable and victory so far off at the beginning of the movement that apparently no one considered how victory would be handled, or that by the end the movement would be making far more demands than just the one point about a multi-party system (although the expansion of objectives characterizes the general development of mass movements). As a consequence, the Left Front, which initially planned and called the movement, allowed the initiative to be taken over by the Congress Party, and the younger Congress leaders the elders through default.

Planning ahead and insuring decisions by consensus should have been a lesson learned through the course of the last forty years of struggle. The regime had always disarmed more progressive initiatives by probing among various leaders and pulling them apart from each other one by one. This time it was only partially successful due to the much greater awareness and organization of the masses, with little thanks to the leaders, although the latter were heralded as the 'Fathers of Democracy'. Nevertheless the masses were successfully circumvented in the actual process of creating a new constitution.

The demobilization of the people and their removal from the political process is a common pattern in revolutions. Commonly, while political movements arise from mass involvement and initiative, after the initial objectives are obtained fearful leaders become wary of actually letting people participate, for fear the a movement might end up someplace else than they wish or else it will oppose the interests that they represent. By the end of the Democracy Movement, the original leaders had become superfluous. Whereas most of them had gained their position due to their having progressed through their respective party hierarchies, new leaders and initiatives were emerging through organic ties to the lower levels of organization and to the local communities. For the first time in Nepal's documented history, women and peasants emerged as a vanguard force, with immense potential power. Since these two groups represented an overturning of two of the oldest divisions in the history of humanity—of gender against gender and city against countryside—these two groups posed a special threat to the leaders, who based their personal and party positions in the perpetuation of these divisions. Democratic initiatives thus were aimed at quieting or redirecting these newly self-conscious forces.

Almost invariably, in revolutions, bourgeois or socialist, demobilization of the masses has ended in disaster not only for the masses but for the original leaders, either through the piecemeal erosion of the gains made by the revolution and the assertion of an emergent ruling class over the state in alliance with the old ones, or else through violent counter-revolution. In Nepal, the leaders of the Left Front and the Nepali Congress have understood leadership in terms of *representing* the people, even though there is no real organic connection between most of the leaders and the people, especially those sitting in the interim government. They do not understand that a good leader speaks not for people but rather encourages their organization, passes the power to them, and enables them to speak for themselves. The argument is that provision of a democratic constitution will effect this. But historical experience shows that people must be involved directly in the process itself for it to have truly democratic results, since the institutional framework is less essential than consciousness and participation. Without the latter, the framework is easily co-opted by whichever classes control property and production in the society, and furthermore, by being presented as 'democratic' the process can actually make people complacent.

The biggest mistake of the individuals and parties which were calling for an interim constitution and constitutional convention is that they failed to offer a means for the masses to assert themselves in this regard. Their strategy was one of reaction to the moves by the party leadership, interim government and palace rather than taking over the initiative. They should never have submitted to the Nepali Congress's decision to draft the constitution by committee without calling their own alternative constitutional convention. Whether such a convention would have successfully created its own alternative constitution is less material than that it would have kept the people in the political process, preserving their initiative. It would have forced the committee-created constitution to confront the existence of an alternative, and manifestly more democratic, claim to legitimacy. Self-appointed leaders were allowed to direct the movement, forgetting that if people were going to participate, this could only happen by their taking their own initiative. Participation is created through practice, not given. By allowing the initiative to shift away from the people to leaders calling themselves 'democrats', the day democracy was won was also the day it died.

The events following the cessation of the democracy movement in Nepal are generally indicative of the class content that underlies the global democracy movements today. Although an expressly 'democratic' constitution has been promulgated, the democracy it frames has mainly to do with allowing greater freedom of action and share of the spoils of the state to a growing entrepreneur class on the one hand and a bulging bureaucratic class on the other—the same groups, subordinated to international capital and transnational corporations, that are asserting themselves in 'democratic movements' throughout the world. The urban workers are presently able to organize themselves within a limited extent. The position of the great bulk of the population, the rural masses, remains essentially unchanged. Democracy for the urban poor and rural masses still remains to be won through further struggle. The lesson from this movement is that people will have to be far better organized and means will have to be created to make leadership accountable.

NOTES

This chapter is a version of a paper presented at the 18th Annual Conference on South Asia, Madison, Wisconsin, 3 November 1990, in a panel entitled 'Democratic Transition in Nepal'. This panel occurred simultaneously to the promulgation of the new constitution and also included the spokesman of the Sanyukta Jana Morcha (United People's Party), Baburam Bhattarai, and his wife, Hisila Yami, among its participants.

1   The seven divisions of the Communist Party of Nepal (CPN) which com-
    bined into the United Left Front for the purpose of the movement consist of
    the (1) CPN (Marxist) led by Shahana Pradhan and Man Mohan Adhikari,
    (2) CPN (Marxist-Leninist) or 'Jhapali', led by Mohan Chandra Adhikari and
    Radha Krishna Mainali [originally founded in Jhapa in the spirit of the Naxalite
    movement in the neighbouring Naxalbari, the party changed its name from
    Jhapali Khand to CPN(ML) when it united with a number of other parties to
    become the largest party of the CPN], (3) the Nepal Labour and Peasant
    Federation of Comrad Rohit, (4) Manandhar CPN, consisting of the lowest
    caste Newars and others of the Kathmandu Valley, (5) Bhim Bahadur Group,
    (6) Tulsi Lal Amatya Group, (7) Verma Samuha, led by Krishna Raj Verma.
2   The Communist parties of the United National People's Front include Masal,
    Mashal, and Proletariat Party.
3   The unequal marriage status in which women married to foreigners were forced
    to move abroad due to inability to obtain visas for their husbands was changed
    in the spring of 1993 when it was successfully challenged in court. However,
    rather than providing permanent residence to foreign husbands in the manner
    of foreign wives, it extended the previous four month non-tourist visa given to
    foreign husbands to twelve months, while reducing the permanent residency
    given to foreign wives to the same twelve months. As of August 1995 women
    continue to lack inheritance rights in family properties, and the maternity of
    women is only recognized through their husbands, meaning that children are
    not citizens except through a Nepali father. However, in the first week of August
    1995 the Supreme Court ordered that new laws be drafted making men and
    women equal.
4   6–8 April.
5   Various articles having to do with the Panchayat regime were suspended, yet
    the constitution remained in effect, leaving the king with powers that were only
    minimally diminished. Legally, he could still reactivate these powers.
6   In subsequent years these women were excluded from entry into the
    Pashupatinath Teej festivities due to this incident which was not even of their
    own doing.

CHAPTER 8

The Local Government Law and Participatory Democracy: A Comparison of Opposites

> When it comes to democracy, the placing of political power in the hands of the mass of intelligent people, there are many who regard this step as philanthropy and withal dangerous philanthropy. They think of the right to vote as a concession from the cultured elite to the inexperienced and irresponsible mass, with the threat of slowing up or even attacking civilization.
>
> —W.E.B. Du Bois (1985a:242)

INTRODUCTION

MUCH OF THE legislation implemented in Nepal in the name of democracy over the last four decades actually extended bureaucratic structures downwards into the communities, neutralized local organizations and initiatives, and made human and natural community resources more easily accessible to exploitation by powerful, narrow interests, both within and without the community. In the last three decades, the growth of widespread, effective popular initiatives throughout the world (including liberation theology, popular committees and councils, culture circles, Delegates of the Word) and parties which are based on such initiatives (such as the Workers Party of Brazil or the United Slumdwellers Committee of Chile) that have risen to confront exploitation and repression have encouraged international donors to rethink their support for bureaucratically implemented plans and introduce initiatives to conceptualize, if not effectively implement, their aid goals in terms of community participation and self management of resources.

Within Nepal, government planners and non-government sectors have not remained ignorant of this shift in the metaphors that hold the key to development aid. The new local government law has appropriated this terminology, showcasing ideologically loaded words such as 'participation', 'autonomy', 'decentralization', and 'development'. However, despite its participatory rhetoric, the local government law was hurriedly introduced and passed late in the spring 1992 parliamentary session, precluding any substantial airing or discussion, except in five-star hotels among lawyers. Close analysis of the logic of this new law and the projected form of its implementation shows that the participatory terminology is mere window dressing for a law that devolves no new substantial governmental powers to the people, while reintroducing institutions that extend bureaucratic control further into the villages. The law gives with one hand but actually takes with the other. Where a mechanism is set up to effect these words at one place in the law, an office or agency is created at another place that takes away the power or negates the attempt. It gives with one hand, but actually takes with the other. The law seems to be driven more by the ulterior motive of extending central power into the villages and urban neighbourhoods and centralizing control than any sort of internal logic of working for the purposes that it expounds. The poorly constructed circular reasoning and logical fallacies needed to effect this end makes the law obtuse and difficult to understand, particularly for the layman who is supposed to implement it and for whom it is to serve. As far as control over resources is concerned, the law is so framed as to ensure that the erosion of local control will not only continue as before, but be further facilitated.

Looking at the law, the local government consists of 'Village Development Committees' rather than assemblies. The members of the committees are elected by adult suffrage, but they have no governmental powers—neither legislative, executive, administrative, official nor judicial. Though the law calls for participation, its purpose seems to preclude people from participating, as the activities are to be carried out by the elite and the powerful, not by common citizens. The law talks of 'planning', but the plans are already drawn up by the planning commission and central government. It talks of 'execution', but the execution and control of the local administration are carried out by secretaries who are neither elected nor nominated by elected representatives, but appointed by the central government. The only thing that the committees can do is sell off village properties, which leads to the question whether this is the true purpose of the law. If any of the committees attempts to step from the narrow path set for them by the law to implement the goals rhetorically claimed by it (participation, planning, execution, autonomy), then that committee would be liable to dissolution, according to the clause that the central government has the prerogative to suspend or dissolve any committee (e.g. for abuse of authority). This clause indeed not only negates any sort of governmental functions locally, given the restrictions and qualifications of the law, it suppresses political plurality at the local level.

Rhetorical democracy is one thing, a practical one is another. Here in Nepal, as elsewhere, it is being designed by people with little practical experience of or commitment to democracy, especially amongst those who are the least empowered, even within their own homes (women relatives, house servants, etc.). Rural poor, indigenous peoples, and residents of shanty towns and ghettos everywhere in the world are discovering from fifty years of experiments and empty promises the hard fact that democracy, by definition, cannot be given from above but must be created from below. Thus we see in barrios and villages of South and Central America, in ghettos of the United States, in the Philippines and elsewhere the use of participatory, grassroots forms of government at the local level.

The Trabalhadares Party of Brazil

The Trabalhadares Party (PT), which has won the municipal elections of more than 30 major cities of Brazil, has taken as its primary concern the democratization of decision making at the state level. 'Democratizing the state means institutionalizing mechanisms of popular participation for drafting and implementing public policy' (Alves 1991a:25–6). These include 'popular committees', in which people from each street organize themselves 'by neighbourhood and issue of popular concern' to elect representatives to neighbourhood committees which work out solutions to their problems and make decisions by common consensus (Alves 1991b:242).

The urban areas are divided into districts, or bairros. . . . The residents of each bairro organize into a committee, usually with one representative for each street, to discuss and draft proposals for issues of immediate importance to them: street paving, lighting, running water, sewage systems, the building of schools, daycare centers, playgrounds, health clinics, etc. (Alves 1991b:243)

These Brazilian popular committees differ in essence from the 'development committees' of the Nepali local government law, because they are built upon and elected from organizations of the people themselves, around issues of common concern. In contrast, the Nepali 'development committees' are imposed from above, to address issues decided at the level of the central government according to its own programme and within the narrow confines set by it. The Nepali committees, furthermore, represent population areas that are too large (i.e. entire municipalities rather than *toles* or 'urban quarters') and thereby lose all participatory significance. Because there is no organizational basis for the development committees within the communities, they have no necessary substantial connection to their constituencies through which they can be held accountable or engender participation. The Nepali law contains some of the elements of the Brazilian committees, but the Nepali committees are generally designed to ensure that local level accountability and participation do not take place.

The Brazilian 'popular committees' in turn elect representatives to 'popular councils' which, unlike the Nepali committees at all levels, carry out actual legislation.

The residents of the bairro committees elect people to a conselho popular, or popular council, whose size varies according to the number of people in the bairro. . . . [S]ome have incorporated a recall vote to increase their accountability to their constituency. (Alves 1991b:243–4)

The popular councils draft their own statutes and meet regularly with members of the municipal government to discuss and draft public policies. Budgetary constraints are discussed, priorities established, and the difficulties of implementation of programs are handled together. For the first time in Brazilian history, citizens, especially poor citizens, participate directly in budgetary decisions and policymaking in a regular manner. Direct participation results in distinctly different programs to deal with development and social problems. (Alves 1991a:26)

Even the shantytown, or *sukhambasi*, communities are organized in this way.

With the encouragement of the PT and the municipal administration, the citizens of the favelas [squatter settlements] organize conselhos de vavela (shantytown councils). These are composed of elected members of the community and also have their own statutes. They are responsible for much of the work involved in planning and implementing programs. The local favela councils are only accountable to their specific units and work in a limited area. High-level representatives of the municipal government and PT officials are present only when invited.

The municipal governments under PT control hire engineers, urban planners, geologists, architects, sociologists, and other technicians to work on urban revitalization projects. They liaison with the counselhos de favelas and provide them with technical assistance. They meet together, draft plans together, and work collectively to implement programs. (Alves 1991b:244)

The Brazilian 'popular councils' are actually at the same organizational level as the Nepali village and municipal development corporations, but the Nepali committees, as well as the next higher district development committees, lack the legislative component of the Brazilian councils, just as they lack the popular basis of the Brazilian committees. Accountability, rather than coming from below through recall votes, is imposed from above, through a central government prerogative to suspend or disband the committees at its pleasure. In contrast, the Brazilian councils, unlike the Nepali district committees, are directly accountable to their local committees and thus, due to the organizational basis of the latter, to the citizenry themselves. Through them, Brazilian citizens set their own priorities and pursue their programmes rather than being handed a set of predetermined plans, as is the fate of Nepali citizens.

Programs for better health and education, and self development projects, are urgent priorities. First of all, however, the popular administration is placing enormous emphasis on modifying the administrative patterns that have created a huge state bureaucracy. The need for democratization and decentralization was clear after an evaluation carried out during the first year, when it became clear that the implementation of programs that encouraged direct participation in policymaking was being hampered by the resistance of tenured government employees who had been hired largely on the basis of patronage. (Alves 1991b:244)

The Nepali law similarly identifies the need for decentralization, but its approach is the opposite of the Brazilian Workers Party. It will be shown below that, as in the previous panchayat period, the present law pursues decentralization by extending bureaucratic control downwards rather than building popular control and accountability upwards. The contrast is clearly exemplified by the handling of strikes and civic unrest. Where the present Nepali Congress government met a civil servants' strike and a 'Nepal Bandh' with police repression (a pattern that has continued in the subsequent Communist government as well, although it has shown itself more open and conciliatory and nearly devoid of violence), the Brazilian government introduced more democracy.

This problem [of bureaucratic resistance] was particularly evident in education, where teachers resisted the innovative ideas of Secretary of Education Paulo Freire, and went so far as to organize a large strike against the PT government. The response of the Secretary of Education was not less but more democracy. Freire called on teachers to elect a committee to work with him and his staff. All of the administration's records were opened to the public and the budget made available for reexamination by the teachers' representatives, as well as by the members of the Citizen's Educational Committee. A tripartite group of government representatives, parents, and teachers began to work on solutions. In the end, the teachers voted overwhelmingly to end the strike and to institutionalize a program to educate teachers, school employees, and parents in the new philosophy of education for liberation. (Alves 1991b:244–5)

The result in Brazil was to make the bureaucracy more responsive to the people (until the subsequent military coup), whereas in Nepal the government utilized its punitive dismissal of civil servants to replace them with its own cadres, extending political patronage to its own party members rather than introducing any changes in the bureaucracy. While this has not strengthened the ruling party's control over the bureaucracy, which in its own right encompasses various class forces, it has immobilized it further and made it less responsive than before, creating conditions for wider popular frustration and suffering, and the expansion of civil unrest.

An approach, as attempted by the Nepali Congress government under Girija Koirala in dealing with the 1991 civil servants strike in Nepal, that seeks to assert control over the bureaucracy by forcibly undermining the power of the bureaucrats without creating a popular counterpoising organization and force to fill its place is almost certain to be counterproductive. Rather than giving positive power to the party in power, it leaves a void in which the military or some other agency (in Nepal's case transnational corporate interests and the resurgent palace forces) can step in and usurp power for their own purposes, often undermining or overthrowing the ruling party in the process—as occurred, for example, in Pakistan.[1]

The most positive approach to the bureaucracy is to make it open, accessible and accountable to and working closely with the people, themselves consciously organized as a counterpoising force. Hereby government functions and powers gradually devolve to the people, weakening the arbitrary, independent and unresponsive character of government while avoiding the creation of a void in which a third, unwelcome power can step in. Party leadership is often reluctant to use such a truly democratic approach, because it means giving up their illusory personal power to their constituency and the real base and substance of their power, the people. They mistake their personal power, itself contingent on the bureaucracy (and thus illusory), the power of the party's own bureaucracy and the special interests they represent, as democracy and thus accuse people promoting such an approach with 'undermining' or 'threatening' democracy or being otherwise 'undemocratic'.

Note that the Brazilian popular organization exists alongside of and in addition to whatever national structures exist in Brazil. It was created by a party that has a strong popular basis in order to actually allow all the citizens of its constituencies to participate in running the government, rather than the party arrogating all powers and decision making to itself. Thereby the people themselves are attempting to overcome major shortcomings and unsolved problems of multi-party democracy that prevent people from actually participating in their own governance.

The United Slumdwellers of Chile

In Chile by the mid 1980s, about 220,000 of the 2 million slum dwellers had similarly organized themselves around specific needs into some four types of grassroots organizations. About three thousand people represent these grassroots organizations in regional coordinating bodies. The four types of grassroots organizations are:

(a) associations for subsistence, such as soup-kitchens and urban family gardens; (b) demand-oriented organizations such as committees address- ing housing issues and high utility bills; (c) local coordinating bodies group- ing all community organizations at the local and district level; and (d) organizations for national social and political representation such as the United Slumdwellers Committee (Comite Unitario de Pobladores, CUP)....

The grassroots organizations vary widely in goals, size, and composition, but all of them represent a collective search for solutions, for victory over repression and the isolation which the economic model and official ideology have attempted to impose on the poor. In today's Chile, rediscovering and reestablishing the links of solidarity among the dispossessed has become a subversive act. . . .

Independently of the original intentions of their members, these groupings [therefore] quickly acquire a political character, arising from the simple act of looking for solutions to their problems together. This runs counter to one of the regime's strategic objectives, namely, to create a society devoid of independent, organized individuals. . . .

The collective practices carried out by the urban poor reflect the arduous process by which the dispossessed attempt to constitute themselves into social actors, rather than a process of 'social disorganization' or 'social dissolution' as some writers have mistakenly hypothesized. (Leiva and Petras 1987:114–16)

In the manner that the Brazilian organizations have represented themselves politically through a national party, the Chileans have united as the United Slumdwellers Committee (CUP). It is similarly based on popular committees at the local level, called *coordinadoras* 'unified coordinating committees', which bring together all the grassroots organizations existing in a given neighbourhood (Leiva and Petras 1987:119–20). Representatives correspondingly represent these local committees in district level coordinating committees.

The CUP as a whole is led by an elected 'collegial leadership body, the Metropolitan Council' (Leiva and Petras 1987:120). Just as the CUP itself, like the PT, is kept from becoming separated from its constituencies by requiring that the membership also be members of local organizations, this Metropolitan Council 'was to be "neither decorative nor bureaucratic. Its members must participate in one of the work areas and working commissions"' (Leiva and Petras 1987:120). Thus the CUP (and the PT) is quite different from the bureaucratized parties of Nepal, in which the leadership loses touch with its constituency; the leaders of its Council remain actively immersed within and part of the constituency.

Although during the repressive years of the Pinochet regime the CUP was unable to participate in electoral politics, it did organize its First Metropolitan Congress of Slumdwellers in late April 1986 (Leiva and Petras 1987:118).

This meeting was the culmination of a six-month long participatory process begun at the end of 1985, during which pre-congresses in thirteen Santiago districts discussed the problems of the pobladores and elected delegates to the city-wide event. . . . About 800 rank-and-file organizations were represented by 364 elected delegates. A profoundly democratic procedure was reflected in the composition of the four hundred or so delegates: 40 percent were women and 72 percent were under the age of thirty. Such broad representation was the result of a lesson learned through much sacrifice over the last decade: the strength of national or metropolitan organization of pobladores is directly proportional to the degree of participation and unity at the grassroots level. (Leiva and Petras 1987:118–19)

Ten working commissions discussed the problems faced by the urban poor and presented analyses, root causes, and concrete actions to be taken to the plenary session. The commission on organization defined the structure of the CUP, already presented above. As the organization of the slum dwellers is based on their shantytowns, the most important of the commissions was the one on territory, which, according to its statement, identified in the slum community territories for the expression of 'Popular Power', as '"territoriality allows, in practice, the accumulation of social forces for the achievements of general political objectives"' (Leiva and Petras 1987:120). This popular power was identified both in the role of self-defence and offensive action. This group solution to gaining and controlling property presents a quite different perspective from the populist slogans, such as of 'land reform', which are used by demagogic leaders to manipulate people for their own selfish ends and those of their ruling class or party cohorts. Issues of repression and struggle, which in Nepal have so far been co-opted by the parties, are brought into the sphere of public debate and organized popular initiative.

The Shortcoming of Multiparty Democracy

The key shortcoming of multi-party democracy is a lack of internal democracy in the parties, such that candidates are selected by party bosses (chairmen, general secretaries, 'supreme leaders', etc.) and party bureaucrats, according to the interests of party sponsors (businessmen, foreign agencies, etc.).[2] The candidates who are screened through the internal selection process of the parties become the instrument whereby offices, contracts, monopolies and other privileges are awarded. Since the candidates were selected through the party mechanisms, they have little practical accountability to the people who elect them. Rather than being the representatives of the people, they are their 'chosen masters'. Election promises are purely rhetorical, lacking substance; they are meant to imbue the masses with the notion of the party's power and confidence of victory and convince them of the leaders' charismatic qualifications. The electoral provisions constitute rules of the game for 'peaceful' contests which underwrite continuing violence (economic, political, police, etc.) against the masses of poor and underprivileged people. The bosses of the competing parties, be they Communist or socialist, conservative or liberal, will combine against popular claims made against the parties in order to protect their own privileges and positions, the privileges and benefits of their party bureaucrats, and the interests of rich and powerful sponsors. Unless the constituencies of the parties can exert themselves through popular organizations, multi-party democracy will continue to represent a dictatorship by the various interests controlling the party in power.

In Nepal this subordination of the election process to the party machinery and election victories led to the seeming absurdity of the Nepali Congress Party recruiting ex-Panchas (the elected representatives of the old regime who had sworn allegiance to 'partyless' or one party Panchayat system) as a large portion of its candidates in the local elections, even though its leaders had previously lambasted the Panchas as non-democratic and set themselves up as *the* democrats in contrast. A Nepali Congress Member of Parliament swaggering over the Congress victory in the local elections of summer 1992, said smugly, 'where we ran our own candidates, we lost more than 50 per cent of the elections; where we ran Panchas, we won more than 50 per cent'.

People throughout the world are making their claims on their governments and their parties through the creation of popular forms of government organization such as the Brazilian neighbourhood organizations and committees and councils.[3] This is in part a result of the emergence of transnational forces that dwarf nation states in power and resources and which are underwriting and supporting, directly and indirectly, non-government organizations in order to develop groups no longer beholden to their national governments in order to share their own interests and further their goals. But it is also in part a result of people receiving education and entering into international interactions on a hitherto unprecedented scale. Presently the former tendency seems to dominate, particularly in the surging NGO movement. The local government law in Nepal also seems to be more a product of this tendency, as local ruling class groups and their international sponsors are wary of returning control of local resources, community and the state to local peoples.

PREAMBLE: HIGH SOUNDING WORDS, FALSE PROMISES

The preamble of the local government law states that the goal of the Village, Municipality, and District development committees is to maximize participation. The word 'participation' is used to make us believe that the law provides for people's participation in their own governance. But the subsequent words are 'in development activities' not 'government'. As clearly evidenced by other sections of the law, 'development activities' are imposed on the development committees from above. 'Participation' will be seen to mean that the people do not oppose or struggle against this imposition but help it along.

The Municipality and District laws, furthermore, specify provision of local autonomy to the people. However, as will be demonstrated below, the laws are crafted in order to ensure that no autonomy occurs. The village law further specifies that it is to usher the development of local-level leadership, but this too can only be interpreted as placing power within a limited number of hands out of the reach of the majority. Further recognizing donor priorities, the village law in particular specifies that it is to usher the development of local level leadership, 'under the naive assumption that one can promote the community by training its leaders—as if it were the parts that promote the whole and not the whole which, in being promoted, promotes the parts' (Freire 1972:112).

This is not a law for local government at all. Even in the preamble there is no mention of legislative powers, no policy making, no execution, no control over local administration. What is government without these? Careful inspection of the rest of the law bears this out. It is the same old Panchayat government with the same old names, 'decentralization' and 'development committee', but decentralization of spoils, sharing the loot, not participation and autonomy as framed in the introduction.

'FUNCTIONS AND RESPONSIBILITIES': 'PARTICIPATION' AS PROGRAMMES DETERMINED FROM ABOVE

Village Development Committees

The functions and responsibilities of the village development committees are in the first place merely those of the different ministries of the central government: education and culture, health and population, agriculture and irrigation, forest, environment and energy, drinking water, works and transport, social welfare.

The law means basically that the function of the local government is to carry out programmes already determined in the ministries. We already know that the ministerial programmes have not worked for forty years. Thus the manifest purpose of the creation of local governments should be to allow people to invent new solutions. But this law still limits innovation and autonomy and alternate solutions to those of the bureaucracy. It seems that once again people are being asked to do what the groups controlling the government determine for them. Note that the functions of the key ministries which determine all the other ministries, finance, planning, justice, home, defence, foreign and palace, are carefully omitted. The people who control power are evidently afraid of actually allowing people to share this power.

Municipalities

The same can be said for the functions and responsibilities given to the municipalities in the municipality law:

1. Maintain inter-sectoral coordination in the municipality administration. There is nothing about actually engaging in administration, only coordinating administration, making it work better, etc. There is no need for defining administration, since as will be seen, the local government actually has no control of administration.

2. Pass the town development plan. There is nothing about proposing the development plan, only passing it, because this

development plan is already proposed and designed by the central government.

3. Determine the rates of tax, fees and service charges. But finances from the central government are not under autonomous local government control.

4. Undertake development related functions. This, however, is merely implementation of predetermined development related functions in the manner of the Village Development Committee.

These committees are not governing bodies in which people legislate local laws. What constitutes the domain of their activities is already predetermined. The local government is nothing more than a new level of bureaucracy designed to extend ministerial power down to the local levels, and thus it is a repeat of the of the 'decentralization' of the Panchayat era, even using the same term. In contrast, a law aimed at participation would define its function as *enabling* participation by giving powers of legislation, planning, administration and execution to the people. It would not limit functions by idly discussing plans, policy and legislation imposed by the central government.

'POWERS' THAT ARE NOT POWERS

Next, in the Village Development Committee Law, there is a list of 'powers', making it seem that the powers of government are being handed over to the people. But these are not 'powers' of governance, they are just procedural rules. Since the local governments have no powers, there is obviously no power in the procedures. The first of these procedural 'powers' is the 'power to form necessary sub-committees'. These committees are restricted to 'local intelligentsia, NGO representatives, social workers' who will be nominated by the development committee. In other words, now the real meaning of 'participation' is disclosed. Participation means that only local elites and contracting NGOs can participate. If you are not educated, do not belong to an NGO, or are not a social worker, then you cannot participate; you cannot decide or act for yourself. This means most villagers will remain unable to participate, especially women and other disenfranchised groups.

The second power is the 'powers and functions of the village development committee secretary'. As it turns out, this is not a power of the elected development committee at all. The section on 'administrative staff and recruitment' determines that the administrative secretary is appointed by the central government. As listed below, all the powers of execution and implementation are then given over to this secretary, which effectively means that the central government not only can determine what the development committee does, but it then goes ahead and does it itself. Observe the 'powers and functions' of the secretary:

1. The secretary executes the decisions by the development committee. Decision making, however, was not one of the functions given to the development committee. As defined earlier, its role was merely to execute planning and policy made by the central government. But now it turns out that this executive function goes to someone nominated by the central government. The central government retains executive powers just as it retained the administrative ones.

2. The secretary maintains the records of the NGOs and the projects implemented by the village development committee. Hereby the bureaucratic functions are now also retained by the central government. Furthermore, 'projects implemented' is a misnomer because according to the previous point, the secretary, not the village development committee, implements.

3. The secretary carries out the guidance given by the local development officer. This merely calls the lie: plans and policy come from the development officer, another official of the central government, not the development committee.

4. The secretary investigates the complaints filed in the village development committee and submits the report to the committee. In other words, investigatory powers are returned back to the central government. Furthermore, below we see that the complaints that can actually be brought to the development committee are totally circumscribed.

5: The secretary records vital statistics on birth, marriage, death and maintains registration. Hereby, control over data and any sort of official recognition is thereby put back into the control over the central government.

The secretary of the municipal development committee is similarly nominated by the central government. His functions, called 'rights' (thus individual rights are no longer rights of the people but of an office filled by an appointee of the central government!) are as follows:

1. Administration. The secretary undertakes administrative functions in concert with the mayor. Since no administrative functions are specified for the mayor, it appears that the central government controls municipal administration.

2. Execution. The secretary executes the town development programme, whereas the elected mayor merely 'arranges' for execution of development committee decisions. In other words, execution of development, which is the only function given to municipal government to start with, goes back into the control of the central government.

3. Official functions. The secretary keeps and maintains minutes and records, and takes overall responsibility to carry out the internal administration. The secretary, that is the central government, takes over all the official functions of municipal government.

4. Miscellaneous activities. In case the municipal government finds some unanticipated way to assert its autonomy from the secretary cum central government, an additional catch-all category was created in which government can pass bills to take this away as well.

It is strange that a law that proposes autonomy, participation, and decentralization places executive, administrative, investigatory, and official functions at the local level into the hands of an official appointed by the central government in the form of the secretary. Since legislative power, policy, and planning were also never given to the village and municipal development committees, it is difficult to understand how these constitute a local government. From the point of view of the citizens, the committees are powerless and insubstantial extensions of central government into the village. From that of the ruling party and transnational interests, the committees disarm and expose the local level to exploitation, not transforming the local level situation but extending the erosion of local autonomy and initiative that was associated with the Panchayat period.

Following the establishment of the governments in 1992, we found that the Congress government refrained from appointing the secretaries in the opposition VDCs such as Tokha, north of Kathmandu, and Bandipur, south of Dumre, effectively preventing them from undertaking their work. It furthermore distributed funds in those areas directly to local NGOs rather than having the funds pass through the opposition-held local governments. As an official election observer in the Farm Labour Party stronghold of Jumla, I observed the Nepali Congress government use the secretary's power over registration to prevent blocks of poor voters from registering.

In contrast to the secretaries, the elected chairmen or mayors of the development committees have basically no power. Given the manner in which the pradhan panchas (chairmen of the local assemblies) abused power previously, it may have been prudent not to give authority to locally elected individuals. But turning over the powers of government to centrally nominated government officials promises even more individual abuse and central government interference than before. Instead, powers should reside in the committees themselves, and the committees should be securely rooted in community based organizations.

PLANS WITHOUT PLANNING

We have shown that the central government takes away whatever it was supposed to give. The question arises what meaning planning can have if people cannot carry out the plans. Indeed, the sections of the law on plan formation and execution of plans are meaningless formulae and contradictory statements to give an illusion of something where there is nothing.

The law determines that local planning, of both the village and municipal committees, 'must adhere to the instructions given by the government and the National Planning Commission in respect to plan formulation and implementation'. What can this mean except that the planning commission and government, not the villagers or municipalities, do the planning? Furthermore, though the village committees cannot formulate their own plans, the plans should give priority to 'income generation, agricultural productivity, indigenous resource utilization and the interest of backward classes and women'. In other words, the priorities of the planning have already been predetermined and set out by the planning commission's funding priorities and rhetoric. Finally, before selection of the plans (which cannot be formulated anyway), feasibility studies should be undertaken, ensuring that only those who can afford feasibility studies will select plans (nothing is said about implementation). The 'execution' of the plans merely delimits the sources of resources for the 'execution' which also cannot be done.

The section on 'guidance' says that the village development committee must comply with the National Planning Commission on plan formulation and execution. In other words, if the committees could formulate and execute plans (which they cannot), these must be those of the central government. It is evident that planning means planning by the central government and compliance of the villagers with the central government planning and directives.

PARTICIPATION OF BOSSES, BUREAUCRATS AND PARTY SPONSORS IS NOT POPULAR PARTICIPATION

The plans, as they are, are not to be implemented by the development committees at all but by Non-Government Organizations. The municipal directive is similar to the village one, as follows:

The Village Development Committee should encourage the non-government organization to identify development activities, implement and evaluate them. The NGOs should undertake the local development activities in coordination with the village development committee. The village development committee can implement local development activities only through non-government organization.

If the local governments are supposedly based on popular participation, why do they need to utilize non-government organizations to implement their development activities? Remember that the village development committee secretary controls registration; thus he, and through him the central government, controls the official recognition of NGOs. In this way, even through reference to NGOs seems to provide a means of implementation separate from the government, the government yet exerts its control over identification, implementation, and evaluation of development activities. However, a direct linkage between NGOs, the government and international agencies already exists.

To wit, international agencies which have been underwriting the expansion of the Nepali bureaucracy for the last forty years through development loans, aid, and advisors, found that the client bureaucracies they themselves created take on their own existence and interests and fail to respond to the needs, not only of their own people (not necessarily the agencies' primary concern) but also of powerful international interests. The latest agency and donor government strategy, therefore, has been to shift aid funds to NGOs, through which international agencies and powerful foreign interests can create an urban client class directly dependent upon and subservient to themselves and no one else. The rapid and enthusiastic growth of thousands of NGOs in the urban areas following the fall of the Panchayat regime is evidence of this process.

In Nepal, it turns out that this client class is the same one that controls the top positions in the government. The people controlling the government and the parties—the opposition to a lesser extent than the Congress government—have opportunistically utilized this international strategy to extend their domestic political agendas. Thus it is no surprise to find the emphasis on NGOs as the implementing agency in the new government law, since the same people writing the law will be those who benefit. Giving power to NGOs does not necessarily mean creating popular participation or empowerment, and it cannot anticipate the future forms that popular effort will take: it has more to do with extending the ruling class and foreign influence, and control of villages in yet another, more direct form.[4]

DEVELOPMENT COMMITTEE FUND:
EXPROPRIATION OF COMMUNITY RESOURCES

We have observed that the development committee is unrepresentative and powerless. One thing that it can do, however, is raise money. There are diverse means of doing this.

1. Grants from HMG (His Majesty's Government) or District Development Committee. Much is being made of the allocation of 70 per cent of the national budget to the village level, but how this is to be allocated and spent is unspecified. Given the nature of this local government law, there is no accountability or insurance that the funds actually serve the people. You can imagine that government grants will only be forthcoming if the development committee members are loyal to the government.

2. Proceeds from the sale of properties. Putting control of the sale of village or municipal properties within the hands of the development committee means that this group of people, especially the powerful elements that gain power over the committees, will easily rob the community as in the past. There is no mechanism in the local government law to make the committees answerable to, or ensure that they remain under the control of, their constituencies. There is nothing to prevent all the communal resources of the villages and municipalities from being sold away, with the rural and urban populations becoming more impoverished and powerless than before. Community forests, water resources and plots of land will become private property, and the development committee members will be able to enrich themselves off the bribes and profits as before. The destruction of rural society, agriculture, forests, and industry will continue. (Witness the way that the present Congress government and the national assembly is giving away water, business rights, public enterprises, and so forth in order to finance their programmes without reference to their constituency.)

3. Proceeds from the income-generating activities launched by the village development committees or internal mobilization of municipalities. How can more be done here than in the Panchayat period, when the local government is legally essentially no different than the Panchayat one, except that interests are exerted through parties rather than the government? Without the means to exert popular will, the only income generation will be for the committees and their friends, not for the communities.

4. Fees, tolls, octrois, etc. Will there be enough popular control to make this progressive?

5. Fines and fees. Will there be enough popular control to make this progressive?

6. Funds allocated by HMG. This will become a means of forcing obedience and subservience on the people, as in the past.

None of these are to be levied contrary to law, which may have different interpretations. The local law does give the government certain additional control. Note that there is nothing said about foreign or domestic independent grants, such as are supporting the NGOs. The Nepali Congress government avoided providing the funds to some Communist local governments and routed them directly to local NGOs run by their supporters.

ADMINISTRATION

HMG appoints the village development committee secretary. Given that the secretary is in charge of execution, as shown above, this means that the government returns executive powers back to itself.

JUDICIAL POWERS WITH NO TEETH

The judicial authority of both the village development and municipal development committees entails a specific, limited set of jurisdictions. The village committee figures purely as a conciliator without binding jurisdiction; actual jurisdiction belongs to the courts of the central government. The municipality's jurisdiction allows it to punish tax defaulters and those encroaching upon roads, but no crimes more significant than this, particularly not those conflicting with ruling class interests (for example, embezzlement, bribery, or procedures for making complaints and claims against higher offices and authorities). The complaints set out for the village development committee deal with insignificant management problems which are already carried out within communities through consensual processes anyway: (1) encroachment of roads (2) borderline disputes (3) farm wages (4) pond and protection of public property (5) various use rights (6) cattle grazing, grass and firewood. It seemed that the writers of the laws looked hard for things that would have no significance to give the appearance of judicial content when there was none.

ULTIMATE POWERS MEANS NO POWERS

The 'right of the government and district development committee in relation to the village development committee' is the most significant part of the entire law. It is the right to issue instruction and guidance, to inquire into irregularities, and to suspend and dissolve the committees. The significance of these points is that the village development committee has no autonomy, and if it attempts to exert such autonomy or go out of its narrow guidelines, which have been shown above to ensure that the people's power is limited, then the central government has the power to suspend the local committees.

DISTRICT COUNCIL AND DISTRICT DEVELOPMENT EXECUTIVE COMMITTEES: ILLOGICAL INDIRECT REPRESENTATION

Essentially everything said here can be said as well for the District Councils and Development Committees, except that the control of the central government at the district level is even more direct; and since many of the district functions are in the district government's interaction with the village and municipality committees, the District Council and Executive Committee become another means that centralized control is brought to these levels. The following specific observations can be made.

The members of the District Council are selected from the Village and Municipal Development Committees, but as determined by their positions or offices within these committees (that is, chairman, vice chairman) and not by election from them. The District Executive Committee is elected, again by the local development committees, but there is no provision for making the members of either the District Executive Committee or Council accountable to the villages or municipalities, just as there was no provision for making the latter accountable to the citizens. The only accountability is imposed from above onto the Committee and Council, as well as on the local committees, by the central government. Thus the whole law is merely democracy in form, which we have shown is the dictatorship of bosses, bureaucrats and special interests, not participatory democracy as in the Brazilian case.

Furthermore, there is a basic contradiction in that the members of the District Executive Committee, which submits policy and budgets to the Council, are also members of the Council. It is difficult to perceive the logic of this set-up, except to create something that appears democratic when there is no democracy in substance. If the council were actually representative, the executive committee— or temporary committees formed for dealing with particular problems—could be selected directly from the council by its members to carry out the actual work, which then could be voted upon by the council as a whole. There would be no need for all these various manipulations and complexities.

The initiatives for the District Council all come from the Executive Committee, thus the latter must be analysed in order to ascertain the substance of the powers of both. The Executive Committee Secretary again has broad powers, including executive, supervisory, administrative and evaluative, and furthermore, he is directly linked to the ministries. This again ensures that the central government will be able to exert itself through the workings at the District level at the local levels. As if there were not enough controls on the village committees, the district secretary also supervises the village committees, lessening their autonomy even further. Obviously, the district government does nothing to provide autonomy, except for the personal autonomy of officials and elected representatives by their lack of accountability.

CONCLUSION

Finally, as pointed out in the Introduction, people's participation is neither an inevitable nor even common feature of multi-party democracy.[5] Such participation necessitates that people (workers, peasants, women, squatters, etc.) build their own organizations from below in their places of activity: the work place, community, squatters' settlements, and urban slums. Here I do not mean exhuming the government sponsored organizations of the Panchayat times or emulating the largely urban based NGOs of today, but encouraging the emergence of organizations from the issues, problems, and perspectives experienced at the grass roots level. In recent years, such community levels of organization have arisen when people found that avenues for other forms of political expression are closed, such as in autocratic, single party (or partyless) states, or when they feel that they cannot express themselves through existing multi-party systems. Such situations have led to a flourishing of such organizations in Central and South America, the Philippines, Indonesia, parts of India, and even among the American Indians, Afro-Americans, Hispanics and men and women feminists and other colonized peoples within the United States.

In Brazil and Chile, decades of extreme oppression in which people had no alternative means of political expression led to the formation of a multitude of such organizations in the work place and community. In Brazil, following the institution of democracy, these organizations formed the Workers Party (PT) and in Chile they formed the United Slumdwellers Committee in order to exert themselves politically. Individuals can only belong to either organization if they participate in one or more of these grassroots organizations; and with its base in such organizations; the membership of both transcends the usual party alignments.

When people are wilfully organized in groups, they become accustomed to dialogue and working together. Such organization consequently creates a truly 'democratic culture' unattainable by internally undemocratic parties in single or multi-party systems. Furthermore, working together with neighbours and fellow workers necessitates listening to others and respecting their views. Such movements consequently tend to counter the hatred, sectarianism, intolerance, and parochial nationalism that continues to be a tool of power within multi-party democracy. This sense of human solidarity, dialogue and purpose develops across national borders as well, as groups communicate and recognize common conditions and problems. In a world in which production, commerce, finance, recruitment of labour and communication of ideas have become fully global, such organization and popular participation originating from community and workplace seem to pose the best potential for bringing people together to deal with social, political, economic and environmental problems that know no boundaries.

Top down government and planning as represented by Nepal's present local government law, whatever its pretensions and rhetoric, will do nothing except hinder such democratic development. It will raise the potential for sectarianism. However, the increasingly broad communication and participation of Nepali rural and urban workers in world markets and a world community, in contrast to the nationalist pretensions of the various ruling groups, may encourage them to search for new ways of expressing themselves through organization, dialogue, reflection, solidarity, and taking action and the future into their own hands. I leave off with the completion of the W.E.B. Du Bois's quote that started this piece:

Such retrogression has occurred and may occur in the progress of democracy; but the vaster possibility and the real promise of democracy is adding to human capacities and culture hitherto untapped sources of cultural variety and power. Democracy is tapping the great possibilities of mankind from unused and unsuspected reservoirs of human greatness. Instead of envying and seeking desperately outer and foreign sources of civilization, you may find in these magnificent mountains a genius and variety of human culture, which once released from poverty, ignorance and disease, will help guide the world. Once the human soul is thus freed, then and only then is peace possible. There will be no need to fight for food, for healthy homes, for free speech; for these will not depend on force; but increasingly on knowledge, reason and art. (Du Bois 1985a:242-3)

NOTES

This chapter was originally published in a slightly different version by the Nepal Law Society in the *Law Bulletin*, Vol. 54, No. 6, 1992, pp. 14–33. A substantially revised version, presented at the International Conference on The Anthropology of Nepal: Peoples, Problems and Process, organized by the University of Sidney in Kathmandu, 7–14 September 1992, and also to 20th Annual Conference on South Asia, Madison, Wisconsin, 3 November 1992, was published as 'The New Local Government Law: Diluted Raksi in an Old Bottle' in Michael Allen (ed.), *The Anthropology of Nepal; Peoples, Problems and Processes*, Kathmandu: Mandala Book Point. 1994. pp. 287–303.

1   'The bureaucracy . . . was presided over in Pakistan by the CSP (the Civil Service of Pakistan), successor to the colonial regime. It was the senior partner in the military-bureaucratic oligarchy that has ruled Pakistan since its inception. . . . It was powerful enough to keep the military at bay even during the Martial Law regimes of General Yahya Khan. The situation changed radically after Bhutto's reform of the bureaucracy which effectively broke its back. Ironically that removed the main barrier that had stood in the way of hegemony of the army which is now supreme' (Alavi 1989:242).

2   Max Weber, in 'The Meaning of Election and Representation' and 'Excursus on Party Control by Charismatic Leaders, Notables and Bureaucrats' (1978:1128–33), observed these characteristics in American politics and predicted them at that time for the nascent Soviet Union. He described parties as bureaucratic organizations which are controlled by party bosses and bureaucracies. On the one hand, the party bosses ('chairmen', 'general secretaries', 'supreme leaders', etc.) usually make their claim for leadership on the basis of some real or constructed charismatic qualities such as embodied by the creation of cults around rhetorical promises of some future Communism, party founders and leaders, like Nepal's B.P. Koirala, the 'Father of Democracy', or Gandhi or Nehru. On the other hand, party and government bureaucrats have a substantial interest in obtaining offices and other opportunities for themselves. They justify their positions, privileges, and usurpation of governmental functions from the people by reference to their expertise, educational certification, business qualifications, etc., just as previous rulers made claims based upon purity of lineage and birth with which these attributes were associated. The party bureaucrats control party policies through their systematically maintained relations with ward leaders and cadres and their control over the official operations and functions of the mechanisms necessary for running the party machine, such as voters' lists and files. The

candidates are their tools, who award government contracts, tax farming, monopolies and other privileges to party sponsors (e.g. businessmen, foreign agencies, etc.), fattening the resources of the party.

3   The Brazilian example basically contains the elements identified by Max Weber (1978:1127–8) in early Athenian democracy and the early British House of Commons, which made representative democracy democratic in substance. These early forms of democracy were based on popular assemblies with full participation of the citizens, as in the Brazilian neighbourhood organizations, which elected individuals to the councils, such as the Brazilian committees and popular councils. 'If this principle is radically applied, the elected person is formally the agent and hence the servant of his voters, not their chosen master, just like in a system of direct democracy' (Weber 1978:1128).

This also is the spirit originally envisioned by Lenin for the soviets or workers' assemblies in the Soviet Union (Lenin 1970:283–367). However, the extremely unfavourable conditions—domination of old interests, prevalence of corruption, extremely poorly educated populace, famine within the country, and the general ineptness of party cadres—despite the immense enthusiasm and high moral quality of many of them, and resolve of other countries not to give this important historical experiment a chance from without made realization of the model impossible.

A problem of socialism generally is that Communist and socialist parties have failed to 'maintain their separateness from social movements so that the autonomy of the grassroots could be preserved. One of the lessons learned from the populist period [in Brazil] was that grassroots movements die when they become purely a base of support for politicians, easily manipulated through the co-optation of the leadership: it was time for the people to learn where and how to swim themselves' (Alves 1991b:234).

4   Gervasi (1991:92) writes that through the course of the last 30 years, over a hundred million dollars was spent annually to build such NGOs in the Soviet Union to destroy any possibility of the popular development of a true socialist alternative by co-opting the party bureaucrats and bosses and forcing the Union to open fully to transnational corporate and banking interests. According to minimum figures, in the 1980s the National Endowment for Democracy (also operating in Nepal, Nicaragua, Costa Rica, and so forth) was spending $5 million, the CIA $80 million, and businesses, private organizations and other governments were spending another $15 million to support pro-'democracy' NGOs in the Soviet Union.

This strategy is summed up by an influential Washington journalist, David Ignatius (1991) in an unusually frank statement: 'Preparing the ground for last month's triumph [the fall of the Soviet Union] was a network of overt operatives who during the last ten years have quietly been changing the rules of international politics. They have been doing in public what the CIA used to do in private—providing money and moral support for pro-democracy groups, training resistance fighters, working to subvert communist rule.'

5   Indeed, as shown by other pieces in this book, democracy originated as a means of controlling and excluding the populace's participation.

CHAPTER 9

Charisma and its Routinization: Co-optation by Party Leadership in the Recent *Andolan*

> Do not cry, do not laugh, but understand.
>
> —Rosa Luxemburg

WITH THE BREAK-UP of the civil servants strike of in the summer 1991 and yet another left-led movement into renewed divisions between the left factions and recriminations among their leaders, the problem of party leadership arises. The left leadership bases its position on past roles and recognition within the party, not selection by the people. This leads to the question whether their change of roles from organizers into representatives of the people is legitimate. Legitimacy implies consensus and accountability. The selection process, however, is decided by vague intra-party mechanisms in which the people of the constituencies the leadership supposedly to represent have no participation or means of making the leaders accountable. This implies that when such leaders start making decisions *for* the people, they are usurping authority from them.

Lacking a popular consensus and departing from a popular basis, the Communist parties attempt to justify the selection of their leaders by referring to extraordinary personal qualities or 'charisma'. If leaders have such qualities, these arise from the extraordinary or charismatic quality of a movement that aims to shift control of people's lives and human destiny into the hands of the working masses, and not the intrinsic character of the individual. It is contradictory for individuals to place themselves over others in the name of such charisma, as the goal of Communist struggle is to create a society which liberates individuals from such domination. Recriminations and backbiting among the leaders will continue to divide and plague the struggle until the focus shifts back to those who live and work among the workers so that the latter may educate and take over this decision making themselves. The revolutionary process must be one of building the conditions which we wish to create *now*, in this world, not making ideal promises of some better future. This means a process in which workers take their situation into their own hands, not one in which they fight like a bunch of Brahmans over who is following the most pure line.

Extraordinary needs, caused by the combination of exploitation, war, and abuse by expanding empires and decaying regimes, have incited people to rise up time and again in history. These movements 'heterogeneously'[1] break the routines of everyday life and shear away the legitimacy of old authorities. The participants of these movements base the legitimacy of their call to act on the authority of the extraordinary or charismatic promises of a new life given form by the energy and power of struggle.

'"Natural" leaders' emerge in these 'movements of distress', who are 'neither appointed officeholders nor "professionals" . . . but rather the bearers of specific gifts of body and mind that were considered "supernatural" (in the sense that not everybody could have access to them)' (Weber 1978:1111–12). These leaders are able to marshal, or somehow seem to embody, the heterogeneous elements that unleash the movement. People follow such leaders solely on the proof of powers in practice, powers whose effectiveness have to be continually demonstrated or else the followers will soon abandon him.

In radical contrast to bureaucratic organization, charisma knows no formal and regulated appointment or dismissal, no career, advancement or salary, no supervisory or appeals body, no local or purely technical jurisdiction, and no permanent institutions in the manner of bureaucratic agencies, which are independent of the incumbents and their personal charisma. Charisma is self-determined and sets its own limits. Its bearer seizes the task for which he is destined and demands that others obey and follow him by virtue of his mission. If those to whom he feels sent do not recognize him, his claim collapses; if they recognize it, he is their master as long as he 'proves' himself. However, he does not derive his claims from the will of his followers, in the manner of an election; rather, it is their *duty* to recognize his charisma. (Weber 1978:1112)

In Nepal, all parties claim charismatic properties for their leaders in order to draw support and allegiance for their parties. The dead Congress leader B.P. Koirala and the Communist Pushpa Lal Shrestha have been given the status almost of deities. Others have been made by their parties into *mahamanab* ('supreme leaders') or *jaana neta* ('people's leaders'). An aura of charisma is constructed around these individuals in order to attract obedience to party objectives and to impose party discipline. Such mystical claims may in one sense be inevitable, but they present a contradiction for Communist parties, which claim to be fighting to end the exploitation of the working classes and to give power to them through their conscious organization.

Arrogation of decision making by the Communist Party leaders and the exclusion of their party members, allied parties, and the mass base of people from the decision making can be seen as a bid by the leaders to establish themselves as 'new masters' rather than provide revolutionary empowerment to the people and create popular rule. Reference to charisma to legitimize and justify the ascendancy of leaders *over* the people from *beside* them is just a continuation of such claims as those made in the name of Prithivi Narayan Shah, King Tribhuvan, B.P. Koirala, and the present 'Supreme' Leaders of the Congress Party.[2] It is done to co-opt struggle and use the sloganeering claims made in the various movements to advance the narrow interests of ascendant ruling classes, not to preserve a democracy which never existed or advance a Communism which they know will never be.

Usually the new classes which have arisen in the name of Communism have consisted of educated groups, generally with identifiable origins in other exploiting classes, which aim to extend their power by means of control over bureaucratic offices, and which limit entry into their ranks through the means of differential access to schooling and use of examinations as gates to instrumental roles and positions in society. We can identify the development of such a professional class or 'intelligentsia' (a term coined in nineteenth-century Russia) in contemporary Nepal, along with its boarding schools, its standardized and universalized curriculum and examinations, and its use of bureaucratic machinery to subordinate alternative revolutionary initiatives—for example, independent mass organizations—and penetrate and intervene in every sector of national life. Most of the major Communist (to say nothing of other party) leaders hail from the elite and the high castes, while cadres are drawn from the great masses of village young people who have been educated enough to turn against the old life and responsibilities, but not enough to pass examinations and qualify for instrumental positions in the state (see Mikesell 1993).

A common tendency is for leaders to appropriate and 'routinize' the charisma of human collective struggle and make it seem to be their own charisma and the struggle their own doing. 'Routinization of charisma' means removing it from the extraordinary situation and turning it into a means of perpetuating newly established routines of everyday life (Weber 1978:1121). Currently in Nepal it is the routine of party leaders representing the working class in the parliament rather than building the organization of the workers to allow them to represent and make decisions for themselves. The problem is that it is not a leadership—either Communist or Democratic—which is the true instrumental actor of revolution; it can only be the workers themselves. Communist leaders are the product of the Communist movement, their fate and fortunes are tied to it, but they are *not* the movement. When the leaders have disconnected their purposes from the common purposes, charisma leaves them.

They are then forced to sustain an appearance of charisma with periodic agitation (the 'movements' since 1991), formula speeches, banners and slogans, claims of having greater ideological purity than other leaders, and obligatory rituals. When Communist parties gain control of state power and turn the 'revolution' into an obsession with holding onto power, rituals are taken to absurd extremes. Communism, like Lenin's carefully embalmed body, was preserved in massive state rituals in the Soviet Union, while the councils or soviets, in which the industrial workers and rural peasants were supposed to rule themselves, were sucked dry of all autonomy and power.

Though it pretended to be 'democratic' rather than 'Communist', the previous Panchayat government in Nepal basically made the same claims and gave us a strong taste of this ersatz ritual Communism. It engaged in the same kinds of state rituals, so much so that it came to a point that every government official was forced to attend them and sign his or her name in attendance books at these rituals. Those who failed to show up were black listed for promotion, those who did were quite aware that the whole thing was a farce and laughed about it. As the Panchayat regime was crumbling in the face of the 1990 movement, it organized these rituals on an unprecedented scale all over the country, draining the treasury to truck in paid audiences from the villages to present a face of mass democratic support.

When the Congress government attempted to re-institute such a ritual on 18 February 1992, to celebrate the beginning of the 'People's Movement' and sustain the pretensions of the mass uprising which brought the party to power, few except their toadies showed up. What is the use of democracy based on intra-party autocracy and captured ballot boxes? people asked. The UML leadership also, now that the party has abandoned grassroots, cadre-based organizing and revolutionary struggle for the Parliamentary Road, dismantling or letting the cell committees wither in the grass roots, hang onto the mysteries of Marxist-Leninism, demanding obligatory belief in its archaic and unwieldy formulae to make up for their own inaction. They too have their rituals, such as their national convention guarded by ushers dressed in green Red Guard uniforms and a podium adorned with murals celebrating an abandoned militancy and the yearly celebration of the party founder Pushpa Lal's birthday in which his pictures are displayed like religious icons.

How can political leaders claim they represent the people when they exclude them from decision-making within the party? From a perspective of long-run strategy, prosecution of the movement must involve organizing the people in their *toles* (urban quarters) and villages so they may not only participate in planning and execution of the movement, but also be consulted to any negotiations. Such organization and empowerment of the people must take place not just as the primary strategy of the movement, but as the foremost goal. If such strategy had been followed in the movement of the summer of 1991, the ten demands of that movement would subsequently have been fulfilled as a matter of course, becoming inconsequential among its eventual accomplishments. Such full participation by people in their governance through the creation of communal organizations in which they can exert themselves *is* the meaning of Communism (and *real* democracy),[3] after all.[4]

Marx, Engels and even Lenin pointed this out,[5] yet as experienced in experiments in France (1848–50), Germany (1919–20), the Soviet Union, China (1930 and 1949 onwards, respectively), Hyderabad (1948), Indonesia (1946), Iran (1905–9 and 1970s),[6] Nicaragua (1977–90) and many other places, there are many lessons to be learnt. Communist victories have too often become the instruments of new stultifying bureaucratic classes and glowering central committees in consolidating their own positions rather than providing for the full release of the human capabilities and spirit, with a deep respect for each individual—as promised. And movements have too often been sold out for parliamentary opportunism. For revolutionaries committed to Communism and thus democracy (meaning real popular democracy and not the mockery that is made of it today), it is necessary to disclose how the popular purposes of struggle are undermined by the very people who claim to be its leaders.

Each period has seen its own revolutionary ideologies give the promises of struggle a form appropriate to the social constituency and conditions of the time. Communism has grown up as the ideology of such movements during the industrial period. In this period, the toilers, wrenched away from small property holdings and personalized relations of exploitation that characterized previous eras, for the first time developed a consciousness of its existence as a class. The worker sees solace not in obtaining his own small private plot of land or establishment of a craft shop, but in taking over the factories, land and other means of production, and owning them collectively for the benefit of the class as a whole. This collective ownership reflects the socialized character of production which has been brought about under industrial capitalism.

Such critical consciousness and its necessary concomitant organization do not appear merely by virtue of the workers' position as part of the global working class (as they themselves are confronted by the transnational corporations, but have not yet become conscious of and begun to act upon themselves). Their understanding and position is mediated by the immediate conditions that they face: landlordism and debt, relations of patronage in the factories and parties, market conditions, nationalism and ethnicity, regressive religious ideas and schooling that domesticate young people rather than encourage them to build a critical consciousness and integrity in living, a culture of commodities and slick advertising, and so forth. This is especially true for Nepal, where workers are drawn mostly from rural areas and find themselves confronted by conditions of bondage that seem feudal, but from which they are recruited to the fields, sweatshops, factories and brothels of the plantations and cities of the world. Their situation is so bad that their immediate concern is to fill their plates with food. Abstract ideologies and slogans are not lentils and rice, and while revolutionary slogans can incite the masses for momentary periods, they cannot sustain a prolonged struggle—especially not in the rural areas where most of the working class resides.

The struggle must start with organizing people in the places where they live and work, around immediate and concrete issues such as food and water, health and child care, wages and working conditions, literacy, and so forth. The focus must be on the process and not on these issues in themselves, or else it will lead just to economism or reform (i.e. getting better wages or other arrangements without changing the basic situation). Educating and organizing people around questions of literacy, rents, getting water taps in villages, setting up community run pharmacies and health programs, building collective marketing associations, and so forth will bring the villagers into immediate confrontation not only with local village patronage, but with the powerful interests nationally and internationally which depend upon maintenance of the local exploitative situation: international marketing, industry, finance and so forth that presently control all these needs worldwide. The consequent struggle takes a social or collective form because the people have organized themselves in groups to assert their demands, and only by extending and interlinking these groups can they confront oppressive conditions that extend far beyond their village and even the borders of their country.

Presently the Communist parties in Nepal conceive the struggle purely in terms of fighting over control of the immediate nation state conceived as *the* state, even if in the name of 'smashing' it they aim to control it. However, oppressive forces and the state machinery (if we take the state to mean the instruments of exploitation and oppression) extend far beyond Nepal, and they take many more forms than just an overtly political one: everything from pharmaceuticals, education, and advertising to international aid and finance. These will never be conquered or even significantly challenged by a purely national political struggle, certainly not by struggles limited to urban *bands* (strikes), noisy demonstrations, bombastic speeches and other forms of reactive politics. They require building a subaltern or counter culture, critical consciousness and organization that reach into every village and every household.

Initiative must be taken to create the conditions of positive change.[7] To date the Communist leadership seems to have held the belief that somehow capitalism will cave in from its own internal contradictions. While it is true that the internal contradictions are there, the crisis and collapse will go to the hands of groups that have built themselves up in the course of it. Presently, this is taking the form of ever greater concentrations of capital, confronting an ever more divided working class. '

To set the workers up to take class power, initiative must be taken at every stage; but in Nepal, the Communist parties have failed to take the initiative. They only react to every move that the Congress Party and its national supporters and international patrons are making. They allow the people's movements to be taken from their hands and agitate ineffectively against the results. They wait for a reactionary constitution to be written and then can do nothing about it. They wait for public corporations to be sold off without organizing the workers to resist or take them over before the policy can be enacted. They organize and agitate around the issue of the death of a couple of their leaders, as if the party exists for the leaders rather than the other way around, rather than addressing the problems of long-term struggle, unity, and the arduous process of conscientization and organization.

The parties, if they are revolutionary, must put forward there own initiatives which then the ruling groups and ruling party must deal with, not the other way around. When the Congress Party used the state machinery to prevent the formation of a constitutional convention, the Communist Party [United Left Front, Unity Centre, Masal (M.B. Singh) and other groups] should have called their own convention and challenged them instead of making half-hearted complaints and futile demonstrations and finally caving in on the issue. When the government put off forming local governments, the so-call opposition missed the opportunity of organizing the people to build its own local assemblies and councils. The CP-UML deceived itself that the Congress would set the terms and then it (the UML) would capture power at the local level. The Congress Party is aware of its weakness at the local level. It had no plan to build a local structure that would allow power out of its hands any more than the king allowed the Panchayats to have a chance to become an effective tool for the people. And indeed, the Congress government drew up a local government law that insured that power remained centralized.[8]

The struggle must form local learning groups, termed 'cultural circle' by Paulo Freire (1972), which have arisen in hundreds of thousands throughout South America, since a struggle that is based on slogans rather than critical consciousness and understanding will always lead to another form of domination in terms of these slogans. Organizers must work with villagers and urban slum dwellers to educate themselves in a manner that leads to action and challenges the tyranny of the school system and advertising propaganda. As these groups confront immediate forms of domination and come to understand them as originating in much larger relations, they will link together and elect popular assemblies in which the people rule themselves through discussions, consensus and popular action locally. These assemblies in turn elect individuals to popular councils with recallable representatives and direct accountability to the local assemblies. Extend these organizations through relations with similar initiatives internationally. They must make whoever is in power in the formal government of Nepal, in the offices of international agencies, in ruling centres throughout the world, confront the initiative of the Nepali villager and urban worker as a powerful force, and not the other way around.

NOTES

1 Used by Max Weber to mean convergence of a whole combination of varied elements, as opposed to the forced uniformity imposed by the ruling regime. This can also be seen as an argument against the divisive sectarianism characteristic of the Left.

2 The author showed how such claims were made by Prithivi Narayan Shah as the basis for harnessing the efforts of the people in the name of national unity to establish a new order of landlordism in 'Marx's Ethnological Notebooks, Feudalism in Asia, and Strategy in Nepal' (chapter 17, this volume).

3 The word 'democracy' is based on the root stem 'deme' (tribe, among the Romans) which is the name of the basic units of the community in Greek society, represented proportionally in the polis. In principle democracy means the rule of the community, not of private interests, although in Greek and Roman society from the start the character of the community, which excluded slaves, foreigners, freemen and women from political participation, greatly limited actual franchise. And even within this small group the content of the demes and tribes was gerrymandered to ensure actual control within a much smaller group of powerful and entrenched interests. All these machinations and more characterize democracy today.

For example, with a global regime of capital, such disenfrachisement is obtained, additionally, through the division of the world into nation states in which limited groups of citizens, themselves divided, unorganized, and generally domesticated and manipulated—such as those of the United States or any West European country—are able to vote upon issues affecting peoples in other parts of the world and for leaders making decisions affecting people in other parts of the world, while these other people directly effected have no say at all.

4   Paul Frölich (1972:xx) writes in his 1948 Preface to *Rosa Luxemburg*, 'The goal of socialism is man, i.e. a society without class differences in which men working in community, without tutelage, forge their own fate. It is —in Marx's words— "an association where the free development of each individual is the condition for the free development of all". It is not socialism if the means of production are socialised and set into motion according to a plan, but a class or a special stratum autocratically controls the means of production, regiments and oppresses the working masses, and deprives them of their rights. No socialism can be realised in a country where the state power breaks in and gets rid of the ruling classes and property relations but at the same time subjects the whole nation to a ruthless dictatorship which prevents the working class from being conscious of its particular role and tasks and acting accordingly.'

5   Marx and Engels in *The German Ideology*, Marx in his works on the Paris Commune and class struggle in France (*The Class Struggles in France 1848 to 1850, The Civil War in France*, and *The Eighteenth Brumaire of Louis Bonaparte*) and late in his life in his vast unfinished project represented in *The Ethnological Notebooks of Karl Marx* (1972), and Lenin in his *State and Revolution*.

6   The so-called 'Islamic Revolution' in Iran and Khomeini's rise to power in the 1970s resulted from the determined and cynical support of imperialist powers in order to destroy the active Communist movement in Iran at the time. More than ten thousand Communists were subsequently executed.

7   Dialectic is often treated as *merely* negation, as in the Maoist slogan 'smash the state', but negation without affirmation turns the struggle into nihilism. If this affirmation does not occur through the working class building its own consciousness, autonomous organizations, and alternative forms of life, the fruits of struggle will be taken over by other groups already organized and poised to do so; in today's world the transnational corporations, corporate bureaucracies, national professional classes in their pay, and so forth are imminently poised in this way.

8   See 'The Local Government Bill and Participatory Democracy: A Comparison of Opposites' (chapter 8, this volume).

CHAPTER 10

Democratizing Tribhuvan University

THE SITUATION of Tribhuvan University, the national university in Nepal, exemplifies what is generally happening in the state-run institutions of the country. Almost everyone has suggested in the ongoing discussion on the problems of the University that it must be democratized. They complain that the university is over-centralized and top-heavy with bureaucracy, the curriculum is outdated and restrictive, the campuses have been politicized by the political parties, there is lack of commitment of the professors to their classes and students to their studies, the university is treated as spoils of victory for whoever comes to power, and throughout the whole Tribhuvan University system there is a general lack of accountability or sense of responsibility.

I have been impressed by the general level of enthusiasm and the sincerity, though justifiable frustration, of the students and many of the faculty. Tarnished though it is, Tribhuvan University makes higher education accessible to the great mass of less privileged people in a way that will never be reproduced by the new private campuses that have been ushered in on the coattails of 'democracy'. Politicization can be seen in the positive light that the university community has not given itself over to despair, although a creative and positive commitment to discussion and working together would be preferable to the mistrust, beatings, stone throwing, and strikes, lockouts and *gheraos* (encirclements) that often occur. With lack of accountability to the bottom, with a custom of issuing of bureaucratic directives from the top down and passing responsibility from the bottom up, and with the top immobilized by politics, this sort of desperate reaction is forced upon people. But with faculty and students divided along party lines, particularly between the Nepali Congress and various communist groups, it is impossible for them to confront and solve even the most basic problem of decentralization which in the long-run would benefit them all. The various groups of students and faculty have far more in common than they might acknowledge, not only in relation to their shared personal problems of a generally poor level of academic preparation and the general problems of the University (buildings in poor condition, lack of finance, low salaries, poor library and research facilities and so forth) but also in the face of the great forces at work in the world which affect every student equally (here I am thinking of the internalization and bureaucratization of industry and finance and the immense threats to the viability of our planet and human society which have arisen in the last half century).

Unfortunately, the solutions so far offered by the administration have been, not surprisingly, administrative. They depend upon enforcing regulations and pouring in yet additional foreign aid prior to addressing the more important issues of democratization and building of accountability. There is a general refusal by the party in power or the administration to relinquish power and initiative to the faculty, students and the communities in which the campuses are situated, with the justification that these groups are too politicized to take responsibility for themselves. In reality, the upper levels of administration want to protect their perks, privileges and power, and they are supported by the sycophants among the department chiefs, as the latter could never enjoy the positions they hold—with their automobiles, telephones, personal assistants and delusion of authority—through democratic means. Those who complain regarding the abuse of power by the ruling party when they are in the opposition, become must reluctant to devolve power within the university when they come to power.

Mere emphasis on more stringent enforcement of administrative regulations without changing the basic structures of the University is like forcing unwilling goats to graze on barren pastures: it destroys both the goats and what remains of the pasture. The current Nepali Congress administration has turned to the World Bank and USAID for assistance, as foreign aid seems like an easy shortcut: it allows people in power to make decisions and take action without consulting the people who they are supposed to be helping. There is a great interest in foreign aid all through the administration and among the various interests that attach themselves to the University, because of the commissions, kickbacks and sinecures that it promises. But aid de-legitimizes the University's procedures and undercuts accountability. It will not be used effectively until autonomy and accountability are built into the system, if then. The foreign grants and loans, which Vice Chancellor Mathima is presently chasing, without making the top accountable to the bottom and dismantling much of the bureaucracy and shifting power to faculty and students, will aggravate the problems and inequalities and lead to throwing good money after bad.

STRENGTHENING THE FACULTIES

The excuse that the university cannot be decentralized due to politicization is an empty argument because knowledge and their reproduction by their nature are political. Prime Minister Chandra Shamsher Rana acknowledged this when, as he opened Trichandra College in 1918, he said, 'I am sowing the seed of revolution today'. The struggles among the students, faculties and parties in part reflect the political character of both knowledge and the institutions in which it is controlled. The centralized power within the university system, and indeed the centralized curriculum at all levels of the government education system from primary school upwards, is a legacy of regimes who, with the compliant collaboration of foreign governments and agencies, wanted to gain the benefits of technique while suppressing the critical character of knowledge. Critique, however, is inseparable from technique, as technique is always applied within a social context. Effective application of knowledge requires inventing it anew and remaking both the society and the technique, as well as ideas regarding what the whole project is about. Without the critical component, technique loses its dynamism and vitality and becomes oppressive. In order to retrieve the dynamism of the university, control must be shifted from the bureaucratic and ruling class groups that want to maintain the society along the old lines to groups with an immediate interest in teaching and learning. If decision making and accountability are devolved or removed downwards to the faculty and students involved in the actual day-to-day functioning of the university, and if close ties are built with the surrounding communities, then the ineffectual and self-destructive character of politicization will largely disappear. Contention will certainly continue, and must do so; but it will have more chance to become creative, address more substantive issues, and produce positive changes and growth in the university and society.

As in the past, faculty seats, chairmanships, and administrative positions are being given as sinecures by the ruling Nepali Congress government in reward for overt displays of flattery and fealty, institutionalized in what Bista (1991) calls *chakari* and *afno manche*, respectively. Under the interim government also all the temporary seats had already been made into full-time ones without any sort of internal review of the fitness of the people for the positions or the need for them. This giving of sinecures is filling the university with self seekers and sycophants who are good neither for the university nor the ruling party. Democratic structures and practices must be introduced which prevent outside manipulation and interference, whatever party happens to be in power.

The first step that needs to be taken is to shift the control of the departments over to the faculty and to make the faculty accountable to their peers and students. Certainly, some departments and faculty in the various campuses will not do as well as the others. But this is a problem encountered elsewhere, and it can be handled on a case-by-case basis. It should not be an excuse for continuing suppression of the development of the University and its campuses.

Faculty members must be selected by the members of the departments, with administrative interference limited at most to review and final approval according to formal requirements. Selection must be open and transparent. There can be advertisement of the position and open acceptance of applications, nomination of an initial long list by a faculty and student selection committee elected by the department faculty and students respectively, reduction to a short list by the entire faculty, oral presentations and interviews with the short-listed candidates, and final selection through faculty (and student?) voting through secret ballot.

The selection of chairpersons of the departments, despite a veneer of formality, depends upon patronage and ingratiating servility, and expressing cynical fealty to whichever party is in power. Often the appointments leave great bitterness, and the inability and disinterest of the chairpersons to work with the faculty members compromises the functioning of the departments. Instead, the chairpersons must be nominated and elected by secret ballot by the faculty of each department themselves, rather than appointed from outside the department.

Decision-making power within the departments is presently concentrated within the chairpersons' hands. As the chairpersons often receive their appointment through patronage or favouritism from higher up in the University, they furthermore are compelled to defer decisions and bow to the wishes of the administration or various political powers rather than serve the needs of the department and the discipline. In addition to placing the selection of chairpersons with the departments, the chairperson's role needs to be reduced to an administrative one, decision-making must take place in faculty meetings—either by oral consensus or secret ballot, depending upon its nature—and many of the departmental functions must be turned over to faculty committees.

Presently faculty promotions are heavily controlled by the administration. Faculty promotions need to be deliberated and voted upon by senior faculty members within the departments, with independent reviews by other departments and only finally by the administration. Promotions must be based on a combination of publication, research, teaching record, and commitment to participation in committees, to the educational process and adhering to basic standards of personal integrity (no plagiarism, sexist behaviour, etc.). The teaching record must be judged in terms of formal evaluations by students, which will make faculty members accountable to the students.[1] Decisions on promotions and other matters should be appealable to the senate.

REBUILDING THE CURRICULUM

The faculties of each campus need to determine their own curricula rather than having one imposed on all the campuses from the centre. The caveat that I have heard made is that if curricula are left to individual faculties students will receive incomplete training. However, I have found that the curricula are presently being taught merely as formality, with neither interest nor substance. Centrally determined curricula ignore the weaknesses and strengths of the faculties of individual departments. Especially in the social sciences and humanities, the boundaries of different fields and what makes up the field are contested domains. Imposition of heavily centralized curricula suppresses the dynamic reinterpretation and re-creation of knowledge—the critical, teleological aspect—that is an essential part of learning. It turns learning into a mechanical process and domesticates it to serve the purposes of various competing oppressor interests in society.

Most of the curricula have been developed in industrial countries according to their own realities. In these countries the curricula and the systems of higher education are currently in a crisis as never before, due to the basic changes that are taking place in the global social and political economy and the fundamental changes in the relations of these countries and their peoples among themselves and the rest of the world. The old ways of organizing people and knowledge are necessarily falling by the wayside. Thus there should be no assumption that there is an essential curriculum that makes up a subject, or that particular subjects exist autonomously from other kinds of knowledge and activity. A constant critical reappraisal in the context of each campus and its particular faculty and student body is essential for Nepal. There can be regular reviews of the various departments, and if problems arise these can be worked out individually with the faculties of those departments.

There is a gross misconception that the creation of knowledge and its transfer are two separate things in the University. This has led to the establishment of separate teaching and research institutes, and a separation of on-campus teaching and off-campus consultant research. Limited budgets are stretched among too many departments, teaching faculty moonlight in extracurricular research contracts often taking time from their university activities without bringing any overhead to the university. Teaching and learning are not only interrupted by the teachers divided responsibilities, but teaching is separated from the making of knowledge. Depending on the situation, the research departments must either be reduced to or interconnected with teaching departments in interdisciplinary programs, or else teaching must be brought into the research departments, or both.

THE SOLUTION: A UNIFIED STRUGGLE

Whereas during the Panchayat period the Vice Chancellor of Tribhuvan University was appointed by the king, who still is designated as the Chancellor, now he is appointed by the Education Ministry. Each succeeding VC makes the same mistake of trying to take an administrative shortcut to solve the problems of the University. The VCs, perhaps under the illusion that administrative office provides real control, rely on administrative means to avoid confronting and dealing with the wide variety of conflicting social interests contesting for control. This emphasis on administration adds more and more layers of bureaucrats who are oriented towards administrative directives and extending their own individual and group interests through what Max Weber (1978) calls 'bureaucratic domination'. They orient themselves and the university processes towards administrative directives and extending their own individual and group interests rather than really finding solutions. The bureaucrats exert their power through control of files and specialized administrative knowledge. Any power held by the VC and other posts is illusory as the bureaucrats insulate them from the people and functions of the University.

The solution is rather to devolve as many of the administrative functions and responsibilities as possible to departmental, interdepartmental, and extramural and intramural faculty and student committees. These committees would be democratically selected within and accountable to the departmental faculties, councils and senates. Specialized offices which impose unnatural divisions, such as the Research Division, need to be dismantled. This would shift power to the teachers and students—rather than remanding them to the hands of a burdensome parasitic element that has very different priorities than the alleged purpose of a university as a teaching and research institution. This and the other solutions could also provide an inexpensive and cost effective framework of decentralizing administration of the many campuses, and they must be taken before pouring large sums of money into an institution rife with privilege and corruption.

The way that this transformation is going to be effected will be through the students and faculty themselves, not through the chimera of bureaucratically initiated 'decentralization' which has been the theory and practice of decentralization in Nepal to date. Such 'decentralization' has reflected the assertion of a growing cadre of middle elements in the bulging bureaucracy in the manner that the growth of the early administration in Nepal, starting with the estates, has always meant this group exerting themselves against the centre. In the past this administrative class aimed for private estates, but as it transformed itself into a specialized bureaucratic corps according to the modern-day demand for more and more specialized knowledge, it aimed for 'socialization'. Nowadays this class frames its continued ascendancy in terms of nice sounding words such as 'decentralization' and 'democratization' and developing 'participation' and 'autonomy'. But these words have little to do with devolving real power and authority to the actual functioning components of the institutions and the society; it reflects more the expansion of the sway of this bureaucratic class and its administrative machinery into every domain of the social life of the people and communities, through both the state and the NGO sector. The party struggle within the University reflects the various attempts of components of this class to control this process of bureaucratic expansion, using slogans and other mechanisms, to gain control over the University as the spoils of this struggle—not to effectively run the it according to its purposes. Thus we have seen since the culmination of the democracy movement in 1990 and the institution of multi-party parliamentary democracy the further decline of the University as an effective teaching and research institution, which was already moribund to start with, as the parties have aroused their faculty and student supporters and cadres to fight it out while sacrificing academic standards and integrity of the University in the process.

Stopping this process is going to take mounting a strong counter-force to the bureaucratic interests of the administration on the one hand and the contractor-commission agent interests, as well as the party-bureaucratic interests, in control of the parties on the other hand. The faculty and students of all flags are going to have to organize themselves around decentralizing and developing the autonomy of the university as a position that they can minimally agree upon. This could be possible if people are made to see that such an authentic decentralization is in their long-term interest. Once they have gained this minimal position with some or all of the elements I have described above, then they can fight out their various positions. Such a change will lead to entirely new and productive issues replacing the former ones, because the agenda of the bureaucrats, which hides behind the current fighting and undermines effectively addressing real issues, will have been pushed aside.

NOTES

This chapter was originally published in slightly different form as 'Democratizing the University' in *The Kathmandu Post*, 27 September 1993.

1   Due to poor preparation and an overly formalistic and authoritarian lower school education which emphasizes blind adherence to the curriculum, there is a tendency of students to only study the material given in the lectures and prepare for exams according to the curriculum. Faculty who demand more than this of students are met with strong protest. Thus weighting of student evaluations must be balanced realistically against the tendency of students to demand minimal requirements and realize that good faculty, who demand the most of their students, may be poorly evaluated by the students.

PART III

South Asia, Nepal, and Strategy
Following the People's Movement

CHAPTER 11

Marx's Ethnological Notebooks, Feudalism in Asia, and Strategy in Nepal

THE NEPALESE Left starts with the premise that the countryside of Nepal, if not the state, is feudal. Although this is a more critical stance than many works which describe the country in terms of being timeless and 'traditional', it is theoretically, historically and comparatively incorrect. Moreover, it seems strategically unwise. Although this interpretation is based on materialist theory, it misreads Marx's analysis of feudalism [e.g. in Marx and Engels' Introduction to *The German Ideology* (1983) and 'Forms which Precede Capitalist Production' (1973a)]. Moreover, in the last years of his life, Marx (1972) strongly opposes it.

In the first place, that relations take feudal forms does not necessarily mean that they are feudal in content or that the state is feudal. A study of feudalism in Europe shows that it arose from the disintegration of the Roman Empire, a highly centralized state controlling the entire Mediterranean, Western Europe, and a large part of Asia. This is not at all the experience in Nepal.

Over the course of five centuries that the Roman Empire developed in Western Europe (from the first quarter of the first century BC to the last quarter of the fifth century AD), not only did Roman society drastically change, but the relations in the countryside under the Roman rule among the tribes which eventually overthrew it also transformed. Consequently, it is important not to too quickly attribute feudalism to other areas of the world without accounting for and comparing conditions that presupposed its development in Europe.

As one of the driving forces of the expansion of the Roman empire, its citizens set themselves up on landed estates in conquered provinces worked by enslaved captives. Simultaneously, the Romans established cities across Europe as seats of administration and trade. The rule of these cities over the countryside was essentially political, meaning that production itself did not in substance change. On the fringes of the empire, the various German tribes were forced to organize for war against the Roman expansion. In the later centuries, this took an increasingly aggressive form. Since the development of the Ancient city was characterized by territorial expansion with its citizens becoming a landed class, Marx spoke of this expansion of the Ancient European city as 'ruralization of the city'.

In the late empire of the fourth and fifth centuries AD, developments led to the appearance of a number of conflicting interests which increasingly weakened the empire from within while the threat from without grew ever stronger. The long years of war against increasingly powerful German tribes placed a heavier and heavier tax burden on the countryside, causing an ever larger split between the strong landholding class and the city. These developments were compounded by a growing class of restless landless citizens and freed slaves within the cities, and growing restlessness among slaves working in the countryside, with their sympathies for the Germans. The landless proletariat remained an unorganized rabble, threatening the rulers (inducing subsequent rulers to promise greater amounts of 'bread and circuses' to sedate the masses) but never posing a threat to take over state power.

Due to the long history of expansion and centralization, when the Western Empire eventually fell at the end of the fifth century the collapse of the state machinery was so complete and widespread that it reduced political power into many small estates and individual landlords organized according to the militarized order of the invading tribes. Although much weakened and depopulated, the cities stood in opposition to the countryside. Throughout the immense area of what was once the Western Empire, cities for the first time had become relatively independent of the control of landed property interests over the state. Feudalism was then characterized by a gradual process of exertion of the independence and extension of control of cities over the countryside and eventually the state. Thus, unlike before, the expansion of the feudal cities took the form of 'urbanization of the countryside'.

At no time in its history has Nepal, however, been characterized by either the great centralization that provided the historical basis preceding the rise of feudalism or the complete collapse of the state that defined it. In the West, at least, where Rajputs had been establishing themselves from the beginning of the millennium, the state in Nepal was always characterized by increasing centralization, and at no time has control of the landed classes over it been relinquished. Unlike in feudal Europe, towns and cities never emerged in opposition to the landed property classes and the countryside. Rather, they developed as seats of control of these landed property classes. Consequently, instead of exerting their independence, the urban industrial and mercantile classes remained subordinated to the landed classes, taking their hegemonic form, caste.

The centuries from the time of King Prithivi Narayan Shah, the first king of modern Nepal (d. 1775), have been characterized by unprecedented centralization and realignment of production and development of social interests, in Nepal, India and globally. Prithivi Narayan's 'unification' of Nepal assumed already great inequality in the countryside which caused hill peasants to rally around him and his promise of agricultural land to his followers.[1] The contingency of the plots on ruling interests of the state, and the subsequent centralization, both of control by landed property within the country and the growing strength of industrial capitalism without, neither alleviated conditions in the countryside nor helped establish industry as an independent force. And while bazaar merchants became a strong force within Nepal, this has been primarily due to their role in the circulation of industrial commodities from without. The conditions of feudalism as a form of state or in the content of the general relations of the people simply never existed in Nepal.

MARX'S ETHNOLOGICAL NOTEBOOKS AND THE INDIAN SUBCONTINENT

We know quite well Marx's understanding of the global process from his earlier works, especially *Capital*. But there seems to be a continuing debate about how he interpreted developments in the Indian subcontinent. Best known are his writings in the New York *Daily Tribune* on India during the Great Revolt of the 1850s, when Marx first began to familiarize himself with India and characterized

British rule as far more despotic and destructive than was ever previously experienced in India. However, he also saw this rule as representing a revolutionary force that would introduce contradictions to bring the subcontinent out of its assumed stagnation. He developed this understanding in the *Grundrisse* (Marx 1973a) with the addition of an 'Asiatic form' to his Hegelian schema of property and modes of production in the history of the world that he had previously developed in his introduction to *The German Ideology*.

Some scholars particularly reacted to this understanding of Marx, especially in its subsequent unilinear interpretations and formulations unintended by Marx. Aware that characterizations of Asia as stagnant have been an aspect of expansionist western colonial and imperial ideology, these scholars try to show how Indian and other Asian Empires were indeed feudal and thus contained dynamic contradictions in the sense of feudalism in Western Europe (Berktay 1987; Alavi 1980).

While agreeing with the critique of Western European Orientalist theory, I have been unsatisfied with these authors' attempts to use particular feudalistic characteristics in order to characterize entire regions or eras as feudal. For Marx and Engels (1983), the general character of a society or stage of social development is defined foremost by the general underlying relation of city and countryside at the basis of the division of labour characterizing the society. Selective focus on the appearance or lack of specific features can cause this essential relationship to be overlooked. Such a focus on the presence or lack of particular characteristics, such as of guilds in India (Alavi 1980) or large estates in Nepal,[2] cannot in itself define a modal difference.

Marx seems to have been reassessing his ideas on the subject when he turned to the newly emerging ethnological literature in the last years of his life.[3] First, in applying his knowledge of ancient and feudal Europe in his reading of Lewis Henry Morgan's *Ancient Society*,[4] Marx shifted his focus from an abstract hypothetical typology of the forms of property to a historical and comparative study of the development and transformation of clan-based states into states representing private property (with the subsequent subordination of the clan to the patriarchal family).

While previously Marx had developed a theory of the rise of the city in terms of a typology of production relations based especially on his knowledge of Europe, in the Morgan notebooks he shifted his focus to the particular histories of this transformation as it occurred variously throughout the world. His focus was less on essential, ideal Hegelian framed differences, as previously, than on how the same processes took different forms and represented various interests in different places and periods throughout the world.

In particular, Marx's notebooks on Edward Phear's *The Aryan Village* focus on the substance of British colonialism in rural India. Here we see that Marx does not attribute the conditions of rural India to feudalism. To the contrary, he castigates Phear for making just this interpretation.

So small the accumulated capital of the villagers and this itself is often due to the mahajan = merchant, money dealer—one who makes it his business in the villages to advance money and grain to the Ryot on the pledge of crop. Extreme poverty of by far the largest portion, i.e., the bulk of the population in Bengal (the richest part of India!) seldom rightly apprehended by the English people. (Marx 1972:249)

(This ass Phear calls the Constitution of the village feudal). Outside of this Village Constitution the Mahajan, the village capitalist. The village ryot has to periodically pay money; e.g., to build new or repair hut of the homestead, to make a plow or another instrument, to purchase a pair of bullocks, the seed required for planting, finally, travel for himself and his family, several kists of rent to be paid before all his crops can be secured and realized. In the western part of the Delta, his savings seldom suffice to tide him over; the period which elapses before his yearly production realizes payment. Thus he must go to the Mahajan for money and for paddy as he wants them. Customarily it takes the form of a transaction between both sides: the paddy for sowing and for food and also other goods, become supplied under the condition that he return an additional 50% in quantity at the harvest time; money is to be repaid at another time, also at harvest time, with 2% per month interest either in the form of an equivalent of paddy, reckoned at bazaar prices, or in cash at the option of the lender. As security for execution of this agreement the Mahajan frequently takes mortgage of the ryot's future crop, and he helps himself to the stipulated amount on the very threshing floor, in the open field. (63, 64)

The Zemindar—this false English landlord—merely a rent-charger; the ryot a field-labourer, living from hand to mouth; the mahajan, who furnishes the farming capital, who calculates the labor and pockets all the profits, is a stranger, having no proprietary interest in the land; a creditor only, whose sole object is to realise his money advantageously as possible. After setting aside his golas (hut in which grain is stored) as much of the production come to his hands, as he is likely to need for his next year's business, he deals with the rest simply as cornfactor, sending it to the most remunerative market—and yet he has not legitimate proprietary status in the community, while those who have—the ryot and the zemindar for different reasons are apparently powerless. Hence, the unprogressive character of an agricultural village, as described by a young zemindar. (Marx 1972:256–7)[5]

Here it is evident that at that time in Bengal, Marx sees that the substance of relations of the landed property classes was not feudal. He saw instead that the merchants dominated the countryside and castigated Phear for interpreting the relations of the country as feudal. Under feudalism rent takes the form of the entire surplus, under capitalism the rent portion taken by the landlord represents only one part of the surplus. The rest enters into circulation as interest and profit of merchants. Even when the landlords physically collect the entire surplus in the form of rent, if conditions force them to enter it into circulation controlled by merchants (or transnational corporations), then in effect the merchants deduct the profit portion and reduce the landlords' share into the rent one.

Marx's previous typology that presented India as 'stagnant' no longer seemed relevant in his *Ethnological Manuscripts*. Indeed, he recognized later in the text that significant changes in landowner-ship, including subinfeudation, had been going on prior to the entry of the British into India (Marx 1972:262). The British totally transformed the system by converting land into private property, in effect favouring the development of merchant class interests over and against those of other classes (to say nothing of the labourers).

The conversion—by the English rogues and asses—of the Zemindaris into private proprietors made by itself (if also not in the idea of the former asses) all intermediate interests into rights in land, and the owner of such interest could encumber the land or alienate it within the limit of the right; he could receive his ownership itself against the complex Hindu joint-parcenary form. (147, 148) (Marx 1972:263)[6]

The implication is that by making property alienable, the British laid the ground for the full alienation of the land by *one* of the dominant classes in the countryside, the merchants, allowing it to become the *primary* dominant class under the British. This obviously served the purposes of the English, because it meant that land and labour could be concentrated under capital and the surpluses easily alienable to enter into the circulation of industrial commodities. These processes were also taking place within Nepal from at least the time of the Ranas, and they were greatly accelerated from the beginning of the twentieth century.

The full history of this mercantile class was described by Ray (1988) as originating in the handling of the credit operations of the Mughal armies. The merchants' domain of operation was the bazaar. With the entry of the British into the subcontinent, the merchants served to link between the European dominated organized business and industry on the one hand, and the artisan and peasant economy on the other. The members of the Indian capitalist class acted as servants of the colonial economy (thus coming under the term of comprador capitalists),[7] allowing them to displace the control of landed property over the countryside and extend their strength through control of up-country markets. The string of crises of the first half of the twentieth century (the world wars and Great Depression), allowed the bazaar merchants, with their much smaller and more flexible operating margins, to push the European interests out of the organized economy and establish their own control over the state in alliance with the transnational interests.[8]

In the Himalayas, the conquest by Gorkha of the various hill states in the last part of the eighteenth and early nineteenth centuries allowed a nearly simultaneous expansion of merchants from the conquered cities of Bhatgaun and Lalitpur into the hills west and east of the Kathmandu valley, respectively. They built bazaars throughout the middle hills, first on the basis of trade in indigenous products such as homespun fabrics and other goods, but increasingly of fabrics, salt, cigarettes, thread, kerosene, and other goods imported from British India and other foreign countries. This, combined with usury, allowed them to exert increasing control over the land. They entered the surpluses extracted through whatever means in Nepal back into circulation, now global in extent, contributing to the realization of values, employment of labour, investment in new means of production, and the accumulation of industrial surplus in Europe, the United States and Japan.

Thus the production and reproduction and the activity of the ruling classes within Nepal became increasingly committed to the expansion of industrial capitalism without the country even prior to the date usually set as the watermark of foreign influence, the (misnomered) 'Democracy Revolution' of 1950–1. Despite the continued existence of landlordism and patronage, key elements of the dominance of landed property were eclipsed. The combination of agriculture and industry was broken as factory-produced cloths, shoes, cigarettes, etc., displaced village-produced ones. Consumption and production in the village became another step in the circulation of industrial commodities. A large portion of the social product was put to reproducing mercenary soldiers whose purpose was (and is) to police the new global rule being established by capitalist interests. Increasing amounts of labour are being recruited into India and elsewhere. And finally, the landlords themselves enter surpluses, collected in the form of rents, into the market.

Even previously, surpluses were not entered into an estate economy characteristic of classical feudalism. Rather, they were controlled, if not directly, by a centralized state in the service of landed property distributed in the form of prebendal estates. Subsequent changes in distribution of surplus have depended upon the ability of various classes to assert their control over the state. This has in part taken the form of assertion of monopoly control by ruling families in alliance with transnational interests—a position analogous to that of the Birlas, Tatas, and other large houses of post-independence India. In opposition to them, in addition to the bazaar-based merchant and contractor interests, is a growing bureaucratic and intelligentsia interest. Although the ruling families were trying to consolidate their hold over the countryside with unprecedented expansion of state mechanisms into the villages, they instead succeeded in creating yet another class interposing its interests over the direct producers. Up to now, the radical opposition forces have failed to capitalize on this failure of the government; and they now necessarily await for a spontaneous uprising to deliver the state into their hands.

Unlike the pattern under feudalism, the expansion of the indigenous capitalist class was facilitated by increasing centralization, not breakdown of the state. Whereas in feudalism the functions of government devolved to estates and other local polities; in the Nepal state, offices and a growing bureaucracy have increasingly absorbed not only the estate functions but social ones of all kinds in the name of rationalization. Growth of industrial production and monopoly centred in other countries provided the force behind the expansion of the merchants. Presently, so-called 'development' means the increasing assertion of transnational corporate control over society and state. The form that this process takes is less consequential to the transnational corporations than the end result—who controls use of the natural environment, markets and surplus labour.

Certain strategic implications follow from this reinterpretation of feudalism in Nepal. If the present problems of Nepal are interpreted in terms of a persistence of feudalism, the problem of change is merely one of disposal of the feudal classes and the capture of state power by a more progressive emerging national bourgeoisie. But when the problem becomes understood in terms of the transnational class relations which have subordinated Nepalese society and interests to their own, then the solution becomes of another order entirely.

Transnational capital is extremely well organized. For example, it brings sugar estates in Honduras and cocoa estates in Peru, oil in the Middle East, shipping transport from Korea, computers from Japan, and media in Manhattan together to produce and distribute cola beverages in Kathmandu. Compared with the means available to the people of Nepal, its resources are bottomless, its presence ubiquitous, its class character complex, and its ideology as many-faced as all the Hindu gods and goddesses (and incorporates them into its pantheon, needless to say). Second, even within Nepal it works through a myriad of occupations and statuses—including bureaucrats, consultants, contractors, merchants, industrialists, educators, doctors, movie producers and movie hall owners, Brahmans, and even Communists; its influence and the people who see their interests and aspirations aligned to it are everywhere. In order to capture state power, where does one start? And what does it mean to capture state power? Even the leadership of the political parties is easily purchased and co-opted.

While agitation at the level of the nation state is important, an increasingly important strategy would be to educate and organize people to recognize and confront capital in its various and changing forms and strategies. The problem is not so much one of leading a universal class, as it has often been framed in the past (usually with the aim of using this class for particular purposes), as obtaining universal engagement by that class in struggle. Even if the leadership is decapitated or sells out, as happens again and again, resistance can then continue. Mere capture of a particular nation state cannot change the present alignment of forces in the world and the general hegemony of capital. In a world where the nation state has been subordinated to a truly global form of state, where presidents and kings are merely beribboned, bemedalled and bespectacled executives of its interests,[9] where production is shifted to wherever labour and bureaucrats are most pliant; popular change (especially a revolutionary one) necessitates the development of a broad-based local, to say nothing of international, consciousness and organization reaching to the lowest levels. Otherwise, the hoped for spontaneous uprising, if it comes, may be co-opted by one or more of class interests in league with transnational capital. Struggle must be a continuing one, dependent on people more than leaders, met in ways that are even more imaginative and diverse than the many guises of transnational capitalism.

NOTES

This chapter was originally published by the Jhilko Pariwar in *Jhilko*, Vol. 10, No. 3, 1990, pp. 3–13. It is republished here with the generous permission of Hisila Yami.

1   As Marx pointed out in the case of the founding of Rome, this process laying claim to soveriegnty has been repeated throughout history: 'old trick of the founders of cities to draw to themselves an obscure and humble multitude, and then set up for their progeny the autochthonic claim. . . . "From the neighboring places a crowd of people of all kinds came for refuge, without distinguishing freemen from slaves in quest for novelty, these were the first to come, because of the (city's) greatness." (Liv. I, I.) . . . Shows that the barbarian population of Italy was very swollen, discontent among them, want of personal safety, existence of domestic slavery, apprehension of violence' (Marx 1972:226–7). Probably much the same can be said for Nepal, especially its western region.

2   In fact the existence of guilds prove nothing, since in Europe guilds were the form taken by commerce and industry under the dominance of landed property in self defence against it, prior to their assertion of their hegemony and conquest of the state. Thus guilds can be expected to exist wherever landed property is dominant. The key experience of Western European feudalism, however, is that landed property had lost control of the centralized state and as a consequence the city stood in opposition to the countryside and landed property, eventually to subordinate it.

3   Some authors, such as John Mepham (1978), argue that in the course of writing *Capital*, Marx dropped his earlier Hegelian categories and turned to scientific ones. (A secret that seems to have eluded even Marx in his prefaces to *Capital* where he described the manner that Hegel, albeit inverted, provides the methodological basis of his analysis.) Beneath this argument lies the motive of substituting a positivist, ahistorical approach for a dialectical, historical one, removing the revolutionary implications from Marx's work. It allows Marx to be used for establishing new forms of class power, such as that of the

bureaucratic intelligentsia under Stalin (which also is why Stalin argued that it was unnecessary to read the first chapter of *Capital*) or according to Althusser and the Frankfurt School of Marxism to further the ends of liberal bureaucratic intelligentsia in the west (Mikesell 1992a).

Teodor Shanin (1987) in his study of the late Marx argues that in his *Ethnological Notebooks* Marx turned from a unilinear theory of history, supposedly espoused in the preface to *Capital*, to a multilinear one. However, Marx had already developed this multilinear theory in his *Grundrisse* (1973a). If in a rhetorical flourish he wrote that England represented the future of Germany (and other countries), it was because he saw capitalism as spreading over the world and subordinating all other forms, not because he saw all forms of society as naturally evolving towards capitalism. He was already far more sophisticated than many of his epigones, who subsequently interpreted his categories unilinearly. Marx turned to intensive study of the histories of other societies late in his career to ascertain how private property and states representing private property developed out of or subordinated clan organized society (in his notebooks on Lewis Henry Morgan's *Ancient Society*), and how industrial capitalism subordinated states with already well-developed forms of private property, such as India (in his notebooks on Edward Phear's *The Aryan Village*). A careful comparison of the *Ethnological Notebooks* to his early works such as the *German Ideology* shows him using the same dialectical methodology, but with more depth, sophistication and knowledge.

4   Marx discarded important flaws in Morgan's work which Frederick Engels (1983) later went on to use as the basis of his own misrepresentation of Marx. Chief among them was Engels' reliance on Bachoven's theory of the 'mother right', which Marx disdainfully dismissed with two paragraphs in different parts of his *Ethnological Notebooks*. The 'mother right' presented society as originally matriarchal, due to the certainty of the natural linkage of mother to child, but eventually men imposed the patriarchy in revenge for the previous domination of women.

Anthropologists generally never accepted this thesis, but probably for the wrong reason—i.e. that it seemed too speculative. Basically, it represented the dominant Victorian ideology of the newly emergent monopoly capitalism in the late nineteenth century (and more generally an ideology of the rule of middle classes that had been emerging through the course of the development in feudal Europe) that women must be 'put in their place'.

Marx, in contrast to Engels, saw in his Morgan notebooks that it was the rise of private property and the subsequent subordination of the clan to the patriarchal family that led to the subordination of women. Among the middle classes of feudal cities, the position of women worsened as property, increasingly in the form of capital, became more concentrated. Subordination of women was one way of keeping property from being dispersed among other families or lineages, particularly of wives, as happened under the communal ownership represented by the clan.

This oppression of women reached its extreme in Victorian Europe, where on the one hand capitalists were fighting to prevent their capitals from being dispersed among other capitalists. On the other hand among the workers, first, more poorly paid women were being used to force down the general level of wages among the labour force, second, the cost of reproduction and maintenance of the labour force was being thrown entirely onto the wives and mothers of the workers rather than being born by the factories. These different strategies of capital reached their extreme during the latter half of the nineteenth century because of the immense competition resulting from the concentration of capital in monopolies (see Lenin 1975). Although now the oppression of women among the ruling classes is becoming irrelevant for capital (though it certainly continues in the form of male monopoly, as a class, over ruling and high status positions), the history of the oppression of women among the working classes is still relevant in the context of the spread of factories into the Third World and a concentration of national capital into transnational corporations in a manner analogous to the early rise of monopoly capitalism (see Magdoff 1969; Mitter 1986).

5   German part translated by the author with minor editing, italics removed.

6   See note 5.

7   The term 'comprador' has been used to denote the merchant classes in Nepal. I am not entirely comfortable with the term, because it was originally used in China to refer to Chinese agents in foreign firms who handled the Chinese employees and business of the firms. It was used by Mao to refer to a class that along with the landlord class existed as 'wholly appendages of the international bourgeoisie, depending upon imperialism for their survival and growth', which 'represent the most backward and most reactionary relations of production in China and hinder the development of her productive forces'. He contrasted these to a 'middle' or 'national bourgeoisie' which 'represents the capitalist relations of production in China in town and country' (Tse-Tung 1975:13–14). Due to its own interests in independently monopolizing state power, revolutionary strategists have thought that they can initiate revolution in alliance with the 'national bourgeoisie' and then subsequently break the alliance to complete the revolution. This strategy succeeded temporarily in Russia due to the war-induced upheaval at the time of the revolution. In China in 1927, Germany in 1920, and India in 1947 this strategy set back the revolution in the former and destroyed it in the latter two countries. In all three cases, as generally, it effectively delivered power to the bourgeoisie class.

Dependency development theory or so-called 'neo-Marxism' turned this strategy into an unabashed theory of development of the national bourgeoisie, which still appeared revolutionary and somewhat daring to liberal intellectuals due to the retention of Marxist terminology and its apparent challenge of transnational interests. But even in 1926, Mao saw that, given the international character of production and the division of labour, the independence of these classes was an illusion.

8   The real content of the transfer of power in India (see Ghosh 1985).

9   Even in the 1989 presidential election in the United States, the main issue besides 'presidential appearance' was over which candidate was the best executive. Intelligence and vision rarely entered into the discussion. Unfortunately, the immense economic and military power that transnational capital gives to the 'national executives' makes them immediately dangerous, in the long-term destructive, and in the short run at least, marginally accountable to their own national populations.

CHAPTER 12

The Class Basis of the Movement:
Historical Origins and
Present Significance

In transforming Hegel's revolution in philosophy into a philosophy
of revolution, Marx stressed that he was breaking not only with
capitalism as an exploitative social order, but also with what he called
'vulgar communism'—that is to say, people who thought that all you
needed to do was to abolish private property in order to have a new
social order. Marx's point was that a new society was not a matter of
form of property, private or state, but of new relations.

Marx called for a 'revolution in permanence' which would abolish
and transcend all exploitative relations and see in place of either the
profit motive of capitalism or the state-form of property in vulgar
communism, the self development of man, woman, and child—with
all humanity in the process of 'the absolute movement of becoming'.
—Raya Dunayevskaya (1975:53–4)

HISTORICAL PREMISE

NEPAL PERHAPS more than others is a country where anthropologists
have had more than the usual difficulty of linking intensively focused
community study with the historical study of class, state and global
relations. Nepal's formal political isolation and lack of overt
colonization, to say nothing of the seemingly exotic character of the
society in the preconceptions of visitors, has made it extremely
difficult for anthropologists to rise above the assumption that Nepali
society consists of unique, isolated, and timeless cultures.
Consequently, only recently has there been a change from village
studies which, assuming that an entire linguistic or caste population

shares a common culture, represent their observations as normative for the entire population, described as a 'culture group'.

Meanwhile, ongoing developments in the state and the world have not been addressed, even when large numbers of people from the villages are engaged in trade and work in other countries. Such migrants usually only enter into the anthropological study in terms of normative behaviours or formal religious or constitutional categories made problematic in terms of particular individual or family experiences not in terms of their historical origins and present manner of reproducing themselves. Official history, described in terms of the events in the Durbars, is accepted as the only relevant history. Since Nepal only opened its borders to anthropologists in 1951, most studies accept that there was no significant foreign influence in the village at that time. Only afterwards did 'change' and 'development' begin. Until then, the countryside is assumed to have remained virtually unaffected by outside influences, further reinforcing the belief that the villages represent a picture of life that is virtually unchanged and that they can at the same time be studied in isolation from the rest of the world as representative of entire linguistic populations.

During the period of the British empire, perpetuation of a vision of a pristine, untouched, traditional countryside conveniently hid the costs born by villages supplying military manpower ('Gurkhas') for the British imperial armies. It also obfuscated the widespread up-country penetration of foreign industrially produced commodities and the vast transformation that these were bringing to the countryside, cities and state. Presently, perpetuation of the idea of a traditional culture serves to present the immense input of foreign capital positively in terms of 'developing' previously, stagnant relations for the good of all. Sweat shop owners, carpet and craft industrialists, exporters, foreign retail chains, travel and hotel businesses, and the narcotics and flesh trade gladly perpetuate the idea of the persistence of an exotic 'traditional' culture. This preconception lends the products of these businesses an added market advantage, be it in the travel agencies and expensive boutiques of Europe and America or the red light districts of Bombay and Calcutta (where the services of 200,000 Nepali women are supposed to be highly preferred commodities). By disconnecting the broader context from the village culture, the basis of this exploitation within the village is also hidden.

Instead of describing village culture in normative terms, categories that anthropologists have accepted at their face value must be separated from the preconception of culture as totality and analysed instead in terms of their historical origins and content. This leads to the discovery that culture, tribe, caste and nation state are not neatly bounded entities which can be comfortably placed beneath the microscope of participant observation. Rather, in a world where intercourse is global (paraphrasing Lukács), each part cannot help but contain the whole, and the object of study takes on subjective proportions in anthropological knowledge. They are part of the history that is giving rise to anthropology, and the anthropologist is a participant in producing and reproducing what is observed. Thus, while I was warned in my undergraduate study that the anthropologist should not go native, since it would presumably disturb the comfortable illusion of scientific objectivity, we are all of us native participants and must see ourselves as building not just detached objective knowledge but a subjective consciousness.

In order to analyse the present situation of revolutionary struggle, it is necessary to break down the immediate categories in which struggle presents itself and show how these arose historically through the development of production and intercourse. Thus we cannot simply accept that feudalism has given away to bourgeois democracy or despotism to multi-party democracy, as currently viewed. Nor can we accept that the political developments of the state and the present movement have little or no organic relationship to what is happening in the villages or urban neighbourhoods, as has been assumed by many anthropologists.

ORIGINS OF CASTE, PRIVATE PROPERTY, AND EXPROPRIATION OF THE SEGMENTARY STATE

The 'People's Movement', as the uprising of February to April 1991 that brought down three decades of king's rule or the Panchayat system in Nepal, may be understood as a maturation of contradictions in a long process of social development and struggle. The present ruling Shah dynasty originally established its sovereignty over Nepal in the mid-eighteenth century under Prithivi Narayan Shah, the Raja of one of scores of small kingdoms in and among the Himalayan mountains at that time. Village peasants were subject to heavy exploitation, abuse and slavery by a collusion of elements of a landed property class consisting of petty Rajput princes, allied families, and priests, who from the twelfth century began to spread the hegemony[1] of exploitative class relations based on private property (which had developed over the millennia in the urban civilizations and empires of South Asia) to the hills of Nepal. Although this process took the ideological form of the introduction of the pantheon of Hindu deities and 'respectable' caste relations, behind this there was the subordination of previous kinship-based forms of organization and communally-held property by classes basing their power in private property, particularly landed property.

The pre-Hindu states, such as Magarat (sixth to twelfth centuries) to the west and those of the Kirati peoples in eastern Nepal were organized on the basis of kinship.[2] These states were based on inclusion. People were brought together and organized within the metaphor of increasingly extensive kinship organization, in the manner of the segmentary state formulated by Southall (1956, 1974, 1986). The state organization was segmented along the dominant lineages, but unlike caste, these lineages were inclusive, expanding their control and dominance by means of marriage and adoption of other groups into lineage structures. Land was communally owned, and everyone had the right to cultivate it by virtue their membership in a lineage. Although inequality existed, it did not take the form of private ownership of property by particular families. Since the entire system brings together people and their labour, in large part by marriage, both men and women held political roles, and women were not disenfranchised from the community. These states were extremely dynamic, and they changed greatly in extent and character from the time of their first appearance to their final subjugation.[3]

In contrast, private property, imposed by the Hindu conquering groups, is based on exclusion of particular classes of people by limiting or excluding their rights to land or, under capitalism, from all the means of production. Thereby their rights to the products of their labour are limited, disenfranchising and alienating them politically and socially.[4] Globally, private property initially appeared in association with the increasing productivity that resulted from the development of agriculture, domestication of animals and appearance of the city. It necessitated destruction of the inclusive, communal property forms that characterized the kin-based states and thus also subordination of the lineage forms of organization to the family. As a general rule this was accomplished by the gradual limitation of the rights of women, as well as youth, within their patrilineal clans and transformation of the state to patriarchal rule. This prevented the redistribution of property and labour power to wider associations of lineages, represented in the relations of and through women (e.g. with affinal kin), and limited it within a class of property owners that traced descent and inheritance patrilineally.

The early city states at first took a theocratic form, based on the sacred position of the previous clan elders, which established the rule of a class of urban priests over rural cultivators (Southall 1984). The prominence of female goddesses in the early myths of ancient Greece (Marx 1972) and in the ruins of Harappa and Mohenjo-daro indicate that the position of women, and possibly, the matrilineage, may not have yet been fully eclipsed as the main form of descent in the initial development of new forms of the city (although the deification of women often tends to mean their objectification and subordination as well). However, with increasing expansion of private property, women became more fully disenfranchised, not for biological reasons but because their particular disenfranchisement was the means for broader disenfranchisement and exploitation represented by the development of private property. Subsequent expansion of cities into empires was accompanied by the further development of the division and distribution of labour and its products between the city and countryside, commerce and industry, and within various branches of industry (Marx and Engels 1983). Increasing militarization led to the eclipse of the monopolistic power of priests by that of secular rulers, while increasingly wider intercourse led to the growing influence of mercantile class interests.

In South Asia the perpetuation and expansion of these divisions of labour took the form of caste. Caste is not class, since particular castes may contain people from different positions in the division of labour. Caste was rather the South Asian equivalent to citizenship in the ancient Mediterranean city states. Both caste and citizenship enfranchise certain groups of individuals according to membership in particular lineages. Thus they have their origins in the early segmentary state that preceded the city. Yet they each addressed quite different histories of the expansion of private property.

In the Greek and Roman city states, the dominant lineages came together with the town as their seat. The coming together was based initially on the 'premise' of the principle of the lineage, in which each citizen (male) had right to use a plot of land from the territory of the city for cultivation. Expansion of the founding lineages, or the practical 'affirmation' of the founding lineage principles in production and reproduction of the society, led to the conquest of the surrounding segmentary states, expropriation of their lands, and uprooting and enslavement of their peoples. In Greece this took form in the spread of urban colonies, each with its territory; in Rome it led to the creation of an empire. The descendants of the founding lineages were all citizens of the city from birth, which gave them the theoretical right to set themselves up as landlords on privately owned estates in the conquered lands. Control over slave labour and the opportunity to accumulate large fortunes led to the shift from the lineage to the family as the basis of property ownership, and the change in the form and content of lineage institutions, such as the assembly, council of elders, and ritual and military leaders, so as to serve the reproduction of classes based on private property. This led to the expropriation of the great bulk of citizens and concentration of land and power with a landlord class that made up a small portion of the citizenry as a whole.

In contrast, the expansion of private property into the Indian subcontinent initially took form with the spread of Aryan pastoral peoples and not with the founding of urban colonies. While the Aryans were not an urban people to start with, they provide an example of the great changes taking place among the peoples of the segmentary states in the periphery of the West Asian, European and north African urban civilizations. Growing opportunities for trade and interaction with the cities led to opportunities for accumulation of wealth and replacement of communal property by private property, to the eclipse of the lineage by the family, and to the rise of property owning classes. It led to accumulation of knowledge, the growth of priesthoods, and the elaboration of production and social organization far more complex than that of the segmentary states that had proceeded the rise of the cities. Constant warfare with the encroaching urban empires and other groups also led to refinement of military skills and development of military classes.

The writings of Tacitus, Caesar and other contemporary writers provide much better documentation, if filtered by their own viewpoints, for the peoples in the periphery of Mediterranean cities. Yet the prior social development of the Aryan peoples who entered the Indian subcontinent, as evidenced by the early Vedas, indicates that such processes had probably taken place among these Aryan groups as well. Their experience was part of the great expanding reverberations that took place among the peoples in peripheries of new urban civilizations, which themselves have given birth to new arrangements of urban civilization and the eclipse of old centres (Southall n.d., Chap. 1).

Among pastoral peoples property was in herds rather than land. As the means for control of labour and wealth of the society, it is no surprise that the cow was held sacred by the Aryan peoples. The sacred cow has the same significance for that time as the enshrinement of capitalist private property in today's world. It sets the life and well-being of the primary means of production of wealth, and thus the relations in which wealth is produced and controlled, above that of the people who produce the wealth. In this way, it is no less irrational (and much less destructive) than the present enshrinement of capital (used to justify mass genocide, ethnocide, subversion of human struggle, bombing of cities, and the general wasteful squandering of the world's resources).[5] This is a much simpler explanation of the sacred status of the cow than the long arguments over hidden functions or manifest malfunctions of cow worship found in the 'sacred cow controversy' in the pages of the journals *American Anthropologist* and *Current Anthropology* in the late 1960s and early 1970s.

Although the origin of the private property forms represented by Aryan civilization was tied up with the growth of cities, the Aryan expansion into the subcontinent did not proceed in the manner of the Mediterranean city state with the coming together of the lineages in the city as their seat, followed by the uprooting and enslavement of peoples by the urban descendants of the founding lineages. The descendants of the original Aryan lineages initially spread and established themselves in the Indian subcontinent according to the lineage principles of the segmentary states that they had subordinated (as formulated by Aidan Southall among the Alur and elaborated by Burton Stein and Richard Fox in India). The Aryans used the pre-existing rankings within the indigenous communities and transformed these into a caste hierarchy. They attached ritual impurity to the people, prescribed lower status and labouring occupations, leading to complete disenfranchisement of the people of these communities. Thus rather than limit the lineage principles to a particular community in the manner of citizenship, caste facilitated expansion of lineages over other communities in a more developed form of segmentary state, prescribing a lower status and labouring occupations to persons of lower status, in which they had to give up their surpluses to the conquerors.

Reproduction of the hierarchical ranking was ensured by attaching purity-pollution principles in which transgression of hierarchy led to demotion for higher caste individuals, especially women, and to sanctified violent retribution against lower caste transgressors.

The ritual leaders of the segmentary state were replaced with Brahman and Kshatriya landlords locally and kings on higher levels, while disenfranchisement of the indigenous peoples took form in consignment to labouring occupations forced to give up their surpluses and attachment of ritual impurity. Marx (1972) notes time and again that as clan principles lost their original egalitarian content in practice, they became increasingly elaborated ritually and ideologically. Even if the non-Aryan indigenous groups did not immediately accept their new status, the Aryan groups increasingly encroached on the communal lands and progressively limited the ability of the indigenous groups to autonomously reproduce themselves. This forced them to submit to the division of labour represented by caste. We can see that the Aryan castes served to establish a certain form of property or unequal distribution of people in production and of their products between them. Only the high caste groups could be landowners. This was similar to the principle in the ancient city states in which only citizens were landowners. Rights in the land were furthermore mediated by the state as landlord, probably resulting from the strong priest class—as directly evolved through the elaboration of the ritual element of the ritual leaders of the segmentary state, though probably all members of the high castes had relatively equal rights in the nascent states. This differed from the ancient city states, where citizens received portions of the territory as private property, ultimately leading to a quite different trajectory of development with the dissolution of ancient Rome. However, both in the ancient city states and in South Asia, as the city states evolved into empires, land and power became concentrated among an increasingly small portion of the enfranchised lineages (citizenry and high castes, respectively), effectively disenfranchising the majority of the populations.

While the Aryans did not uproot communities and replace them with estates worked by slaves, they did introduce much more intensive forms of agriculture to serve the enthralment of the people within the context of their own communities. Agricultural innovations provide increasing amounts of surplus in the form of tax rents, allowing development of an increasingly complex urban civilization and expansion and elaboration of the landed property class— including both its sacred (Brahman) and secular (Kshatriya) elements. The sacred status of the cow was further reinforced as it gained importance as drought power in agriculture and thus, along with the irrigation and its sacred waters, a main means to increase the productivity of agricultural labour.

Class, the unequal distribution of labour and its products, is based in the division of labour. It coincides with neither citizenship nor caste, although both serve to reproduce it. As production, urban civilization, and the state developed in the Indian subcontinent, increasing numbers from the upper castes became relegated to the status of small marginal farmers economically undifferentiated from the low castes. The most productive land, wealth, and power became concentrated in the hands of a class making up a small percentage of the upper castes. Cultivator, industrial, and commercial classes all remained politically subordinate to these landed property interests. This subordination was reproduced ideologically and ritually in terms of the class position being relegated to specific castes.

Industry, associated with agriculture, was characterized by subordination to landed property as reflected in the out-caste status of the artisans. This political disenfranchisement and social alienation served to prevent the growth of the sort of control over the means of production that would have allowed the artisans to gain independence and become a class force in opposition to the ruling landed property classes. Thus, in contrast to the guilds of Europe, the artisans did not develop significantly as a lasting and independent urban class that was able to exert itself within the state.[6] Rather, they remained for the most part analogous to peasant artisans on the estates of feudal lords, where the distribution of labour and products of the Shudra industries remained a mere adjunct to landed property and thus were totally subordinated to it.

In contrast, the merchants, as traders and usurers appropriated the product of agriculture and industry by means of mercantile and money-lending capital, were able to establish a high caste status for themselves. As evidenced by religious endowments, temples, and so forth that were financed by them, the merchants, like the military groups, shifted a part of the surplus to priests. The priests obliged the merchants by legitimizing the latter's particular capitalist exploitation through the commodity form in terms of the caste framework, which insured a continuing powerful role for the Brahmans as mediators of exploitation (albeit, the mediation was presented in the form of a false consciousness in terms of mediation between the merchants and gods). It also ensured that the merchant capital served to reproduce itself in terms of caste, contributing to the continued ascendancy of landed property, and preventing capital from asserting itself as a class over the state. Because the landed property class never lost control over the state to the extent that occurred after the dissolution of the Roman Empire, the cities and urban merchants never received the opportunity to rise as an independent force, and capital in general and merchant capital in particular remained subordinated to landed property.[7]

SIGNIFICANCE FOR THE FORMATION
OF THE NEPALI STATE

When he set out on the road of conquest in 1746, King Prithivi Narayan Shah of Gorkha premised as the basis of his conquest and unification of the disparate Himalayan states that came to make up Nepal the previous destruction of the kin-based state and the spread of private property in land over the western and southern regions of Nepal.[8] The Kirats in the far west had long been subordinated to Rajput kings, and the segmentary states of the Magar and Gurung speaking peoples in the west-central region of Nepal were in large part already subordinated, with their communal, kin, religious and other institutions having lost their original content, persisting ultimately to serve landed property. Thus already subjugated and disciplined according to the needs of property-owning classes, the Magar and Gurung speaking peoples who resided in the area around Gorkha provided the core of the manpower to the Gorkha army (subsequently an important force in the army of British India). In the east, although kin-based segmentary states continued to persist among the Kirati groups, they were already somewhat transformed and weakened by several centuries of eroding influence of Brahmanic and Rajput infiltration. Furthermore, these states were no match for a greatly expanded and centralized state which, based on private property, could mobilize significantly large combinations of labour. Thus they proved much easier to conquer than the Rajput states in the west. Once conquered, however, it was much more difficult to subordinate their communities to exploitation by a new class of private proprietors.

Nepali history presents the unification of Nepal as arising from the charisma and actions of Prithivi Narayan Shah and his successors. Thus in ethnography this history is treated as having little significance for everyday lives of the villagers beyond giving background and colour. In general, however, the Gorkhali conquest in Nepal had more to do with the continuation of the dialectic of expansion of private property than with the particular charisma or vision attributed to the person of Prithivi Narayan. Developing conditions prepare the way for the possible appearance of people with a vision of the times.[9] From this perspective, the unification itself arose from the history of the development of the community, and it must be understood in terms of it.

ROYAL SOVEREIGNTY AND POPULAR DISENFRANCHISEMENT

Due to their previous subordination to landed property, it was a discontented, obscure and humble multitude that Prithivi Narayan Shah confronted in Rajput areas. In an old trick of dynastic founders, he drew them to himself with promises of land and personal safety to conquer and create a unified nation. However, rather than using this conquest to liberate the peasant conquerors according to the vision that he had used to inspire them, Prithivi Narayan expanded and centralized the state and set up the autochthonous claim for his progeny over it.[10] By means of the proselytizing of Brahmans, to say nothing of the creation of a Rajput pedigree for the House of Gorkha in terms of the Gorkha Vamsavali (genealogy), the state was made to appear as though it had been created and sustained by chimerical gods and goddesses rather than by the armed might of a hopeful people.

In the eastern Kirati areas, where Prithivi Narayan Shah had not been preceded by proselytizing and expropriation by Hindu priests, the going was tougher. He was unable to establish the full sovereignty of private property interests over the community lands. He instead had to compromise with existing powers set upon quite a different material base, allowing continued communal ownership of the land in exchange for recognition of his ultimate suzerainty. It has taken the expansion of Brahman families in combination with urban mercantile capitalist interests into the Kirati areas to alienate the lands and spread the hegemony of private property over these people, albeit not without social tensions and conflict.

In 1846, Jang Bahadur Kunwar, the head of a lesser aristocratic family massacred most of the competing members of the aristocracy in a court conspiracy (the Kot Massacre), allowing himself and his family to seat themselves in the prime minister's office, set himself at the head of the state machinery, and banish the weak monarch to the palace. That this could happen was a consequence of the manner in which the expansion of the Nepali state had turned the people's efforts against them in the form of their disenfranchisement. This disenfranchisement had shifted the base of the monarchy's legitimacy from the people to the consensus of the various nobility, so not only was the palace weakened by a series of intrigues among the nobility, but when Jang Bahadur annihilated most of the them, no countervailing base of power remained, neither in the palace nor elsewhere.

The only lesson that the Ranas (as Jang Bahadur and his family called themselves in deference to their new position) learned was not to trust competing elements of the nobility or the palace. They collaborated uneasily with the British Raj in India to increase the oppression of the people and to insure perpetuation of their family's monopoly of power in the face of growing opposition within and without the country. This collaboration included using state monopolies and concessions to facilitate and mediate trade within Nepal and supplying military manpower (the 'Gurkhas') to assist in imperialist expansion outside the country. In this way the rulers of Nepal shifted the cost of British economic and military expansion from the British people in the Nepali communities, with devastating effects for the latter.

The trade and infiltration of foreign industrial commodities and export of Nepal's forest and other resources was handled by a growing army of merchants, who in the late eighteenth century had initially followed the sword and ploughs of the peasant conquerors to establish of market towns and bazaars across the new nation. This national merchant class enjoyed a trade monopoly protected by the Rana government's isolationist policy that allowed them to become middlemen between growing industrial empires and the Nepali hill producers. They destroyed peasant artisan and household industry, especially in textiles, and profiteered from the growing poverty by means of usury.[11] They ruined and displaced many of the old landlords to establish themselves as a new class which entered land rents into circulation of industrial commodities and profits. They thus assisted the growth of foreign industrial capitalist preponderance over production in Nepal by impoverishing rather than transforming it, while establishing the international interests they represented in alliance with the village priests and state bureaucrats as an opposition or counter hegemonic force[12] within the country.

The penetration of foreign capitalist interests by means of bazaar merchants was an extension of the process by which foreign capital also extended simultaneously into other up-country areas of South Asia under British colonial rule, as described by Ray (1988). Except for a short period during the first half of the twentieth century, the activity of foreign merchants was limited to the predominantly white enclaves of the urban centres of India, and they never penetrated directly into the subsistence sector. Nepali merchants had become very much a part of this economy and cannot be said to be an independent national bourgeoisie, but rather one very much committed to the expansion and reproduction of international capitalism.

In extending their counter-hegemonic position, the merchants continued to use Brahmanic religious institutions that had previously served the hegemony of landed property, except now for the purpose of wrenching away state control of landed property and establishing the dominion of capital. The use of religion by capitalists to consolidate their position and ensure market sovereignty also occurred in Europe during the development and colonial expansion of the capitalist classes.

Outside the country, opposition sentiments found fertile ground among a growing number of exiles in Banaras and Darjeeling. Studying in Indian schools and obtaining valuable experience in the Indian independence movement, members from the elite classes— particularly the landlords—emerged as opposition leaders who developed ideas of independence and democracy and created the first large body of secular Nepali literature. This group, not surprisingly, was schooled and domesticated in terms of the limited demands of the Indian independence movement. This movement, under the sway of Indian Congress leaders, Muslim chauvinists of Pakistan, and of Hindu and Sikh chauvinists of India, had destroyed the workers' movement in India. In a settlement acceptable to British interests, they placed Gujarati and Marwari businessmen of north India, such as Birla, Dalmia and Mafatlal (very much in partnership with transnational corporations) in control of India and a group of 'robber barons' over Pakistan (Gosh 1985).

THE SO-CALLED REVOLUTION OF 1951 AND ITS AFTERMATH

In 1947 B.P. Koirala and other liberals from a group of landlords, state servitors and intellectuals who had fled to India founded the Nepali National Congress, calling itself a social democrat party (although the current leadership make no more pretensions of following the socialist and Gandhian ideology of its founder). With the British gone, the Indian government withheld interference in opposition activities sufficiently long for the Nepali Congress to mount in 1950–1 a campaign broadly supported by merchants and, to a lesser extent, the peasants. This 'Democracy Revolution' brought down the Rana government. But fearing the rise of a republican regime that might disturb the situation for the large domestic business interests that dominated post-independence India in alliance with transnational capital (as described by Ray 1988 and Gosh 1985), Nehru negotiated the Delhi Compromise between the revolutionary leaders and Ranas under the previously powerless King Tribhuvan, who had fled his palace in the confusion.

As characterizes compromise, despite the epithet 'revolution' attached to the period, the alignment of ruling interests controlling the state changed little. A revolution implies a dramatic transformation in the structure of property (and thus the division of labour) in society, resulting from a new class asserting its control over the state. This results from its sufficient maturation in the course of production and intercourse of the society to the point that it can overturn the control of previously dominant classes. What happened instead was a shift of state power from the Rana family as prime ministers under British patronage to the Shah family as kings under Indian patronage. Opposition leadership, itself for the most part from the old ruling classes, acquiesced in such an arrangement, because lacking any sort of popular organization and uncertain of their status in the event of real democracy they thought that they could ascend to power through this patronage as well.

Ethnographers and historians, following in the wake of popular and official belief, basically accepted the situation at face value, and thus they have accepted 1950–1 as a watershed in Nepali history. According to this view rural culture was characterized by a changeless, shared tradition. Only with the disposal of the old regime and opening up of the country (particularly to foreign ethnographers) that was brought by the 'revolution', has change, development, or modernization begun to take place. Operating on this assumption, ethnographers have engaged in village studies aimed at capturing this changeless past. In an attempt to find the least changed cultures, allowing the most controlled testing of their hypotheses, they have sought out the most remote, isolated villages. Yet, by following upon this assumption, villages least representative of the situation are picked; and biased by their presumptions, significant factors that fail to fit preconceived ideas are ignored.

For example, the merchant community Bandipur emerged as traders in imported industrially produced textiles. Its entire history, from the beginning of the nineteenth century, was one of entering the products and labour of the surrounding countryside into the circulation of industrial commodities and thereby subordinating production, labour and community to this circulation. Yet previous studies of the community and others like it had attempted to present these villages and bazaars in terms of a cultural continuity with the same past pristine culture, in this case with the pre-modern urban community of Kathmandu Valley. This was a moot point, because these communities kept strong commercial, family, political, property and other ties with the valley; the merchants had similar ties and strong interaction with merchants and industrialists in India; and they set up subsidiary shops throughout the countryside of Nepal. Neither could the merchants be understood outside of what was happening in the factories of Britain and India, nor could the Nepali countryside be understood in isolation from these merchants.

CLASS INTERESTS AND THE 'DEMOCRACY MOVEMENT'

What then are the class interests presently at work in the countryside? The monarchic interests, including the deposed Ranas with whom they intermarry, continued and greatly enlarged upon a career of the unabashed appropriation of properties that characterized the

Rana regime prior to the compromise of 1951. The monarchy has been feverishly engaged in transforming its position of sovereignty, in which land was the property of the monarch as the corporal embodiment of the state, into a capitalist notion of private property, in which all property could be uprooted and converted into other forms of wealth.

Although for the time being the ascendant classes had been confused in their struggle for state power, they did not stand still. The merchants, already committed to the circulation of industrial commodities and the accumulation and export of Nepalese surplus labour, continued to both further extend their trade and directly subordinate labour in the countryside to their capital. In addition to commerce, they have been entering into export-oriented concerns, such as hotels, tourism, and carpet and garment industries, and into contracting and construction. This group of interests supported the 1990 Democracy Movement to the extent that it promised to lessen the monopolistic grasp of palace interests on the state machinery, allowing them more business freedom. However, they are also committed to a capitalist notion of private property and want to see the movement go no further than this. They see the present organization and demands of labourers as directly opposed to their own interests, which, couched both in business theory and sacred religious representations, seem to have universal validity. Thus the demands of the labourers seem totally unjustified. There is a feeling among them that these demands are instigated by agitators and that the current wages and living and working conditions of the working class are adequate—it has been 'traditionally' so, after all—though they would never live under such conditions themselves.

Those in the various export businesses, including tourism, say that their 'industries', as they call them, 'produce' foreign exchange and thus deserve their present rate of profit, despite the misery of the villagers and the progressive destruction of the hill environment that the present general rate of surplus is predicated upon. The necessity for foreign exchange arises because there is lack of will and very strong interest against the release of the 18 million strong Nepalese labourers and the land from relations of bondage to employ them in true *human* and *social* development. The products of their labour, alienated under the old conditions, are used rather to purchase foreign commodities and employ foreign factory workers to change the country according to an alien vision. Render that which belongs to Caesar unto Caesar, so the saying goes, and so must dollars earned today purchase American and Japanese commodities tomorrow (Magdoff 1969), contributing to the employment of labour and reproduction of capital in these countries rather than employing Nepalese labour and reproducing the Nepalese community, except as a part of this circulation.

Who does this serve in the long run? Not the Nepalese small businessman, but the transnational corporate capital—traders, bankers, industrialists, commission agents, etc.—to which Nepalese businessmen, including the palace, have committed themselves. Historically, as monopoly capitalism has expanded, the profits of the small businessmen are undercut by the competition of large capitalists. However, when confronted with the workers' struggle against the tendencies of monopoly capital, the small businessmen interpret the workers' demands for higher wages as the cause of their own decreasing profits—not the competition of the large capitalist which is creating the general environment. Thus they join on the side of large capital within the country against the workers, although such alignment counters their long-term interests, to say nothing of their human dignity.

In revolutionary movements, small businessmen tend to associate with the Social Democratic and Communist parties in initial phases of mass uprisings by industrial and rural workers. After initial demands have been fulfilled and promises made due to the pressure and sacrifice of the working classes, the further revolutionary demands of the workers cause small businessmen to change sides to large capital in order to protect the general order of private property—though usually their small properties are not what is threatened anyway. This however contributes to the further expansion of large capital and the ultimate destruction and absorption of the small businessmen. They are either thrown into the mass of workers or join the great army of lower level civil servants in state and corporate bureaucracy.

In Nepal we see that almost the entire upper level leadership of all the parties, including the Communists, is dominated for the most part by landed property which over the decades has been exerting itself more and more, not only in control over its property, but in control of the bureaucracy. In the villages, the cadres are dominated by wealthier groups and small shop owners. Thus in the east, where I have been associated with education initiatives, resistance against villager education and organization comes from local Left cadres who claim to be the vanguard of revolution.

Nepal's intelligentsia, which had already begun to develop in Varanasi and Darjeeling as well as in schools established by the merchants in some bazaars prior to 1951, entered the national, corporate and agency bureaucracies, the professions, partially employed Bohemian life-styles, and into the struggle as revolutionary intellectuals of various categories. Most of the intellectuals in the upper ranks of the bureaucracy and the professions have been recruited from various upper class groups (especially the urban upper castes), since their class position gave them a better position for obtaining education, passing examinations, and strengthening the position of the bourgeoisie, i.e. in the state in particular.

Within the villages that we have studied, the Brahman cadres of the religious intelligentsia have tended to shift over into a secular role, as school teachers, often in combination with being village priests, to help spread the capitalist hegemony. Education succeeds in this, even when it fails to educate the majority of village children because, if nothing else, it makes their disadvantaged class position appear to be justified by their personal inability to pass examinations. This leads them to believe that they are personally unqualified for deciding how the country should be shaped and run. It is also creating a growing class of what Bayly calls 'angry young men from the hills' who are susceptible to demagoguery. Furthermore, the content and structure of the national education programme, which was designed by US advisors, has been inappropriate, partial, and extremely apologetic to the powers that be. It teaches rote learning and sycophancy rather than the critical view needed to transform the country according to its own situation. It is to secular knowledge what the Sanskrit universities that the East India Company established in India in the early nineteenth century were to Hindu thought and culture, and serving a similar purpose.

The dominant theme of agencies, bureaucracy, the village schools and of the state in general has been the ideology of 'development', *vikas* in Nepali. This was defined in terms of increasing the productivity of the country, with the promise to labourers of less work and producing more, and that everyone will share in the riches. In practice, it has been the theory of the ruling class aggregation of the country's resources and foreign aid funds into their hands. Rather than end the debt bondage, decrease agricultural rents, and transform property and the division of labour in the countryside, it has mean that the floodgates were opened to a tremendous inflow of capital, called foreign 'aid' and 'investment', which was in large part either repatriated or pocketed by the monopolistic interests surrounding and professing dogmatic allegiance to the palace, thereby strengthening their position in the state and countryside.

Popular understanding and state ideology conceive that capital is wealth, and not the relationship that it is, which transfers surplus into the hands of the owners of capital. Although it mobilizes labour and engages it in production, this is according to the priorities and values of the donors, not of the villages—although these values are being internalized by the villagers as well through education and the entertainment and advertising media. And where development has too often failed to live up to its explicit promises, it has created a class of patriarchal and elective officials, bureaucrats, contractors, and professionals, in addition to merchants and businessmen, from the royal family on down, who are beholden and committed to the expansion of the transnational interests and willing to facilitate their invasion of the country and subordination of the people.

From the viewpoint of foreign donors and finance, the concern is to further pry open Nepalese commodity and labour markets. This seems generous and logical enough to them, because according to their free-market ideology they are involved not in exploitation but in imparting the Nepalese people with the benefits of commodities, employment and civilization. They do not perceive development in its actual terms of completing the deindustrialization of the countryside, of the full expropriation of the means of production from the Nepalese labour, and of the incorporation of the country's labour and resources into the global circulation of their capital. In other words, 'development' is the full alienation and disenfranchisement of the labouring population from its means of production, products, culture, life and identity. Generally, it is the subordination of the lives of the people to needs and priorities determined by the market and finance centres of the world, and not the development of the people's own needs and visions. Finally, the entire logic of capital is to force down the proportion of the value of the labour component in production. This has serious implications for the bulk of the population in a country that is rich in labour, community relations and imagination, but characterized by a highly decentralized and dispersed stock of capital.

NOTES

This chapter was originally published by the Jhilko Pariwar in *Jhilko*, Vol. 11, No. 1, 1990, pp. 1–20. It is republished here with the generous permission of Hisila Yami.

1   Hegemony is used here in the sense of Antonio Gramsci (1971:12) to describe the manner that culture serves the social interests represented in the structure of the society. A particular culture takes the form of a hegemony when the group or class it represents comes into power over the state. As opposed to the coercive state power which 'legally' enforces it, hegemony is the manner that the ruling class elicits the consent of the subject peoples to its rule so that they participate more or less willingly in their own subjugation. It is produced and perpetuated through religion, state ritual, education, community organizations, and so forth. In Nepal, Hindu religion and caste are aspects of hegemony of the landed property interests that controlled the country until recently; as demonstrated in India and by the religiosity of the capitalists in Nepal, these ideological structures happily serve a variety of interests through history—similarly Christianity, other religions and even modern positivist science, with its 'priesthood' of scientists and social philosophers.

2   Chemjong (1967) offers an alternative history of the Kirat peoples. For example, first or second century Newar or proto-Newar civilization in Kathmandu Valley, seventh to twelfth century Magarat in the west-central region, and most recently, the Kirati groups in the east, such as Tamang, Rai, and Limbu.

   The anthropologist Aidan Southall termed states based on kin organization 'segmentary' (1956, 1965, 1974, 1988). See also Stein (1977, 1980) for south India, and Fox (1971) for north-Indian Rajputs.

   Ethnographers in the Indian subcontinent, following after the writings of colonial administrators and servants such as Hodgson and Kirkpatrick, have termed groups of people organized along these lines as 'tribes' (Saha 1986). But as Southall (1970) has pointed out, the contemporary definition of the term 'tribe' is framed in terms of the modern capitalist state, which is based on the most extreme development of private property, allowing the attribution of its own totally alien elements to kinship based 'segmentary states' with their communal properties. Thus the term has facilitated and legitimized the subordination of the latter states to the logic and interest of capitalism. In this manner the term 'tribe' is the capitalists' heir to the application of caste categories that occurred in earlier periods, e.g. in the Muluki Ains (legal codes) drawn up by the various Rana prime ministers in the nineteenth and twentieth centuries in Nepal.

   More recently, with the rise of the global dominance of capitalism and the subordination and incorporation of all states by a global form of state, the term 'ethnic group' has displaced the earlier term 'tribe'. It shifts the focus from class struggle to the struggle of groups that contain within themselves elements of dominant classes in alliance with monopoly capital and thus tend to serve the subordination of these groups to monopoly capital. Witness how the division between Hindus and Muslims of India has served the repression of the working classes of both groups (Ray 1988). In the meantime, the elements of the working class turn against each other with the belief that their exploitation and suffering are the result of religious, linguistic, or other forms of ethnic oppression. If they succeed in obtaining national autonomy, they continue to remain subordinated to transnational capitalism. Consequently their frustration leads to further divisions and violence among themselves. Thus we saw in Nepal the constitutional expert and big business lawyer, Blaustein, who was brought to Nepal by the Friedrich Neumann Foundation (representing the German Liberal party) to advise in the drafting of the new constitution, emphasizing 'ethnic rights'.

3   Chemjong (1967) offers an alternative history of the Kirat peoples.

4   This discussion is based on the theories of Southall (1988, n.d.), Krader (1972), and Marx and Engels (1983), and Engels (1983b). Note that Engels diverged significantly from Marx (1972) due to Engels' uncritical reading of early anthropology. Engels consistently quoted Marx out of context and misrepresented him, especially with regard to using Marx to support the theories of Bachoven regarding the existence of early matriarchy and the overthrow of matriarchy by men, ideas which Marx totally denied in two separate places in his notebooks. Marx's interest had been in understanding the subordination of clan organized society and communal property to political society and private property.

5   Take as a particular example the protection given to capital in the form of what David Werner (1989:4, 8–35) calls the 'killer industries' and their yearly total profits: alcoholic beverages ($170 billion), tobacco ($35 billion, USA alone), illicit narcotics ($350 billion), pesticides ($14 billion, USA alone), unnecessary, overpriced pharmaceuticals ($100 billion), arms and military equipment ($300 billion, USA alone), and international banking ($1,000 billion, Third World Debts serviced). Add to these the extremely wasteful private automobile, by which an individual dons a 500 or 1,000 kg metal carapace to get him or herself to the grocer to buy a bottle of milk and loaf of bread.

6   This is not to say that guilds failed to develop in the Indian subcontinent. Rather, urban industry and commerce never generally freed themselves from the forces dominating the countryside to grow as a hegemonic force in opposition to the countryside to eventually become the state.

7   Thus South Asian society, though it contained may attributes of feudalism, cannot be described as a feudal society or mode of production, since a feudal mode of production implies a certain relation of city and countryside characterized by the collapse of control of landed property over the state machinery and the subsequent rise of cities and urban capitalists as a significant opposition force against landed property. However, this is not to say that South Asian society did not have its own dynamics and dialectic, just that one should be careful about using formal terms to identify it.

8   The Chaubisi and Baisi Rajyas, Kathmandu Valley, Makwanpur, Butwal, Janakpur, and Vijayapur.

9   Makunda Sen I of Palpa, who in the twelfth century conquered much of central Nepal and even invaded Kathmandu, was a man of at least equal vision and charisma in comparison with Prithivi Narayan Shah, but he appeared several centuries too early, in conditions where landed property had not yet sufficiently established its hegemony over the kin-based state to sustain a centralized large

hill state. Consequently, he is reputed to have spent his last years in disillusionment and isolation.

10 This statement is rearranged from Marx's observation about Romulus and the founding of Rome: 'old trick of the founders of cities to draw themselves an obscure and humble multitude, and then set up for their progeny the autoch<t>onic claim' (Marx 1972).

11 This is the real source of the of cited 'bravery' of the 'Gurkha' mercenaries. It was not a result of some mythical spirit unique to the Nepalese hill people. They entered the British army by the tens of thousands with the desperate hope of ameliorating their circumstances, and while some did so, most returned to lose their earnings to the same forces that had originally driven them from their homes.

12 'Counter hegemonies', in contrast to 'hegemony' (note 1), are the competing cultures of classes which are not yet able to become a 'state' (Gramsci 1971:52). 'In order to become a state, they have to subordinate or eliminate them ['other forces' in the state] and win the active or passive assent of ["specific auxiliaries or allies"]' (ibid.:53). These subaltern classes attempt to establish their culture as the dominant culture in society in their bid for power.

CHAPTER 13

The Next Step: Cultivating the Roots of Rebellion

The communists try to achieve a perfect society where each one contributes his labour and receives according to his needs. The word 'communist' means community. And so if we all come together . . . we are all communists, all equal. . . . The rich and the poor will be liberated. Us poor people are going to be liberated from the rich. The rich are going to be liberated from themselves, that is, from their wealth.

—Solentiname, Nicaragua[1]

Communism is for us not a *state of affairs* which is to be established, an *ideal* to which reality will have to adjust itself. We call communism the *real* movement which abolishes the present state of things. The conditions of this movement result from the premises now in existence.

—Karl Marx and Frederick Engels

THROUGH history a series of ruling classes have asserted themselves over other classes and groups, due to the specific requirements and relations arising with the growth of the productive forces.[2] As each new class[3] asserted its control over production, its ideas gained universal acceptance in society, until its capture of state power seemed like a natural rather than historical process. The bourgeois revolutions of the eighteenth and nineteenth centuries, in which capitalists took control of the state in Europe, occurred because the merchants, bankers and factory owners had already asserted their control over production and established the primacy of their ideas in society and culture. We now see the assertion of the transnational corporate and financial bureaucracies over the entire world, the merger of the Soviet 'socialist' bureaucrats into this international corporate bureaucratic ruling class, and the effective withering away of the nation state[4] but not the state machinery (the loosely organized global corporate state, various state bureaucracies, and electoral machines the world over), which transnational capital is subordinating and incorporating into itself.

In Nepal, as elsewhere, a great many of the 'national' bourgeoisie and bureaucrats wear the garb of nationalist democratic pretensions and religious piety, while licking their chops and panting in anticipation of the reward of a few crumbs (contracts, commissions, concessions, positions, bribes, overseas trips and junkets) from their new corporate masters for helping to subvert their peoples' aspirations, health, industry, culture, prosperity, independence and autonomy. They believe their own self-serving propaganda that the double *rakshash* ('demon') of self-interest and greed have become virtues, and that true virtues—such as communal effort, shared interest with the great masses of people and the environment, self-sacrifice, intolerance of poverty and suffering, and the promotion of prosperity of the individual by the promotion of the prosperity of all (both humans and their planet)—have been vanquished from the main discourse.

The continuing struggle of the people in Nepal and throughout the world demonstrates that the great masses of workers do not accept this view. While the collapse of soviet bureaucratic socialism has meant the withdrawal of an immense source of support for struggle, it has also meant that there can be a healthy shift away from the tendency to frame struggle in terms of a global polarization between the United States, the Soviet Union and China.[5] There is a shift of emphasis towards intensive local organizing and sharing of information and strategy, combined with growing regional and global consciousness and solidarity and coordination of struggle.

Especially in the context of the withering away or, more accurately, the subordination of the nation state, the local organizing is as important as the struggle for control of the nation state. Transnational corporations have essentially taken over the state as one of their tools of expansion and repression. The people bear the costs of running state machinery while the corporations enjoy the bulk of the benefits. This is at least as true for the United States, a deindustrializing nation, as for the so-called developing countries, or deindustrialized and reindustrializing regions, such as Nepal (a government that has more than two-thirds of its budget financed by foreign aid is not autonomous by any stretch of the imagination).

Simply capture of state power, either by electoral means or militarily, is insufficient when that machinery belongs to other interests. Transnational capitalists will gladly sacrifice the rulers of a regime—whether it be the panchas, a Noriega or a monarchy—in order to salvage their control over their state machinery when 'their' regime inevitably loses legitimacy or no longer serves their purposes. They will even continence the election of socialists and Communists to national parliaments, if this does not bring a significant transformation of the character or distribution of state power and labour power, since this often leads to their being discredited by the impossible situation left to them or by co-optation. Attempts to bring a revolutionary transformation of society merely through the means of state machinery, no matter how well directed, will mean running against the corporate owners of the state, resulting in capital flight, withdrawal of international credit, sabotage from within and counter-insurgency from without, ultimately undermining and discrediting the revolution. Finally, when the masses who provided the basis for the revolution are excluded from instrumental participation in a revolutionary state, the entire socialist experiment turns into a parody of socialism, as demonstrated by the Soviet experience, where socialism was turned into an immense state ritual that hid the consolidation of the control by bureaucrats over the state. Capitalism ultimately wins because the state remains a tool of coercion and the population remains as powerless as before.

A truly revolutionary transformation comes about when control over resources, labour power, technical knowledge, and culture are pried from the control of state bureaucrats, capitalists and other property owning classes. This can occur in large part without a political revolution, although as the shift of control progresses, it will make a political revolution inevitable. A political revolution, on the other hand, cannot be successful without the organization and education of the working classes as its basis. In Nepal, there is an entire range of resources and activities to which people can gain or extend control through organization. Some of these resources, such as forests and pastures, are in the public sector. Many activities that can be effectively organized communally remain in the peasant household, only indirectly controlled by landlords, moneylenders and merchants, such as handicraft production and marketing, child care, food preparation, herding and agriculture. Other activities, such as child education and socialization, drinking water, health care, sanitation, and so forth are provided by the government, but are insufficiently funded or misappropriated, ineffectively administered, or otherwise sabotaged by various groups for their personal benefits. Then there are government properties, such as privately operated mines, which can be captured by organized workers with the support of community organizers and their elected representatives.[6]

Such a shift of activities and resources to communal organization and control is urgently needed. Transnational corporations and their agencies are engaged in the reverse process of shifting control of resources into the private sector. This has been a matter of unabashed policy of the Reagan, Bush and Thatcher administrations in the United States and Great Britain which, ruling over empires in decline, are unable to shape policy independent of transnational corporate domination. International agencies, such as USAID, the World Bank, Asian Development Bank, and the International Monetary Fund, which are engaged in assisting the expansion of transnational corporations, are promoting policies such as 'privatization'. Governments are being pressured to sell national resources such as forests, lands, water, and public services to private owners.

Planners say that this is the most rational alternative to the failure of bureaucracies to properly manage these resources, both in capitalist and bureaucratic socialist countries, even though many of these bureaucracies (Nepal's included) have been financed and built by the capitalists themselves in order to create strong sympathetic client interests within these countries. This in spite of many of these public controlled properties and services having been well managed and the failures of the ones that are not often due to corporate sabotage.

Privatization is supported by the foreign corporations and the rising indigenous entrepreneurial elements aligned with them (contractors, large merchants, and officials who treat their offices as sinecures providing means for personal gain as characterizes much of the Nepalese bureaucracy). This shift of the public domain into private ownership effectively takes the power piece by piece away from the common people, decreasing the possibility of effective reform and revolutionary change. By making a class of private owners of previously public resources, privatization creates strong class interests within and without the country which are antagonistic to any sort of strengthening of popular control over social and political life. In conditions of transnational corporate organization of production, it prepares the way for Nepal's resources to fall into transnational corporate control. Furthermore, when more popularly oriented groups obtain control of the state, they must waste valuable time and effort wresting control of these resources and the organization of production back into the hands of the people just at the moment when they are most vulnerable. This process itself sets off reaction and subversion against the workers movement.

Yet the mass destruction of communities and cultures, and the death and suffering of untold millions of people (especially of women and children, including the deaths of 14.6 million children per year world wide) all demonstrate the extreme irrationality and inhumanity of the present order. The transfer of power and control, from the centralized national control of socialist bureaucracies and capitalist ones alike, is proposed as the logical alternative of state socialism. In contrast, consideration of the transfer of control of the state and production to organized peasants and workers is carefully kept from the agenda.

An essential aspect of the revolutionary struggle prior to capturing state power, and the means to do so, is the shift of production and resources into the communal control of the people. I suggest below a few possible steps that can be taken. The object of organization, the problems to be solved, the strategy and the actual organizing must be worked out by the people themselves, with or without the assistance of Communists and other like-minded organizers. In this way, the process of organizing becomes a means by which initiative is shifted from the bureaucracy, itself aligned with capital, and capitalists, to the people. The people will learn to participate in changing the conditions of their existence.

ORGANIZATION

> With a united people there are no problems. Maybe I won't have food, but my neighbor will. If we're together something [powerful] can happen to us. . . . It seems that's a fundamental teaching . . . : That's the way the world ought to be . . . that we ought to organize ourselves into communities.
>
> —Solentiname, Nicaragua

Successful revolution requires organization, and not just politically. Obviously, the growth of the Communist movement in Nepal has so far been due to widespread organizing by committed party workers.

However, now with their capture of a significant number of seats within the national assembly, the question is *how* to organize the people so as to assert control over the government.

The purpose of electoral democracies is to mobilize the population to vote once every 4, 5, or 6 years (or whenever there is a crisis of confidence), but to keep them out of the actual political process during the rest of the time. The strength of the Communist movement, as well as its goal, is that it encourages people to take direct control over their own governance. In Brazil, Nicaragua, liberated parts of El Salvador and elsewhere, the rural villages and urban neighbourhoods are organized into popular assemblies or councils in which people participate in governing themselves.

In Nepal time has come to create these organizations, prior to the establishment of the local governments. The people holding power will tend to push for a centralized rather than decentralized control. They will want to use state power to control the local governments from the centre and prevent the Communists or the masses from developing their hold over them (although this tendency tends to be self defeating, as evidenced by the Panchayat system). These governing bodies do not replace constitutionally created ones, but they encourage people to relate to them in a collective manner.

These organizations can play a key role in the revolutionary process. Despite their lofty ideals, the Communists' lack of governing experience causes them to grope and blunder when they assume power. Such popular governing organizations provide them with valuable experience in developing and implementing programmes. These organizations can study the conditions of land ownership, labour, resources, and environment to provide valuable data banks on these conditions and develop policies on how to go about handling them. People in the communities learn skills such as accounting, management, legal rights, and so forth. Thereby, when Communists come into power by electoral means or otherwise, a popularly-based governing framework is already largely in place. These are valuable tools in preventing the capital flight experienced after revolutions—sale of tools, tractors, machinery, and so forth from the large estates and businesses. They allow the shaping of programmes from below that address the needs, conditions and realities of the people. And they create a population already experienced and committed to struggle.

These organizations vary depending upon the conditions confronted in each country. In Kerala under the British, for example, the Communists were unable to participate directly in government, but they could create strong labour unions and peasant organizations which provided the framework for organizing widespread programmes for the people. After independence, these continued to exert a strong political role, providing a basis for Communist victories and the general betterment of conditions.

In Latin America and the Philippines, where US-backed regimes have been responsible for extremely violent repression, these organizations could not directly address political issues. Thus some hundred thousand 'base communities' have been organized in villages throughout Latin America. Ostensibly, these began religious discussion groups, but since religion is the vehicle of legitimization, they have been the means for teaching literacy, raising consciousness and organizing around local issues.

Initially, the organization of 'base communities' is not tied to political parties. Usually, the organizing of such communities first addressed the immediate conditions of the urban and rural poor in terms of the religious world view in which the poor already understand their world. However, as the poor people reformulate their consciousnesses, they tend to align with progressive parties. Since Communism and socialism by definition must be based on wilful and conscious participation rather than coercion or superficial slogans, an approach that emphasizes the development of consciousness prior to the political organizing not only seems logical but is far more successful and enduring in the long run. Furthermore, people are thus organized first according to their shared condition, with political affiliation arising subsequently. Starting with political organization first often imposes party divisions upon people who should be united together, undermining their own strength and cutting short the momentum of any general movement. Also, without the strength of their own consciousness, community organization or personal resolve to fall back on, the poor are easily waylaid by demagoguery or otherwise dissuaded by the opposition when difficulties arise.

Berryman (1984:30–2) generalizes a series of steps out of the experience gained from the organization of base communities:

1. The first step is simply 'going to the people,' often by leaving a level of comfort . . . and sharing their conditions: wooden shacks, water shortages, poor bus service, dust and mud of unpaved streets.

2. The aim is recreating consciousness ('conscientization'),[7] understood as

a two-way dialogue, often systematically organized in evening meetings and courses, but also understood as a wider process of interaction in the community.

3. Participants acquire a critical view of their inherited consciousness and take on a new vision, which emphasizes their dignity . . . and their vocation to shape their own destiny rather than to accept passively things as they are. Local communities with their own leadership emerge and begin to act on their own to some extent.

4. At some point there is conflict, very often as people make the step from conscientization to organization. The conflict is typically first at the local level (for instance, people demand their rights of a local landholder, who may denounce them as 'Communists' to the army or police).

5. Conflict brings the organizers to recognize the factor of *class*, namely, the problem is not simply the particular landholder but elites who have economic and political power, which they maintain by force and, if necessary, by violence. From this realization the organizers may become convinced that the problem lies in capitalism as a system (the ownership of the main means of production in private hands) and that only through socialism (the socialization of these means of production) will people's basic needs be met and repressive violence stopped.

It is remarkable how often one can trace the steps just sketched in the experience of individual organizers and teams of organizers working with the poor. The process has often taken years. It is *not* a matter of reading liberation theology or Marxist texts and leaping into political action. In almost every case there is a step-by-step process, even in the case of people who are notionally familiar with the ideas of socialism.

After one comes to question capitalism, there are further steps. 'Opting for socialism' in itself does not tell one what to do, for example, in a rural area where there is no viable national organization. As organized people have come in contact with existing political organizations they have encountered factional and personal disputes, immaturity, and large, unresolved problems of strategy and tactics and have begun a long process of political apprenticeship.

While the experience in Latin America did not lead immediately to any viable project of liberation, it served as a preparation for what was to happen in Central America in the 1970s and 1980s. Without the benefit of those earlier experiences it is difficult to see that the poor people could have taken such an active role in the later struggles.[8]

Nicaragua[9]

In 1968 nine hundred lay priests, called 'Delegates of the Word,' organized 'base communities' throughout Nicaragua. Seeing the success of these base communities, the FSLN (Sandinista National Liberation Front) popular liberation forces further organized 'Committees of Agricultural Workers.' These base communities and committees provided discussion groups in which people dealt with their problems and received literacy education and health care. They increasingly organized the workers to demand basic health services, drinking water, liveable wages and year-round employment. Prior to the fall of the US created regime of Anastasio Somoza, severe repression of these 'base communities' and 'committees' caused them to spread, grow stronger and make more bold demands. The peasants captured estates and established their own communes. In the urban areas, where a large proportion of the men had been murdered by death squads, the women created 'neighbourhood defence committees' in which the women organized and defended themselves.[10] Both the urban and rural organizations eventually merged with the Sandinista Front as a popular militia, helping to defeat Somoza's national guard.

After the Sandinista victory in 1978, areas which had been previously organized were much more responsive to the development of co-operatives, communes, and other forms of communal organizing and initiative.

Brazil

In Brazil, where like in Nepal the progressive forces have won the right to participate in the electoral process, popular governing organizations are created in constituencies controlled by these forces.

Since its founding in 1979, the *partido dos Trabalhadares* (PT) has won municipal elections in more than thirty major cities in Brazil. In these cities, the PT has implemented some important economic and social programs. . . . The democratization of decision making at the state level is a primary concern of the PT, which organizes *conselhos populares* (popular councils) with budgetary power to work with the municipal administrations which the PT now controls. The concept of building socialism in day-to-day struggles is put into practice in the popular organizations, where the PT has won in local elections. . . .

Democratizing the state means institutionalizing mechanisms of popular participation in the drafting and implementation of public policy. One such mechanism has been the development of popular councils which are organized by neighborhood and by issue of concern. The residents of each *bairro* are organized, usually with one representative for each street, to discuss and draft proposals on such questions of immediate relevance to them as building schools, daycare centers, playgrounds, health clinics, etc. The neighborhood residents elect members of each of the committees to form a *conselhos popular*. The popular councils draft their own statutes and meet regularly with members of the municipal government to discuss and draft public policies. Budgetary constraints are discussed, priorities established, and the difficulties of implementation of programs are handled together. For the first time in Brazilian history, citizens, especially poor citizens, participate directly in budgetary decisions and policy making in a regular manner. Direct participation results in distinctly different programs to deal with development and social problems. (Alves 1991:25–6)

Socioeconomic as well as Political Objects of Organizing

These organizations cannot be directed simply towards capturing state power. Political power follows from control over production; democratic power arises from communal, not private or bureaucratic, control. The working poor must organize their own community organizations, such as the 'base communities' in Latin America, to manage and take control of resources from the bureaucracy and pre-empt privatization. As seen in Central America, where the first communal organizations were organized by the Catholic Church, this need and should not be a solely Communist project. These non-Communist organizations enriched the Communist movement, indeed transformed it, giving it a truly democratic character prior to eventually merging with it. The Left must encourage and promote the development of communal organizations, but also carefully watch them, since many such projects are done incompletely, in form only, not fully empowering the people but just making their labour accessible to business and bureaucratic interests (e.g. in the form of 'participatory development').

Women as the Key to Organizing

Much of the shift of control of production into the private domain hurts women directly and, through them, their families. Women's productive activities in Nepal are particularly concerned with the subsistence sphere: animal raising, collecting fodder and fuel wood, food preparation and household crafts. The shift of these resources over to bureaucratic or private control and to cash crop production undermines women's control over production, passing it over into the private sphere. This control is not necessarily alleviated through the 'income generation' activities which train women in craft skills without providing accompanying knowledge and organization necessary for obtaining their raw materials and marketing their products; they fall into the control of middlemen who turn the women at best into extremely exploited wage earners.[11] The result is exploitation and impoverishment of the women, along with worsening condition of the members of their families dependent upon their activities.

These disempowered women are then recruited into lowly paid categories of factory labour. Their desperation allows undercutting of wages and working conditions for workers worldwide. In Nepal some sixty per cent of the jobs in some cotton textile mills near the Indian border are held by women. The expansion of transnational corporations throughout the world is based on recruiting this unorganized and vulnerable element on the factory floor.

In the United States, the response of the male dominated labour movement was to exclude women, and the eventual result was that the wages of male unionized labour has itself been reduced. The split was so great that some women in disgust joined a separatist movement, which divides and weakens the struggle in a manner similar to the communalism in India. Ignoring women leads to loss of the central component of the labour process, in the household, field and factory. Furthermore, as we saw in the movement and during the elections, since women are fighting two interconnected battles, one against private property and the other against gender repression, they are extremely militant and capable organizers.

Globally, the Communist movement has a poor record with regard to women. Where women have been able to assert themselves, such as in Nicaragua, Central America, and Kerala, India, it has been due to their strong, militant organization of themselves and to the Communist party's (albeit imperfect) ability to reflect upon its mistakes. The successes of the revolutionary movements in these areas in turn resulted from the instrumental and powerful role of women. Since women are in the front line in the struggle against capitalism, the success and strength of struggle will depend upon whether they are brought into a central, equal role in the Communist movement.

In Nepal, men heavily the dominate internal hierarchy of all the parties, including the two dominant ones, the Communist and Congress parties, with very few women holding party offices. Yet it is evident that women make up a major if not majority force within the rank and file of the Communist Party, in both village and the city. Therefore, not only must they enter the party organization at every level, they must take an equal role in shaping the strategy, objectives and the course of struggle. The Communist Party must champion women's issues such as equal property rights and full citizenship, as their disenfranchisement underlies exploitation and inequality in general. This will lead the movement into new and innovative directions, it will further the creation of egalitarian relations in all spheres of relations and activity: class, cultural, caste, ethnic, community, and household.

Many tasks currently within the women's sphere can be organized communally as a strategy of the Communist movement. Women weave cloth and produce other handicrafts which they must sell individually to merchants who take the profits and pay them minimal wages. By organizing themselves into groups for purchasing their raw materials and marketing their products, locally and internationally, they can cut out middleman control and decrease the power of merchants as a class force. They can work together to increase the quality of their products and create a demand for handicrafts in the domestic market, replacing imported goods. Much of the drudgery of the household tasks and farm production can be organized communally, reducing the total amount of labour that women have to put into these tasks. They can organize to solve the problems of family and community. They can fight devaluation of the relations of men and women through education and activities such as protest or creation of counter-cultural activities against raunchy Hindi films, beauty pageants, and chauvinist advertising. They can fight flesh trade, alcoholism and other vices which are eroding the well-being of the community. They can collectively work together in the socialization and education of their children, reclaiming them from the cultural oppression of film and television. And of course they can fight for property rights.

All these struggles must be a basis for women to emerge as a powerful and leading element of the party, and not merely as its tool as has so often been the case. These issues must be central to the Communist agenda, and not set aside as a separate 'women's question' as has so frequently happened.

EDUCATION

As observed in the 1991 election in Nepal, the Communists succeeded best in areas characterized by higher levels of education and consciousness (Lamsal 1991). Elsewhere adult education has been key to building the base for the movement. In Nicaragua and Kerala, as well as in liberated areas of El Salvador, the Communists and their allies sent out immense numbers of volunteers throughout the villages to educate children and teach adults how to read.

Within the first four years of FSLN rule in Nicaragua, through community organized schools and volunteers, adult literacy rate rose from under 50 per cent (already higher than that of most low-income countries due to adult education in the course of struggle) to 87.3 per cent; by 1991 it had become well over 90 per cent. The Sandinista realized that if the poor were educated, even if the party lost state power, they could never again be repressed and exploited as they had been under the Somoza dictatorship. Furthermore, they would provide a strong basis for future revival and renewal of the revolution.

In Kerala, raising literacy in the population was a major tactic for raising the consciousness of workers and peasantry. Volunteers formed reading and writing circles in the villages. Prominent authors wrote stories and poems with liberating themes. Workers published their own poetry and narratives in union-sponsored publications. By the 1980s more than 5,000 libraries had been created in the villages. Literacy became an important demand of the movement, with the result that Kerala, despite its great poverty, now has one of the highest literacy rates in the world.

A mass literacy and education programme mediates the role of education as a means of reproduction of class repression. In Kerala, like Nicaragua, the low castes and poor are now entering the bureaucracy (which still, however, is only an advance within the current framework of bureaucratic domination and not liberation from it).

NECESSITY FOR HONEST REPRESENTATION

Success of the struggle in Nepal will have strong implications throughout the world, particularly for its close neighbours, not only in rearranging the position of Nepal's people within the international political-economic order, but in encouraging and re-igniting the revolutionary movement in other parts of the world. It is another experiment which is being carefully watched by the Left elsewhere, in which previous mistakes are corrected and new ideas tested. Consequently, as the movement expands, it will suffer increasing interference and subversion from countries, international corporations, agencies and other forces, such as the Unification Church.[12] In the 1991 general elections in Nepal such forces donated large amounts of money and other kinds of support to certain reactionary political figures (in addition to the usual foreign aid). The progressive elements within Nepal must attend to publicity, spreading the truth of the real situation of the country through publications, and communicating with progressive social movements and elements throughout the world. The silence and wall of untruth that has been constructed around the people of Nepal must be broken.

The ascendant transnational corporate interests are far advanced in this matter. Bookstores are filled with tourist guides, picture books and 'scientific' works which present Nepal as a mystical country, with simple minded, happy people who think only of god and spend their free hours worshipping in temples or dancing in festivals. Or else they are the 'loyal' porters and guides who carry the loads of tourists and climbers up mountains, or soldiers who 'bravely' fight in the British army to repress other struggling peoples. If the people have problems, it is due to natural as opposed to social causes: 'overpopulation', difficult environment, or traditional, backward morale, as if hill people have not been successfully and brilliantly coping with such problems through history or there were not any other human agents in the entire process.

There is little analysis of the previous century's complicity of Nepalese rulers in the East India Company's subjugation of the Indian subcontinent or of the Nepalese bazaar merchants as purveyors of goods from Euro-American (including Indian) and Japanese factories into the countryside, undermining the domestic economy and community. The people of Nepal are said to be 'poor', as if their poverty is a natural condition and not because there are 18 million rural cultivators, urban workers, small shopkeepers, and low level bureaucrats subject to landlords, usurers, importers, smugglers, arbitrary rule, self proclaimed 'experts', corporate infiltration and international finance. Consequently, struggle, and desperate violence, seem to be an aberration described by newspaper headlines as the *New York Times*' 'Trouble in Shangri-La'. The point of view and voice of the masses is silenced, and their consciousness is described as non-existent, requiring 'consciousness raising' programs financed by INGOs and administered by the urban middle class.

Not only do the airlines, tourist hotels, garment and handicraft exporters stand much to gain by this misrepresentation of the Nepali condition and state of mind; as contradictions deepen and struggle grows, the false image of Nepal and lack of sympathizers overseas will facilitate economic, political and military intervention, making real change much more difficult and causing immense suffering for people trying to bring about the change. Oppressed peoples struggling throughout the world find it necessary to demonstrate that their own struggles are interlinked with those taking place within the industrialized or imperialist countries themselves.

For Nepal, there is need to show the role of the state as a tool of landlords, large trading houses, commission agents, contractors, and international corporate and government interests, in widespread day-to-day violence against the people, and not the resistance of people to this being the source of violence. There is a need to expose not only state violence, but economic, political, and bureaucratic violence as well. For example, the deaths of two out of every ten children before the age of five, the premature disability and death of many adults (a disproportionate number of these among the poor and oppressed, particularly women), and a general condition of fear and despair, or the limited and formalistic education forced on the young people that does little to address the real situation of their lives or prepare them to deal with it.

Rebellion must be shown by the people of Nepal as a creative and justified response to this violence. People must understand that rebellion itself only *seems* to be violent because instead of people confronting this violence daily on an individual basis, they all stand up at once and confront it together. Indeed, many lives are saved and many less physically or emotionally brutalized when people stand up together than if they continue in their day-by-day isolated individual confrontations with their oppressors. Nor does the rebellion cause the uprooting of masses of people, erosion of values, and a myriad of other aspects of the decades or centuries of state supported violence. Rebellion has to be shown to be a great celebration of human spirit and resolve. Finally, it needs to be interlinked to the struggle against large hotel interests, soft drink and beer companies, food and drug multinationals, foreign aid interests and the confrontation with the industrial process of which these are part and which people of all countries are engaged in.

Struggle must ascend above the tourist industry propaganda that is being used to silence and exploit people and project a new, powerful, inspiring experience of revolution through the voices of the people, reclaiming and revitalizing their literature, poetry, art, music and film, showing that this struggle is part of the struggle that people find themselves in throughout the world. Finally ties of solidarity with progressive and creative groups, movements and publishers the world over must be cultivated.[13]

Even class struggle must be done with love. A Chilean priest is quoted as saying, 'Only love is revolutionary. Hatred is always reactionary,' and Marcelino [of the Solentiname community] reflects, with frequent pauses: 'If we hate we are no longer struggling against the enemy. . . . The difference between us and the enemy is that we fight them without wanting to oppress them, only to liberate them.'

–Solentiname, Nicaragua

NOTES

This chapter was originally published by the Jhilko Pariwar in *Jhilko*, Vol. 16 (April-June), 1991, pp. 1–18. It is republished here with the generous permission of Hisila Yami.

1   All quotations from the discussions that took place in the 'base community' of Solentiname, Nicaragua, are taken from Phillip Berryman (1984).

2   Productive forces encompass human relations both to the world, including the various means of life that humans have created, and to each other. Productive forces thus also include human language, which arose as the means of human relations and which Marx calls a 'practical' consciousness, and human consciousness generally, including ideas, technical knowledge, laws, religion, etc. When workers develop consciousness, organize and unite themselves, they reshape these productive forces into a revolutionary force by which they take control of and transform the conditions of their existence.

A misinterpretation of 'productive forces' in the limited sense of 'technology' has led to an overemphasis on technological development as the purpose and means of revolution. This is little different from the 'freedom' of bourgeois democracy which means merely the releasing of human labour from control by other classes so it can be subjected by technology controlled by capitalists. Marx, in contrast, envisioned a freeing of human effort and thought from the encumbrances of private property through revolution. Technology also was to be subordinated to the needs and possibilities of a community of humans relating equally as full participants rather than the subordination of humans to the needs of technological development and its accompanying class interests.

3   These ruling classes appeared as follows: first communities of elders in the early clan societies that preceded the rise of the first cities; then priesthoods which developed on the base of the ritual status of the clan elders, but differentiated from the labouring groups by means of control over the new levels of surplus resulting from revolutions in agriculture and animal husbandry; the rise of the first cities (9,000 to 6,000 years ago) and the multiplied social power of greater concentrations of people; then warriors and war leaders who arose through the militarization that accompanied the subsequent imperial expansion of the cities; and finally merchants and various craft specializations encouraged by the expansion of contacts between the cities.

4   There is a reorganization of the world in terms of increasingly regionally unified political economies, in Europe with the European Community, the Central American Common Market, CARICOM, and the North American Free Trade Agreement, and so forth, which are totally changing the entire character of the state, society, and struggle in the world.

5   There is an attempt to create new polarizations, such as between Arab peoples and the West. However, this polarization revolves merely around the extent of control of oil profits. It will be difficult for areas with ascendant economies, such as Germany and Japan, which can assert their control over the world economically, to maintain a consensus with declining imperial powers, such as the United States and Britain, which must assert themselves militarily to maintain their control. As seen in the Iraq War, the United States and Britain were enthusiastically in support of the invasion of Iraq, whereas Germany and Japan were somewhat ambivalent.

6   As an example are the slate mines in Bandipur, Tanahun District, in west-central Nepal. Up until the 'Democracy' Movement of 1990, three mines were worked legally by large merchants, who took five rupees profit for every rupee they paid their workers. Since the Democracy Movement, the mining has been taken over illegally by the previous Pradhan Pancha of Bandipur, whose control of an army of hired thugs has allowed him to push out the previous mine owners. The surrounding community could be organized to take over the mine operations, which could then be worked and managed collectively, paying an ample wage to the workers as well as the due to the government (as opposed to the present bribes to the government functionaries). The immense profits would provide means for a true community-oriented development, reviving and building the local schools, campus, hospitals, agriculture, crafts and services without government or foreign aid. Organization of such a 'base community,' as it is called in Latin America, would take an immense struggle with the local bureaucrats and merchants; it would not be easy, but it could be a tremendous example to show the potential self-sufficiency and inner force of the people.

7   From Paulo Freire (1974).

8   Minor editing has been done to fit the Nepalese context. For a manual on this approach written from the Asian perspective, see Maglaya (1987).

9   In part from Collins (1982).

10   To give an idea of the extent of repression that gives rise to such organizations

of women, in El Salvador nearly every adult woman is a potential rape or torture victim for the military. Husbands and brothers who attempt to protect them are killed.

In Nicaragua, the women in the Sandinista army and the militia consisted of 40 per cent of the military force. With the fall of the Somoza regime, the women saw that a continued role of women in the military was key to their power in society, and thus the women refused to disband these divisions—a position that the Sandinista leadership first resisted but then came to agree with. Presently women also play an equivalent role in the revolutionary army of the FMLN (Farabundo Martí National Liberation Front), the opposition in El Salvador.

11   There are a number of cases of people from the upper classes in Nepal who have obtained funds to develop the autonomy of women who then market the handicrafts while taking the products to support the administrative personnel, for example the Dhukuta Sisters store at the bridge to Patan. Or else the UNICEF programme which pays women about Rs. 450 ($9) per month.

12   As an example of the kinds of subversion the Nepalese people will have to confront in their struggle, the Unification Church is an extremely anti-labour religious cult founded by a Korean, Sun Yong Moon, who claims to be the reincarnation of Jesus Christ. The Unification Church recruits young people, called 'Moonies', by means of intensive brainwashing, and pays them starvation wages for long hours of labour, making immense profit by them. It has widespread business interests and strong ties to the US CIA. It sponsors counter-insurgency efforts throughout the world by supporting reactionary elements, supplying arms, assisting in destabilization, using immense propaganda. President Bush was a regular reader of their newspaper, the *Washington Times*.

13   An example of what can be done is the backing off of the World Bank from funding the Arun III high dam project on 4 July 1995 as a result of concerted pressure from within and without the country, including the embarrassing press the World Bank had received on its backing of the Tehri dam in Uttar Pradesh, India.

PART IV
Bandipur Bazaar

CHAPTER 14

Up-Country Bazaar and Changing Forces

COMMON interpretations frame change in terms of the same obvious political events which are accepted as cumulatively making up Nepal's history. Starting with unification in the eighteenth century these events include subsequent ministerial takeovers by the Thapa and Rana families in the subsequent century, and in the twentieth, the revolution of 1950–1 which brought the fall of the Rana regime, and the People's Movement of 1990 which ended the Panchayat system.

This reduction of history into a document of the careers of regimes allows the complicated lives of Nepalese villagers to fall away from the picture. Their lives are trivialized and formalized in theories that misrepresent them as overly traditional, stagnant and fatalist. Rather than being treated as the force and purpose of change, the villagers' fecundity and conservatism are presented as its roadblock, which must be subjected to the dynamism of 'development'.

The truth of the matter is that rural Nepal has always dynamically interacted with and shaped the flow of historical events. The Nepali countryside of today was shaped by a long, gradual process of the entry of village society into wider spheres of interaction. It is the villager who produced and traded the products of the land, who filled the coffers of kings and fattened the moneylenders, who built the palaces and fought the wars and who bore, nursed, and fed all, from pauper to king.

More significant as markers of change than the rise and fall of regimes is the development of relations among the various peoples which provided the real base and substance of the political forms. Industrialization, marked by the invention of the spinning jenny in 1764, merely confronted an existing dynamic which had been developing over many centuries, or even thousands of years, to subsume and set it to its own purposes. Key steps in the process, for the transformation of industrial and commercial life in Nepal, were the global rise of the conglomerate joint stock corporations, in the latter part of the nineteenth century, and their succeeding expansion into the multinational corporation in the 1940s. These changes were accompanied in the Indian subcontinent by the appearance of indigenous industrialists in the second half of the nineteenth century and their assertion of control over the economy and polity of the subcontinent from the 1920s onwards.

The sudden, successful proselytization in Nepal of 'development', the ideology of capitalism in its multinational form, has been the culmination of a long series of developments in the villages. While colonist adventurers of the late nineteenth century created a picture of a 'forbidden kingdom', still profitable today for marketing exotica (albeit increasingly tarnished by pollution and cultural theft and destruction and the reality of the exploitation behind it), the hills of Nepal were being buffeted by economic and technological changes with origins far from the Himalayan heartland—in the industrial cities of Europe and America and the commercial centres of India.

How did these changes penetrate Nepal's remote valleys? Perhaps the most important agents of change opening the hinterland for expansion and exploitation by outsiders were the Newar mercantile families who managed rural commerce across Nepal from their trade marts such as Dhankuta, Chainpur, Doti, Tansen, Bhojpur, Kusma, Baglung, Pokhara and Dailekh. Scattered through the length of the middle hills of Nepal, these towns were settled mostly by families from Bhaktapur and Patan in the wake of the Gorkha conquests. Although these rural bazaars grew quietly and slowly amidst the swirl of political events, they have been major actors in shaping the countryside of today.

THE BANDIPUR LEGACY

An old genealogy, written on bark in the eighteenth century, records that in 1769 a scion of a wealthy Bhaktapur family, Tekan Singh Piya, left his home following the overthrow of the Malla regime that had ruled for the previous five centuries. He travelled westward and settled in Bandipur, a trade mart on a ridge of the Mahabharat range above the Marsyangdi river. Bandipur, according to the letters of

Prithivi Narayan Shah, had already been taken by Gorkha from the Tanahun king in the February of that year.

Following the complete conquest of the kingdom of Tanahun, Bandipur became the military capital of the new district. Rana Bahadur Shah, Prithivi Narayan's grandson, awarded Jagadev Bhandari, of a prominent Lamjung family, with the post of sardar of Tanahun in 1792 and provided him a large *birta* or family estate near Bandipur as reward for his role in the war of conquest.

Old *tamsuk*, or debt vouchers, indicate that by the 1790s, Tekan Singh's family was trading homespun cloth, ghee, and other goods produced by the surrounding Magar and Gurung villagers. Business records and personal correspondence from the 1830s indicate that Tekan Singh's descendants also continued to maintain property interests in Bhaktapur, where they collected rents and engaged in usury.

Taking advantage of the peasant hunger for credit—arising from the centuries-old inequalities in landholding and distribution of agricultural products which had culminated in and underwrote the Nepali state—the merchants loaned a portion of their profits to peasants in the surrounding countryside. The peasants mortgaged their accumulated wealth in jewelry, farm implements, animals, land, and even rights over their children. Formidably high rates of interest enabled the merchants to slowly alienate this peasant wealth and labour and increasingly assert more direct control over agricultural production, displacing older claims on the peasant labour. The surpluses alienated in this fashion were entered in trade.

Strategically situated between the north Indian plains and the Himalayan highlands, the Bandipur merchants also established themselves as middlemen in the flow of trade from India to the hills and mountains of what are now the districts of Lamjung, Manang and Mustang. Thus, when machine-made textiles began to enter the subcontinent following the mechanization of cloth production in Britain during the last half of the eighteenth century, these bazaar merchants were already positioned to promote the penetration of foreign fabrics into the Nepali countryside and the great changes in rural society this entailed. The establishment of textile factories in Indian cities such as Kanpur in the latter part of the nineteenth century pushed down prices and encouraged further expansion of textile markets.

Previously, traders had been mostly immersed in local commerce, economically exploiting village producers and buyers, but also providing the credit that underwrote and sustained agricultural production and community life. As the bazaar merchants traded increasing quantities of industrial commodities, however, their relationship to the countryside slowly changed. With the new trade, the bazaar merchants of Bandipur became incorporated in the circulation of industrial commodities, in which the sales of cloth to villagers became the last step in realizing the price of the product necessary for sustaining and expanding factory production in India, Britain, the United States and, eventually, Japan. The merchants' orientation and commitment gradually shifted away from the community of the villages around Bandipur, with its moral imperatives and obligations, to the goal of expansion of markets for foreign commodities.

The market underwent a qualitative change following the First World War, nine generations after Tekan Singh's arrival in Bandipur. Large numbers of Magar and Gurung veteran mercenaries returned from the war with their accumulated wages and new desires. At the same time, up-country bazaar capitalists in India began forcing their way into previously European-controlled foreign trade, displacing the large European houses such as the Ralli Brothers of London, Volkart Brothers of Switzerland and David Sassoon & Company of Manchester, which with their higher operating costs and requirement for higher profit margins could not survive the market crises of the period.

As they grew in strength and consolidated their position, the native Indian mill owners were beginning to shift their support from the British colonial government to the Indian Congress Party. Foremost among these were the Birla and Ispahani families, closely connected with Gandhi and Jinnah, respectively. This process culminated, following the Great Depression and the Second World War, in Indian native capital's final assertion over the colonial state apparatus, represented by the Indian Congress Party and the Muslim League in India and Pakistan.

Although the Rana regime in Nepal, along with the remaining Indian princes, was one of the casualties of this process that transferred colonial power from foreign rulers to indigenous ones, the impact was not limited to Kathmandu's rulers. As large Nepali merchant houses were themselves already integrated within the up-country bazaar economy of north India, and through it the world economy, this process greatly benefited their position.

Expansion

The merchants of Bandipur were set to take full advantage of political and economic changes represented in the shift of the administration of colonial states from foreign to native rulers. By the 1930s the bazaar population totalled more than 10,000 people. Tekan Singh's descendants alone counted for more than 4,000 of them.

The eight largest merchant houses, each with large *sangai* 'together' families and dependent retainers, expanded their operations into subsidiary bazaars across the southern slope of the Himalaya and along the Mahabharat east from Trisuli to Pokhara and south to Chitawan. These smaller bazaars with Bandipur outlets included Phale Sangu, Besisahar, Khudi, Tarkughat, Jarebar, Tunje, Changling, Maibal, Rising, Kabung, Sabung, Khoplang, Phalangkot, Thulo Dunga, Kunchha, Chisenku, Gorkha, Trisuli, Pokhara, Narayanghat, Butwal, the yearly *haat* bazaar at Devghat, as well as Bhikna Thori on the Indian border, where Bandipur merchants also had winter shops and large godowns.

While remaining under the ownership of patriarchs of the trade groupings in a manner characteristic of north Indian business houses, these subsidiary shops were managed by sons and poorer, dependent sons-in-law. Other brothers and sons apportioned their time between Kathmandu, Butwal, Bhikna Thori and India, arranging licenses and quota rights, raising finance and transferring money, buying and facilitating the movement not only of cloth, but of raw cotton, thread, cigarettes, kerosene, salt, bangles, shoes and other profitable goods.

The trading house headed by one of Tekan Singh's descendants was largest and wealthiest in Bandipur. According to oral histories, by the 1930s, eight major merchant houses were engaged in a total yearly purchase of approximately 1.5 million rupees of fabric and other goods from India, wholesaling to other smaller Bandipur merchants and to traders walking down from Manang and Mustang, and retailing from their own shops to the agricultural producers in the villages of the region. Members of each household made about five trips to India every year. On these trips, 70 to 100 merchants took along hundreds of porters and carried immense quantities of coinage. They went armed, as protection against thieves in the forests of Chitawan, where they often buried and slept upon the money at night. Avoiding colonial government's inspection points, the merchants surreptitiously exchanged their Nepali coins with Indian businessmen in Narkatiaganj or with returning 'Lahuray' mercenaries in Butwal, depending upon the rates—a constant topic of their letters.

In India, many of the merchant houses had established residences and warehouses, and close social relations (often as *mit* or blood brothers) with large Indian commission agents who provided them with purchasing, credit, money transfer, exchange, transport, insurance and other facilities. They also utilized close relations with important figures in the Rana government to gain control of customs, licensing, marketing quotas, as well as obtaining various government contracts within Nepal. Some of their own family members, positioned as judges, customs inspectors, *talukdars* and other officials, greatly facilitated access to the Rana government. During a period when a son of one of the families of Bandipur bazaar took the contract for the customs post at Bhikna Thori, the Bandipur merchants avoided paying customs duties entirely, causing Kathmandu businessmen to walk the two weeks round-trip journey to Bandipur to buy wholesale fabrics at cheaper prices.

Erosion of Rural Life

The Bandipur merchants' expansion of outlets directly into the countryside meant that they were able to exert further control over agricultural production in villages between Trisuli and Pokhara. It was in this period in the late 1920s and 1930s, with a decrease in the prices of imported textiles and a transition by Indian mill owners to the production of inexpensive fabrics, that indigenous fabric production in the villages of the central hills received its death blow.

The fields of cotton in the valleys and the looms in the households all but disappeared. Peasant agricultural production and the round of village life were by now deeply drawn into the sphere of commodity exchange, and elements of village relations and culture had taken a new content and meaning, or had been transformed entirely. As spinning and weaving had been the domain of women and this same household labour had to be somehow entered into the market within relations controlled by men to obtain the same commodities, this change particularly affected women's status and autonomy in the households and community.

As he lay dying of fever in 1775, Prithvi Narayan Shah of Gorkha had warned of the threat posed by imported textiles. In the years 1939–44 Rana Prime Minister Juddha Shumshere vainly attempted to reindustrialize Nepal by establishing the Gharelu Udyog 'Cottage Industry Corporation'. Although initiated to encourage indigenous village producers, the Gharelu was co-opted by the merchants, whose accumulated capital, control of the villages, and connections to officials gave them an edge over village producers.

A group of major Bandipur merchants, facilitated by a well-placed family member, took advantage of government subsidies to establish the Saraswati Cloth Factory, which fell apart as soon as the subsidized thread became unavailable. Individual merchant houses used a quota system, meant to encourage the producer by allotting distribution of cloth in each district, to establish a monopoly over materials and finished textiles, allowing sale to villagers at exploitative prices.

Soon after the Indian Congress Party, itself linked to the large Indian business houses, took over the state apparatus in India, it forced the Rana government to discontinue the quota system. The Bandipur merchants who, according to their letters, had already been anxiously anticipating this step, dismantled the Gharelu and shifted the capital accumulated under it back into commerce on a scale far larger than before.

As the rural community had been based on the unity of agriculture with household industry, the destruction of the domestic industry in the 1920s led directly to erosion of rural society and culture. Wider and wider spheres of rural production were subsumed in the circulation of industrial commodities by merchants. In part, all this meant the growing subordination, expropriation and displacement of the old class of landlords, as represented by Jagadev Bhandari's descendants, who lost their original *birta* estate piece by piece over several generations through foreclosure to various large merchant houses; many of these, however, moved into new roles in administration.

Shifting Centre of Gravity

Until the 1950s, the Bandipur merchant houses were satisfied in simply establishing themselves as rental landlords over existing smallholder agriculture through various sharecropping arrangements. But with the development of transport and greater accessibility to markets, the merchants and other landlords have been entering their capital into cash crop production and industry using a growing pool of 'free' expropriated peasant wage labourers, thereby minimizing liabilities associated with new landholding laws and maintaining a client labour force.

It was in 1952 that the gradual shift of Bandipur residents into the Chitawan valley to the south started. In Chitawan, facilitated by a USAID malarial suppression and 'defoliation' campaign which inundated the area with DDT and constructed the then largest sawmill in Asia, the Bandipur merchants, especially those from the large houses, used their stocks of capital, alcohol and Tharu hospitality to expel the Tharu villagers from their communally held lands, transform them from hosts into house servants, and illegally clear great swathes of forest for grain, mustard, and vegetable production for sale in urban markets in Nepal and India.

The emigration from Bandipur to Narayanghat, but also subsequently to roadside markets of the inner valleys, increased as roads were constructed linking the region to India, the new agricultural markets of the Chitawan and outer Tarai, and the urban centres of Kathmandu and Pokhara. This process has repeated itself in Tansen, Dhankuta and other hill bazaars.

In Bandipur's case, individuals of one 'new rich' family spirited the offices of the district headquarters to Damauli (on the newly constructed Kathmandu-Pokhara highway) in a night-time *coup d'état.* The town of Bandipur, which meant so much to so many generations of bazaar Newars (and with a somewhat more ambivalent meaning for villagers), remains today little more than a crumbling, though elegant, monument to its economic heyday. It had risen upon and sapped away its own rural hinterland, to itself disappear as roads that followed river valleys took away the *raison d'être* of hilltop bazaars and its wealth, the product of generations of peasant men women and children, moved to more commercially profitable areas and applications.

Recent Events

In the 1980s the transformation to cash crop production extended from the Chitawan lowlands back towards Bandipur and other hill areas to the north. The remaining small merchants and others who could mobilize the necessary resources began citrus plantation and nut orchards. Where the hill farmers had already long served as sharecroppers on the paddy lands, these cash crop plantings, growing exponentially since the beginning of the 1980s, have increasingly displaced these people, through foreclosure on long accumulated debts, from the dry lands which had been the remaining property base of the communities.

The rural labourers have had no choice but to enter directly into national, regional and international labour markets in order to satisfy needs and wants which they had previously supplied themselves (clothing, foodstuffs, energy, transport, entertainment) and to offset their decreasing access to products.

As the members of the bazaar class extended their activity and control into more and more sectors of national life, in their role as agents of regional and international forces, they and associated groups, like their Indian counterparts under the British Raj, began to bid for more direct control of the state political machinery than possible through *chakari* (flattery and sycophancy) or other personalized means of making demands on power. Thus, in the closing days of the overstated 'revolution' of 1950–1, it was the people of Bandipur bazaar, feeling that their widening spheres of activity and interests were increasingly restrained, who launched an attack on the local army garrison (albeit when shot upon they fled, leaving eight dead). They were not the villagers who had lost their land and become dependent upon the bazaar merchants for commodities an finance, nor were they economic migrants.

The subsequent royal takeover and essentially one-party rule from 1962 to 1989 were tolerated by the merchants and the international forces that they represented, because a variety of unpredictable interests continued to contest their control of the Nepali state and society. Foreign governments and agencies underwrote the one-party state's advancement of penetration and co-opting of the remaining local autonomy and control over resources and labour in the name of development, modernization, rationalization and other euphemisms (crowned most recently by the new local government law). This process was augmented by universal education and a certification system that set (and continues to set) formalistic, esoteric and inappropriate forms of knowledge of the Western-oriented specialist over the generalist, practical knowledge of the villager.

By 1989, many of the sons of the Bandipur merchants had become national players in business, the professions and political leadership.

Their power and breadth, along with that of their domestic counterparts and the international interests with which they associated, had sufficiently neutralized the remaining indigenous social organization and culture in the countryside, albeit with disastrous effect on the environment and rural community, leading the one-party government to itself become an obstacle for the full assertion of these groups.

Thus the burgeoning new force represented by the bazaar merchants, nationally and internationally, gave its qualified support to a political upheaval ignited by the images of freedom and democracy. Euphemistically called the 'People's Movement', it was safely halted once the representatives of the emergent dominant groups had set some minimal terms to negotiate their access to state machinery without actually threatening it.

The drafting of the new constitution and laws, such as of local government, which was one of the more visible aspects of this process of renegotiating the relationship between various interests within society, has removed many aspects of the process of industrial expansion and transformation from the domain of state control and political contest to the private one of business relations in the name of 'democracy' and removed control over the country's resources and labour from the village producers in the name of 'free markets' and 'autonomy' of local governments that lack any effective mechanisms of accountability to their constituencies.

This cure for the changes exemplified by the 200-year history of hill towns in Nepal is an even bigger dose of the old medicine, but with new names. It reflects the world-wide consolidation of corporate interests over state and civil society in the far reaches of the globe.

NOTE

This chapter is a slightly altered version of an article that originally appeared in *Himal: Himalayan Magazine*, Vol. 5, No. 5, 1992, pp. 16–18.

CHAPTER 15

Mercantilism and Domestic Industry in West-Central Nepal

INTRODUCTION

THE LAND OF Nepal was never formally incorporated into the boundaries of the British Empire. Accordingly, based on state records, ethnographers have assumed that the community and domestic production remained relatively autonomous until 1951 when the royal family regained control of the country from the autocratic rule of the Thapa and Rana prime minister families. Our work on the merchant town Bandipur in west-central Nepal uncovered a different picture of domestic production and rural economy. We based our historical work on 200 years of business records found in the musty cupboards of the merchants' shops. These records include ledgers, letters, purchase orders and receipts, railroad freight bills, shipping insurance documents, court and other litigation records, and tax and land records. They also include many bundles of promissory notes recording, in addition to loans, credit given to the villagers for purchases of fabric from the merchants.

The usually accepted sources of historical documentation in Nepal have been official government records, inscriptions, and religious manuscripts (ethnographers use oral histories as well). However, if the state is considered in terms of a combination of interests struggling with each other for hegemony,[1] then official records are biased by the alliance of interests in control of the state. They show the struggle of the divided 'subaltern'[2] or opposition interests with their own counter-hegemonies from the standpoint of the politically dominant interest mainly by inference. The merchant records, while generally not 'official' documents, provide documentation for the extension and rise of a major new form of state organization representing the global dominance of capital, as it was experienced in Nepal. The documents give insight into the struggle of capital to establish its control and legitimacy in the countryside. For Bandipur and other Newar bazaars and the surrounding villages that came under their influence, the documents show the content beneath ethnographic descriptions which have too often remained on the level of appearances.

These promissory notes record in increasing detail from at least the mid-eighteenth century the nature of commodities traded, credit and loans, rates of interest, forms of collateral, names of the shopkeepers and their stores, and the names of villager buyers and their villages. In addition to the kinds, values and volumes of cloth sold, the rates of surplus (or exploitation, i.e. surplus ÷ remuneration to labour), profit and rate of profit indicating the changing relationship of labour and capital can also be calculated from the ledgers. The self conscious ideological form of the new hegemony is indicated in the wording of contracts between the producers and the merchants. The letters between the various merchants present a picture of the complex trade relations within Nepal. Letters between Nepali merchants and commission agents in India indicate the manner and extent to which the Nepali merchants were integrated into the bazaars of British India.

The picture painted by the documents is that from the early nineteenth century Manchester textiles were already entering the Nepali countryside from British India. And while one can presently see the extent of the merchants' land holdings in the west-central region of Nepal, the records show that the usury and expropriation of wealth and land involved in the trade of the industrial fabrics increasingly established the merchants as an important force in the state, but in the form of the hegemonic interests of the state and caste ideology, not of their merchant capital. The merchants displaced the control of Chetri (Kshatriya) landlords over landed property, entered some of their sons into the government as officers, used their wealth to influence other officials, and based their legitimacy on notions of Hindu dharmic suzerainty in alliance with Brahman priests. The assertion of a national bourgeois from its base in the bazaars in British India during the last three decades of British rule (Ray 1988) gave birth to a transformation of scale and content of merchant activity in Nepal as well.

While the merchants did not until recently directly apply their capital to production in Nepal,[3] their trade in industrially produced fabrics imported from British and, later, Euro-American, Japanese and Indian factories meant that they no longer existed autonomous of production in the manner of mercantile capital prior to the industrial revolution. Rather, their trade and through it production became increasingly subordinated to industrial capital and its reproduction. These points have been overlooked when the merchants are analysed in their own terms—for example, of 'survivals' of Newar culture or in terms of cultural continuity between merchants of the valley and those who have emigrated.

Lewis and Shakya (1988), as a case in point, write that the industrial fabric trade 'has reduced many Newar trading families to being *mere* middlemen supplying imported goods' (emphasis added), when by definition traders *are* middlemen. The difference between the trade of precapitalist domestically produced commodities and those of industrial capitalists is that in the former case the merchants were merely middlemen who traded goods between various relatively independent communities. Their profits came by exploiting the communities through the trade itself: purchasing cheap and selling dear. In the latter case, the trade becomes the last stage in the circulation of commodities represented in the production process. It is through the merchants that the value of the commodities produced in the factories is realized as money for the factory owners, who then purchase new machines, raw materials, and labour power to continue production on an ever increasing scale. The merchant profits come to the merchant as a share of the surplus extracted from the factory workers in the labour process. For the factory owner, these surpluses that he pays out to the merchants are just another cost of doing business, to be reduced if possible. A destruction of domestic industry that Lewis and Shakya want to emphasize resulted from this subordination of the merchants—and through them, the country-side—to large-scale industry.

This new kind of trade did not destroy the community in form, allowing anthropologists to describe it in terms of a hypothetical traditional culture. However, by the 1930s (two decades before the so-called revolutionary opening of Nepal to the west) their trade had essentially ruined most cloth production in the surrounding villages. This separation of industry and agriculture implied that consumption of cloth and other goods, and therefore production and reproduction of the society within the village, had become incorporated into the circulation of industrial production.

THE GHARELU UNDER THE RANAS AND THE SARASWATI FACTORY IN BANDIPUR

It was in the context of a domestic industry devastated by foreign commodity imports that in the early 1930s the Prime Minister of Nepal, Juddha Shamsher Rana (reigned 1932–44), instituted a last ditch measure to save this domestic industry (Prasad 1975). In a futile effort to develop a measure of economic freedom and self sufficiency and to salvage the collapsing hegemonic basis of his regime in landed property and the village community, he initiated a range of programmes aimed at reviving production in the countryside and laying a basis for large-scale industrial production. In 1939 the Prime Minister formed a 'Cottage Industry Department', the Gharelu, which was to organize and develop both old and new village industries. It was to ostensibly serve the interests and promote the economic well-being of the villagers by reviving the once flourishing cloth weaving industry which had disintegrated in the onslaught of imported fabrics. The Cottage Industry Department was to supply raw materials and mechanical looms to the villagers at cheap prices and on easy payment terms. The villagers were to then sell back the finished products. They were to be organized in industrial co-operatives which would provide the raw materials, tools, and marketing facilities.

Four prominent families of Bandipur took advantage of the establishment of the Gharelu to build a textile weaving factory. The district subba, Bishnu Lal Pradhan, the clerk Harka Man Shrestha, the fabric retailer Krishna Kumar Piya, and the brothers Hira Lal and Shyam Krishna Pradhan (representing a large textile import house in Bandipur) combined in 1942 to build the Saraswati Factory.[4]

Bishnu Lal Subba (Pradhan) was admired by the people of Bandipur, and bazaar Newars say that he seems to have been sincerely motivated by the goals set out by the Prime Minister for the Cottage Industry Programme. But his choice to combine with the three merchants and use their capital to build the factory meant that he had asked people representing the same interests that had brought the demise of industrial production to rebuild it.

According to letters between his wholesaler brothers, Shyam

Krishna and Hira Lal Pradhan, the merchants were interested in the factory because the Nepali government had imposed quotas and was supplying subsidized thread to the villagers in order to encourage the development of domestic production. The letters document how the merchants used their connections, influence, and wealth to obtain bulk quantities of the subsidized thread. Simultaneously with the construction of the textile factory they were struggling to receive import quotas and gain control over wholesale and retail markets for imported cloth in the surrounding countryside. They were also hoarding fabrics controlled by quotas to force prices up. The textile factory was part of their strategy to 'make money any way you can', as they reiterated in their letters —i.e. to make profits and reproduce capital as the overriding purpose of their activity. This also included black marketing, currency manipulation, and hoarding of commodities.

In the factory letterhead and receipt (Figs. 1 and 2) the clerk, merchants and district subba presented their factory as a co-operative association meant to educate villagers and encourage the development of indigenous production, but they themselves took the

---

SARASWATI CLOTH FACTORY
BANDIPUR

In this factory, whoever wants to take the training and, if after training, wants to have a loom in their own home, they will be trained without fee. Whoever wants to work in the factory, they will get paid monthly, according to the factory rules.
In this factory, you can get different kinds of domestically produced cloth and printed Damar Kumari Sari, and many kinds of thread are available.

Pieces	Name of Article	Yards	Cost	Amount
. . . . .	. . . .		. . . . .	. . . .
. . . . .	. . . .		. . . . .	. . . .
. . . . .	. . . .		. . . . .	. . . .
		Total		

Cashier's Signature

FIGURE 1. Translated reproduction of the
receipt of the Saraswati Cloth Factory

In this factory, whoever wants to take the training and after training if they want to have a loom in their own home, they will be trained without fee.

Whoever wants to work in the factory themselves, they will get paid monthly, according to the factory rules.

In this factory, you can get different kinds of domestically produced cloth and printed Damar Kumari Sari, and many kinds of thread are available. Look at the sample and try to contribute to the factory.

Manager—

Bishnu Lal Subbaa

FIGURE 2. Translated reproduction of
the letterhead of the Saraswati Cloth Factory

surplus in the form of profits. This was perfectly in accordance with the logic of Juddha Shamsher's policy, which was aimed at developing an industrial capitalist class. However, his intent seemed to have been to develop this class from among the producers themselves and not to strengthen the already existing mercantile capitalists.

The partners hired a master weaver, Hari Bhakta Shrestha, from Chetrapati, Kathmandu to build the looms and oversee production. Now a small *kinara* ('variety store') owner, he describes how Bishnu Lal Subba was originally inspired by a government run factory in Kathmandu in 1942. He used his position of subba to elicit the aid of the government and organize the factory. It took the four families the year 1942–3 to construct the factory building. It was an approximately sixty metre long, two-story brick structure with a series of rooms opening onto a long porch in front on the lower level (half of which remains). The second story similarly opens onto a long covered balcony which makes the roof of the porch. The weaving master built 37 flying shuttle peddle looms (25 *chaakune* and 12 *pitaa*) which were placed in the long series of rooms on each level.

Hari Bhakta brought six craftsmen who trained the labour force for several months and then returned to Kathmandu. Except for two Brahmans from Chiti, all the labourers were from Bandipur.[5] Initially the numbers of men and women were about equal, but by the time the factory shut down nearly all of the workers were women.

Production in the Saraswati Factory lasted from 1943 to 1945. The fabric was sold both from the factory and from outlets already controlled by the merchants in the surrounding countryside and in the Lamjung hills to the north. Production was stopped in the summer of 1945 due to the Nepal government's reluctance to supply subsidized thread,[6] combined with the desire of the dominant share holders, Shyam Krishna and Hira Lal Pradhan, not to share profits with the other two families.[7]

For some reason, the Nepal government was hesitant about supplying the thread. An appeal in August 1945 to the government claimed that, without the subsidized thread, the merchants would have been unable to continue operating the factory (Fig. 3). As yet we have not found the resolution of the problem in the letters. The weaving master claims that the factory was running extremely well, but the partners fell at odds, disbanded the factory, and divided the looms among themselves in proportion to their shares. The letters of Shyam Krishna and Hira Lal Pradhan show how they connived to obtain subsidized yarn and continue production in their own houses into 1947. For example, the following references are found in a series of letters in 1947.

The price of thread has gone up, so I am not planning to send it. And if you ask for the control thread to weave in Bandipur and sell, they will give it to you. To sell the thread is not permitted now. So, we should take 20 to 30 loads of the thread to weave. If you send them now, because of the winter you can save 10 to 15% on the porter's wages. The government will give

---

Appeal.
Sarkaar [Government]. Everything is okay here. About the factory, because of the shortage of thread, it is difficult to keep the factory operating. The thread is nearly about to finish, so that we will have to close the factory. To close it, we have to send away all the workers. If the thread comes, it will be difficult to get them back. To bring all the workers together, it takes a long time. If we do not terminate them, but give them salary without work it is difficult for the factory. We have written about this many times to the Gharelu [Cottage Industry Department], but up to now we have not heard anything. If you cannot supply a full supply of thread, then you can just give two to four months supply so the factory can keep on going. If you could arrange this thing, it would be very helpful so the factory may not be closed. If I write something wrong, please forgive me.

Na. Subba Bishnu Lal Pradhan

2002 Bhadra 4. [AD 1945 August 20]

FIGURE 3. Appeal from Subba Bishnu Lal Pradhan to the government about the Saraswati Cloth Factory

you a 10% discount in the weaving cloth too. If you calculate all these things, it is profitable. If you send this thread in the summer, it is not profitable. It takes many days. It may get wet. Because of that, I am thinking of taking this thread. What is your idea? Please let me know soon. If you run 8 to 10 looms, the time will not take so long. I will take the permission to sell the cloth in Bandipur.[8]

The thread is coming continuously. Our cloth is little, but growing.[9]

But in India, from the fifteenth of January or the first of Maagh, they are going to discontinue the control system. It is in the news of the Indian government. What is going to happen nobody can say. Whatever happens, take profit and sell whatever you have. That would be the best idea. Even if they abolish the control system, you may not get goods soon. And again, we may not even get (the things) at the same price, because they have increased the price of raw cotton. Therefore, you do not have to sell the goods at a loss. From India, they are going to abolish the control system. But here, they have increased the prices of all the things. I cannot understand anything.[10]

About the control thread, they have sent an order from Nepal to Pokhara to sell it. You may get the news from the post or from the Gorkha Patra. . . . And the wage for *dharni* is 5 paisa per mile. So count the miles carefully. The rate of thread they will fix from Nepal.[11]

Please send me two copies of the finger prints of your left and right hands to get the application for the thread.[12]

Once the Congress Government came to power in India, it forced the Nepal government to end the quota system on fabric imports and stop the thread subsidies, allowing again an uncontrolled flood of foreign and, especially, Indian textiles into Nepal. The letters of Shyam Krishna and Hira Lal indicate that they liquidated their previously hoarded textile stocks in anticipation.

Nowadays the things are not like before. Sell the things that you have at home soon and make a profit. Do not keep in stock. We do not know what is going to happen. The Congress government is trying to break the quota system. Mahatma Gandhi is trying his best, and I do not think that it will take a long time to break the control. If it takes a long time, it still will not last more than two or three months. But even if the control breaks, and then you will not be getting so much material from India because there will not be enough booking on the train. There may not be so many things coming from India. So it is better to sell what you have at home.[13]

Sell the cigarettes. . . . It is not profitable just to keep them. After the cigarettes from Thori arrive, the price of cigarettes is going to fall. Now you do not have so many customers, so I did not think it was such a good idea to send a lot of goods. Now there is rumour that the control may break. The quota things will all be in the market again. That is why we just cannot take the material for Maagh and Phaalgun now. If you can sell things, then I will send them to you. A lot of goods are coming from Lhasa. It does not appear that the price will go up. So it is not a good idea to take things now and keep them. Just take the profit and sell the things you have now. Nobody can say anything tomorrow. The Congress Government is going to break the control. And the quota controlled things will be distributed in the villages pretty soon. After a month you can get 2 and 1 numbered things. After the quota things come onto the market, you will not be able to sell any of the black market goods.[14]

The cloth Controls were abolished yesterday. But from one region to another. In Nepal [Kathmandu], they are still giving by the quota system. Even if the quota system were to break, you would not get the goods. Maybe after one or two months, you can get them. But even if you can get them, you cannot take them from one to another region. And the price may even rise one and one-half times. We got the things at the control rate. The merchants of this place also think the same thing. Even if the control is abolished, it will not make any difference for Nepal [Kathmandu]. But I think that after four to six months, something will happen. So whatever you have, try to sell and get out of stock. The quota goods we have, we will not lose anything on that. . . . The goods we have, try to sell soon. But do not discount them. Even if the control is abolished, you cannot get the things, and it seems that the rate is going to be higher than the control rate. Again, they have not controlled fully for Nepal. So think this over and work accordingly from it.[15]

They were joined in this by all the other large wholesalers in Bandipur. The prices dropped, and the merchants saw larger profits in the fabrics imported from the large factories of India, Europe, the United States, and Japan, if not the futility of continuing their production in the absence of subsidies and controls.

DISCUSSION

Blaikie et al. (1980—see note 4) were essentially correct when they attributed the failure of the Bandipur textile factory to foreign commodity trade and industry, although they did not sufficiently emphasize the merchant participants' willing collaboration in this. Weighing potential surplus against the capital invested (the rate of profit) and not the goals of the Gharelu programme at all times seemed to determine the merchant participation in the Saraswati Factory. Thread subsidies and strict quota controls over imports made it profitable. They had no interest in developing the autonomy of the Nepali countryside as envisioned by Juddha Shamsher.

Blaikie et al. (1980:126) wrote that the construction of the Saraswati Factory had been an attempt to 'revive the once vigorous cotton-weaving industry of Bandipur' (Blaikie et al. 1980:126). But there was no precedent for such an industry. Previously cotton weaving had been a household industry totally in the domain of women. In reality, they were shifting production from the household into the direct control of merchant capital, using the Gharelu plan as its basis, and thereby attempting to transform their indirect mediation of trade of textile commodities into direct control over wage labour as a commodity.

As noted above, the labour force eventually came to consist mostly of women. Thus the factory in particular and, due to the control given to the merchants over the distribution of raw materials and marketing of the products, the Gharelu in general not only shifted textile production into the domain of capital, it took a sector of production controlled by women and shifted it over to the control of patriarchal interests and relations which already characterized merchant capital indigenously and industrial capitalism globally. The production and knowledge of the women come into the control of male owners and managers, and their products as commodities came under the control of male merchants. The factory owners apparently eventually took the gender relations and division of labour within the household and domestic skills of women as their basis.

The new gender mediation of women in the Saraswati Factory underlines the significance of the destruction of the domestic or household textile industry in undermining women's autonomy. In recent decades, this has turned out to be a double-edged sword in Asia. While transnational corporations have presupposed the same conditions as the basis of recruiting a vulnerable and unorganized female labour force in order to destroy organized labour in western Europe, the United States, Japan, and now in the Newly Industrialized Countries, the women of Asia and elsewhere in the third world have begun to organize, often far more militantly than their male counterparts.[16]

The historical experience of capitalism globally has been the expansion of the domain of capital from the products of industry to industry itself, from the products of labour as commodities to labour itself as a commodity, and from mediation between communities to the basis of community. The bazaar merchants of Bandipur were unable to transform themselves into a national industrial class because their trade presupposed and based itself on already developed industrial capital elsewhere. While the large business houses of India used the bazaar as a basis to take the opportunity of global crises in capitalism to enter into direct partnership with foreign capitalists (Ray 1988), the Bandipur merchants only expanded their trade with India (while the Ranas and subsequently the palace has been trying to fill the role of state monopolist).

Their expansion of direct control over the countryside continued to take the form of expansion of land-holdings and usury, not of capital applied directly to production. The mercantile capital presupposed the same direct peasant production assumed by the landed ruling interests of the state. By the time that Juddha Shamsher attempted to implement his plans, the interests represented in the industrial class development in India and a dependent form of mercantile class development within Nepal were already too far developed.

Another important structural difference of the Saraswati factory from domestic production was its dependence on subsidized, imported thread. Thus, from the viewpoint of Indian factories, the Saraswati factory and, for that matter, the Gharelu programme, consumed the thread as the last step in the commodity circulation represented by industrial production that was shown above to have characterized the merchant trade. This point is emphasized by the immense trade of both quota and other threads in the countryside, as documented in merchants' letters. In the latter period, the merchants were constantly calculating whether they could more profitably (or legally) weave the thread on their own looms or merely sell it in the villages.

The significance of this discussion for anthropologists is that community and culture in Nepal cannot be analysed in their own terms. Even prior to the entry of industrial capitalist interests in the form of mercantile capitalism in Nepal in the eighteenth century, the state contained various interests which controlled peasant surpluses. These included, at the least, merchants and the hegemonic landed property groups. After the rise of industrial capitalism in western Europe, the community in Nepal became increasingly mediated by the bazaar and merchants representing foreign industrial capitalist interests in the form of industrial commodities and mercantile profits, usury, and rents. By the 1930s this was a process that even the Rana rulers of Nepal were forced to acknowledge as they found the material basis to their political power and cultural hegemony eroding away. The subsequent change of regimes and development of the state and community have been shaped by this growing dominance. Anthropologists cannot analyse the community in isolation from this larger totality; they must understand the latter theoretically. While every particular analysis need not be a study of the totality, the anthropologist must understand Lukacs's riddle that the part contains the whole.

NOTES

This chapter was co-authored with Jamuna Shrestha and originally appeared as 'Mercantilism and Domestic Industry in West-Central Nepal: Significance for Anthropological Study of the Community' in *Occasional Papers in Anthropology and Sociology*, Vol. 2, 1990, pp. 77–89.

1   The term 'hegemony' is used in the sense of Gramsci (1971) to mean here the ideas of the ruling class are internalized into the institutions of the society so that the ruled participate in their own domination.

2   'The subaltern classes, by definition, are not unified and cannot unite until they are able to become a "State": their history therefore, is intertwined with that of civil society, and thereby with the history of States or groups of States' (Gramsci 1971:52).

3   Control of land as landlords and usury cannot properly be considered as application of capital or investment into production. It merely asserts rights over surpluses without changing how they are produced.

4   Blaikie et al. (1980:126) write, 'Around 1940 attempts were made to revive the once vigorous cotton-weaving industry of Bandipur and skilled workers were imported from the Kathmandu Valley to operate the looms, which at one time reputedly numbered about around 250; but a combination of disputes among the shareholders of the company concerned, and enormous price increases of the cotton yarn with restrictions by India on its export to Nepal, bought about a rapid decline.' The date, numbers of looms, and origins of the workers are corrected in this text. We also differ somewhat from the assessment given by Blaikie and Seddon regarding the significance of the rise and decline of the textile factory.

5   This contradicts Blaikie et al.'s (note 4) description of the workers as specialists brought from Kathmandu Valley. The factory owners assumed the already transformed conditions of the people and their domestic skills, especially of the women, to provide a wage labour force from the Bandipur locale.

6   Rising prices of the thread given by Blaikie et al. (note 4) seem to have only been a factor some years after the factory had been disbanded by the merchants.

7   There are some other examples of attempts by families in Bandipur to organize joint corporate ownership but to have them fail as individual family interests overrode the collective one. Presently capital is also organized in the framework of *sangai* 'together' (or inappropriately 'joint') families, which similarly introduces a contradiction into the tendency of capital to concentrate ownership and production when the families break into *chuttai* 'broken' (or inappropriately 'nuclear') families. Marx pointed out that this is a dialectical contradiction because it eventually leads to a greater concentration as the smaller divided capitals of the *chuttai* families are absorbed by larger ones.

8   Mikesell (1988), Appendix D, Letter 8, Paus 3, 2005 BS (1947), Shyam Krishna in Thamel, Kathmandu to Hira Lal Pradhan in Bandipur.

9   Mikesell (1988), Appendix D, Letter 10, Paus 10, 2005 BS (1947), Shyam Krishna in Bandipur to Hira Lal Pradhan in Devghat, Chitwan.

10 Unpublished letter [09/04/89:1], Paus 14, 2005 BS (1947), Shyam Krishna in Kanpur, India (Address: Purusottan Das Ganapati Ray, Kanpur), to Hira Lal in Bandipur.

11 Mikesell (1988), Appendix D, Letter 11, Paus 28, 2005 BS (1947), Shyam Krishna in Birganj to Hira Lal Pradhan in Bandipur.

12 Mikesell (1988), Appendix D, Letter 16, Aasaadh 22, 2005 BS (1947), Shyam Krishna in Bandipur to Hira Lal Pradhan in Kathmandu.

13 Mikesell (1988), Appendix D, Letter 2, Maagh 10, 2005 BS (1947), Shyam Krishna in Kathmandu to Hira Lal Pradhan in Bandipur.

14 Mikesell (1988), Appendix D, Letter 3, Maagh 11, 2005 BS (1947), Shyam Krishna in Kathmandu to Hira Lal Pradhan in Bandipur.

15 Unpublished letter [8/16/89:2], Maagh 7, 2005 BS (Postmarked 22 Jan. 1948), Shyam Krishna in Kanpur, India (Address: Purusottan Das Ganapati Ray, Kanpur), to Hira Lal in Bandipur.

16 See Swasti Mitter (1986) for detailed discussion.

PART V

Critique of Theory and Practice in Nepal

CHAPTER 16

A Comparative Study of South Asian Caste and Mediterranean Citizenship in the Development of Classes and the State

INTRODUCTION

KINSHIP organized societies have often been seen as being pre-state and acephalous. In the Indian subcontinent, this understanding has taken the form of a dichotomy between the division of 'tribal' society versus 'caste' society, in which caste and tribe are perceived as falling at two ends of a continuum. Often, the transformation from 'caste' to 'tribal' has been conceived within a framework of 'Hinduization', in which societies move not only along the continuum from tribe to caste, but from stateless to state. Along the way, this framework has picked up Robert Redfield's dichotomy between the Great Tradition of the Hinduized society and the Little Tradition of the tribal society. There are often implicit values that disparage tribal society, due their statelessness, while Hinduization is seen as an advance over tribal society.

This paper shifts the analysis of caste from a typological approach and a continuum between opposites to a developmental and comparative approach. It argues that caste arose historically to solve problems that were also being faced elsewhere throughout the world in the transition from a state organized on the basis of kinship to one organized on the basis of property and class. These changes arose out of the growth of productive forces available to humankind represented in the domestication of plants and animals and the accompanying developments of tools, the rise of the city, the accompanying development of new forms of knowledge and so forth. Even before the initial transformations of clan society into the first, 'pristine' urban societies, the elements that underlay caste were well developed. In particular, these were the displacement of communal property and a division of labour organized according to class. Caste was one way that this new organization exerted and expanded itself according to the logic and form of clan organization even while it destroyed it in substance.

Whereas caste and class are sometimes presented in comparison to each other as mutually exclusive, if not opposites, it is argued here this opposition is not an essential one. Caste is presented here as one of the forms taken by the development and expansion of class society and private property. As such, it is not a form essentially different from institutions in western society. And in this, the key is not the ideology of hierarchy, as argued by Dumont (1980), although hierarchy is contained in both, but the manner that people who find themselves in intercourse are disenfranchised or enfranchised in society, and how they are distributed within the production process and enjoy the fruits of their labour. Similar problems were being addressed by 'citizenship', which appeared in the northern Mediterranean while caste was developing in South Asia. Each arose out of the same broad historical processes. Each, initially at least, took the clan as its basis and expressed the rise of interests contained within the city and urban classes, but each addressed different conditions and needs.

PRIOR DEVELOPMENT OF THE STATE WITHIN THE LINEAGE

At the core of the theory of the state is the problem of the origins and development of the division of labour, classes, property and consciousness. Aiden Southall (1965, 1984, 1986) argues that these processes initially arose *sui generis* from within kinship organized societies (he uses the term 'lineage mode of production') in the course of the evolutionary development of human society. Southall calls this early form of state the 'segmentary state', which he sees as a particular genetic stage in the development of society and the state.[1] In addition to being a genetic stage in the development of the state, he also sees the segmentary state as a generic type of the state, applicable in comparisons between different times and places.

This 'segmentary' state form developed primarily through extension and elaboration of lineage relations and institutions. The division of labour within the lineage is based on what have been called 'natural traits', that is, gender and age,[2] although the division of labour in reality is a social product and any natural character given to it is through the lens of society. What has been called the 'first true division of labour', between physical and mental labour, was defined according to age. Within the lineage group, elder women and men who generally had the wisdom that comes with age also usually were the ritual functionaries. They controlled the ritualized communication with the spirits and gods backed with the sanction of wisdom.

In this way these rituals served to preserve or reproduce the division of labour and distribution of the product within and between lineage groups from generation to generation (Meillassoux 1978a:134). Prior to domestication of plants and animals, only limited surpluses could be accumulated, which meant one group of humans could not set itself over others through accretion and control of the products of labour, that is, through private property. Labour thus was controlled or brought together for common projects through relations of kinship, using ritualized sanctions.[3] Just as elders within the lineage group set themselves over youngsters, lineages representing themselves in mythology as having descended from elder siblings (sisters or brothers, for matrilineal and patrilineal societies, respectively) set themselves over those of younger siblings. Using this logic, it was not difficult for groups to invade an area and set themselves over another group by claiming certain privileged relations with spirits and gods, such as for making rain or bringing lots of game. These ritual powers would provide such invading groups with the means to demand various forms of tribute of labour or products. If these failed to materialize, the members of these ritually superior groups threatened to withhold rain or make game scarce, which would bring disaster to the society.[4]

Members of local lineage groups established themselves over an area by making claims to common descent from ancestors projected as elder to the ancestors of other groups, or else to unrelated but ritually privileged ancestors. In order to place these individuals in a comparative perspective, Southall (1956,1986) calls them 'ritual leaders' and their direct power over nearby local lineage groups 'political sovereignty'. Their direct power is limited, due to limited productive forces and a lack of basis in private property in land, which is held communally. But they still have an authority over much wider areas, termed 'ritual suzerainty', through which they can demand certain prestations backed up by sanctions such as the threat of ritual chiefs descending upon recalcitrant villages with their entire entourages and staying as uninvited guests until their hosts' stores of food and drink are gone—in effect looting them of all their provisions by means of the obligatory hospitality that members of lesser lineages must pay to those of higher ones.

Thus, within kin frameworks historically termed 'tribal' in South Asian ethnography, states emerge or exist, even if they may be highly diffuse, decentralized and relatively egalitarian. A division of labour develops which demands transfers of labour from certain lineage groups and provides ritual services in the other direction from others. This division of labour further determines a certain distribution of labour and products between those groups of people who produce and those who enjoy the products of other people's labour. In other words, a nascent 'private property' emerges, which in effect is the same thing as distribution but from the perspective of norms and sanctions.

However, as long as the same productive activities are reproduced within every local group, no matter what its lineage status, we cannot say that these are fully developed class societies or that private property proper exists (this ceases to hold as soon as a lineage organized society has entered into intercourse with a dominant class society, such as in the periphery of developing urban centres and certainly in the colonial situation). The state exists in the form of a set of institutions, in this case the various rituals and associated supernatural sanctions available to the members of the dominant lineage groups through which they enforce the property form. Southall (1954, 1986) termed such a state 'segmentary' because it was segmented both vertically, between higher and lower status lineages, and horizontally, between segments of the same lineage. There were not separate, unitary state institutions which appeared to have autonomy separate from the fractures of the rest to the society, as characterizes the present bureaucratic capitalist state.

In order to explain how members of a clan or caste of ritual leaders could set themselves over other clans, Southall (1986) refers to Godelier's position that the 'relations of domination and exploitation . . . presented themselves as an exchange of services . . . to get themselves accepted, and . . . to obtain the consent of the dominated' (Godelier 1978:767). However, 'exchange' implies interaction between two different communities, which already anticipates not only more fully developed forms of property beyond that found in lineage organized societies, in which large segments of the society existed outside of or are alien to the community as in non-citizen or foreign groups of some sort.[5] It is simpler to propose that ritual leaders would have based their position on the already existing relationships of seniority and gender and their accompanying ritual paraphernalia, all of which have been already repeatedly attributed to clan relations by anthropologists (e.g. clans said to have been founded by elder siblings are attributed higher status than those of younger ones, and those of maternal ancestors are different in status than those of paternal ones, etc.). If dominant clans impose themselves in these terms, with their accompanying ritual status and material rights and obligations vis-à-vis each other (and I think that Southall's data and analysis both point to this), then it is unnecessary to describe relations in terms of exchange.

Finally, women had a prominent, relatively equal and even powerful role in such societies. Production and social intercourse were based within the household and local lineage group, where women were central to all kinds of production. Given furthermore that power—that is, access to human labour—was based in the inclusion of as wide a group of lineages as possible, then unrestricted linkages through both marriage and descent and through wives and daughters as well as sons and brothers were instrumental. As we shall see, this situation changes with the development of private property.

Within Nepal it is evident that such segmentary states existed within the eastern areas of the country, what are called the 'Kirat' areas, until recently. The history from the time of the original unification of the country in the latter half of the eighteenth century can give a pretty good idea of how such communities were subordinated before that. This was also probably the state form that characterized the Gurung and Magar areas from west of the Trisuli River in the west-central portion of the country. Prior to the entry of the Hindu groups, there was a confederation called Bhara Magarat ('Twelve Magarat'), with its 12 divisions, which seem to have represented 12 centres of sovereignty organized within the framework of lineages.

Among the Gurungs, there seem to have been ritually dominant clans versus subordinate ones, although there has been a tendency to characterize them as *jats* subsequent to their subordination to private property and a class society organized in terms of caste. The Ghāto dance drama, which has been attributed as a normative element of a separate 'Gurung culture', seems to have been performed widely by the Magar speaking people as well, although it disappeared sooner due to their earlier direct subordination. Thus Mikesell (1988) tentatively argues that the Ghāto dance drama represented a ritual suzerainty that transcended both groups, providing the means for members of various ritually dominant local lineages to assert a certain sovereignty over other lineages while asserting ritual authority over more widespread areas. With the establishment of Rajput lineages over the west-central areas in the sixteenth and seventeenth centuries, these early ritual forms with their accompanying myths increasingly lost their old content and took on new ones. This process could have resulted from either of two factors. It could have resulted from the influx of actual groups of 'populous clans of warrior cultivators' from India which have been described by Bailey (1983:17) as being involved in a 'slow process of settlement (in north-east India) which set the main features of land-control in modern times from the borders of Awadh to Bengal'. It could have resulted from further differentiation within already established lineage groups through influence from outside ideas. Or else (most likely) it could have resulted from a combination of both tendencies. The manner that this process took place in human history generally, its particular forms in citizenship and caste, and its specific reference to Nepali history are discussed below.

SUBORDINATION OF CLAN TO CLASS
IN THE PRISTINE CITY STATE

The preconditions of the development of the first or pristine cities were represented in these developments of the production relations, productive forces, division of labour, property, and the state, with its ideological and ritual accoutrements, that occurred in the lineage organized societies. Domestication of plants and animals, along with the accompanying developments of the tools and conditions of production, led to increasing surpluses, the control of which meant the control of people. More directly, the control of land or herds meant control over the labour and products of people who worked the land or tended the herds. Due to previous developments described above, it was the members of the lineages of ritual leaders which were positioned to control hand, labour and product, leading to the full development of these lineages into separate, priestly ruling classes in these pristine cities. For the first time there became not just a division between lineages of non-specialists and ritual specialists, but a full-blown division of labour between those engaged in manual labour and those engaged solely in mental labour. This new division of labour first took the form of a division between the city and countryside, a division which has underlain and coloured all subsequent divisions of labour.

Now that there was an actual divide within society, characterized by the increasing disenfranchisement and exploitation of the labouring classes, the services provided by the priest class were elaborated into salvation religions. Since the people's suffering and difficulties were chronically related to the contradiction in the division of labour between those who laboured and those who enjoyed the products of the labour; the priests, unlike the ritual leaders before them, could no longer supply the worker's need without overturning this division of labour, abolishing private property and transforming their own lineages back into a labouring class as well. Thus, in addition to communicating with supernatural powers and formulating sanctions, the priests had to formulate an ideology explaining the suffering and inequality in this world and provide a hope for a better life or release after death (if the sanctions are obeyed).[6] Thus some sort of functional correlate to dharma, karma, and reincarnation or nirvana is found in all of the great religions.

As these cities expanded in their population, wealth and influence, not only did the power accruing to the priesthoods increase, but the basis was being laid for the ascendancy of other classes and the decline of the monopoly of the priests. The conquest of neighbouring cities and the creation of empires led to the rise of military classes and leaders who directly controlled the material forces of subjugation. Military leaders and secular landlords became kings and officers, subsuming and subordinating the priests, who never reappeared with such monopolistic power as they had exercised in the early city states. Nevertheless, they continued in providing the ideological framework in which the rule of subsequent rulers were sanctioned and legitimatized. They also remained a prominent force in the state in administration. And furthermore, as a ruling class based on landownership and collection of rents developed, the interests of the priesthood and of the military groups to a large extent merged, despite a continuing contest for power between the two. The growth of cities and their expanding influence brought also a quickening of intercourse and trade, leading to the development of specialized commercial classes and a division between trade and industry, and further divisions within industry.

Where previously, the expanding linkages of one lineage to another had been the means to multiply the human resources available to an individual, under private property these became a liability. Linkage to other groups meant also the sharing of control over land and flocks, the dispersal of wealth, and the decentralization and equalization of power. Thus the rise of class society also brought the subsumption of the lineage to the patriarchal family. Among the ruling classes particularly, the rise of private property meant the disenfranchisement of women, since the cutting of the woman off from rights within her natal family was a means that the link between affined clans was broken, preventing the dispersal of power and wealth. The effeminization of women (and masculinizing of men) was not necessary or natural, but probably there was a tendency towards it due to the prior militarization of men, for example.[7] Other means to the same end were the strengthening of the power of the patriarch over his wife and sons, reducing them in essence to the status of slavery. Estate slavery found its origins in this slavery of the patriarchal family as, with the expansion of the territory of the cities through conquest, the cultivator was transformed into estate holder.

Even far distant from cities, the division of labour and property relations within segmentary states became much more pronounced in the course of the development of urban civilization. For example, the great expansion of the urban colonies of the Greeks and administrative cities of the Romans led not only to the exploitation of segmentary states through exchange by urban traders, but to the opportunity for enlarged accumulation and aggrandizement by groups composing the segmentary states in the shadow of cities. The Scythians, Mongols, Germanic tribes are examples. Commonly it was from among these greatly transformed lineage organized groups on the periphery of decaying empires where the contradictions stymieing the development of old civilizations were transcended and innovative new urban forms arose. From the standpoint of the changes that have continually taken place among the lineage organized societies in the hinterlands of cities, the delineation of the segmentary state as a generic type became problematic.

EXPANSION OF CLASS: CASTE AND CITIZENSHIP

The secondary civilizations arising from the Mesopotamian pristine cities took two essentially different forms, both shaped by, but differing from, the development of those cities. In the civilizations of ancient Greece and Rome, these developments led to the division of the populations of these states into citizen and non-citizen, while in the upper Ganges River of the Indian subcontinent of the early Vedic period (third and second millenniums BC), they led to the distribution of populations among the various *varna* and *jats*, that is, caste. Both citizenship and caste developed according to principles (though different ones) inherent in the clan itself, even as they subsumed the clan. Citizenship and caste represent alternative forms of organization and ideological representation which appear to have addressed different conditions and needs arising as ruling classes subordinated lineage organized societies to a division of labour based upon private property. As these two forms developed, each continued to be elaborated and transformed to satisfy new needs arising from changing class configurations with the development of society. This is a process that continues to this day.

Mediterranean Citizenship

As discussed in Southall (1984, n.d.), the form of state that arose in the course of the development of the city states of the northern Mediterranean diverged significantly from that of the states that had preceded them. The city states of Ancient Greece and Rome initially formed through the coming together of disparate groups of cultivators on the basis of lineage relations. All male members of these founding lineages were citizens, residents of the city. All citizens had an equal right to a vote within the general assembly which had developed from the assemblies of the collections of lineages (phylae or tribes), which had come together in the city, and, initially at least (if that), they had a right to a plot of land and thus were by definition landowners.

It was due to this enfranchisement in terms of ownership that, though the Ancient community began with its seat in the city, it was associated with a territory which had to expand as the population reproduced itself and grew in numbers and wealth. This expansion initially took the form of the emigration of citizens and establishment of colonies in other locations throughout the Mediterranean region.

It ended in the Macedonian and Roman Empiress, in which the enfranchised citizens became increasingly rural landlords set upon estates throughout territory, leading Marx (1973a) to speak of the career of ancient society in terms of the 'ruralization of the city'.

Even prior to the foundation of the Mediterranean cities, the lineages had been greatly modified due to the influences of urban empires to the east, as well as due to internal pressures arising through their own reproduction and development. Thus the principle of lineage equality had already been transformed in practice in the preceding segmentary states. The civic democracy that lineage equality had evolved into with the coming together of the tribes into the city was in fact a means for a small landlord class to rule with the assistance of dependent clients who made up the large bulk of the members of the lineage groups. Inequality in property holdings increased, and the large property holders increasingly asserted themselves in this democracy. The clan institutions gave way to less democratic forms, eventually falling to the rule of emperors among the Romans. Women were disenfranchised (although this changed in late Rome); immigrants, freedom and the less directly exploited people of segmentary states in the hinterlands were left disenfranchised; and conquered people were enslaved to provide labour on estates and in workshops owned by the small group of wealthy and powerful citizens. Thus citizenship, which had developed on the basis of the clan, served as the ideological category supporting the class rule of a very limited group of people.

The general freedom of thought and action, the balanced cultivation of body and mind, the passion for beauty in life and art have haunted Western man ever since. But at Athens even in its heyday these things were paradoxically only for a minority. Less than a sixth of the population were full citizens, another half were of free but non-citizen status, while over one third were slaves. Only citizens participated in Athenian democracy, which was thus a glorious facade. (Southall n.d., Chap. 3, p. 18)

In reality, however—granted that many poor citizens were supported in a degree of leisure by political attendance payments at councils and assemblies . . . , as well as a by the free food which both they and destitute non-citizen could share—a minority group of the relatively wealthy and privileged citizens monopolized power and leisure, despising the disenfranchised merchants who generated most of the wealth, collectively oppressing and taxing the peasants who grew the food and standing on the necks of the slaves who did the mental jobs. (ibid. 20)

Caste in the Indian Subcontinent

In the Indian subcontinent, the segmentary state, or lineage organized society, gave rise not to the division of citizen versus non-citizen, but to caste. Like citizenship, the ideological categories of caste were based on characteristics of clan categories. Unlike citizenship, caste originated not from a coming together of tribes in an urban community and the transformation of their members into a citizenry defined in terms of the clan principle of equality. Rather, caste developed as further elaboration of the ideology and ritual of the lineage inequality of the segmentary state, but with the same effect of displacing communal property with private property and transforming the organization of labour in the lineage into that of classes.

Marx (1972:183), in this notes on Morgan's *Ancient Society* (1877), in what the anthropologist Karl Krader (1972:15) calls 'the most explicitly dialectical of all Marx's formulations . . . in the Morgan notebooks', hypothesized that caste arose from the ranking that developed among various groups of clans.[8] As the ranking that developed between lineages in the segmentary state came to assure control over increasing amounts of labour and greater accumulation of its products, higher ranking lineages could no longer intermarry with lower ranking ones, since such intermarriage would lead to a dispersal of property. This led to what Marx identified as a conflict with the principle of clan exogamy, resulting in a 'petrification' of exogamous clans into endogamous caste, a clearly Hegelian elucidation of the problem (see the quote from Hegel in note 8). Like citizenship, the clan increasingly existed only in abstract principles, while the concrete relations give way to caste relations.[9]

It is proposed that this process occurred among pastoral peoples living in the periphery of the early cities of West Asia. Breeding of domesticated livestock (particularly cattle) along with trade and other forms of intercourse with the growing cities provided a basis for the accumulation and differentiation of wealth, division of labour and product, and therein the full development of private property. Consequently, some form of caste ranking seems to have existed even at the time of Aryan entry into the Indian subcontinent, although it may have been closer to the sort of ranking found among the segmentary states. As this ranking grew into a means of preserving and extending subjugation of sedentary peoples, it took on other characteristics presently associated with caste, depending upon the development of class interests therein. This is a process that has continued to evolve and seems to have been distorted by the British Raj, which exaggerated the importance of caste in order to facilitate the expansion of the domination of capital, and it continues to be used by elements within the nationalist successor regime in India.

This position is supported by existence of the four *varnas* (Brahman, Kshatriya, Vaisya and Shudra) in the early Vedas,[10] indicating ideological categories corresponding to the same main divisions that matured with the growth of cities: mental labour, estate holders, commerce, and physical labour, respectively. As in the cities, this differentiation started with the maturation of a priesthood that fully differentiated out of the ritual leaders of the segmentary state. The other groups and categories must have arisen more or less simultaneously with the creation of a separate priesthood, since the existence of such a priesthood would depend upon much greater productivity, trade, and accumulation of wealth. Militarization occurred in the face of military pressure from the cities; traders became increasingly prominent in the intercourse with and between the cities; and specializations within production arose with an increasingly complex aggregate of productive forces.

While caste represents and extends class interests, like citizenship caste is neither class nor do its divisions correspond to class divisions. Class initially arises 'in itself' as divisions of labour develop within production and commerce due to the exigencies and possibilities extending from growing productive forces. As consciousness develops among groups of people due to their position within the division of labour, class also comes to exist 'for itself' and in the process assumes an ideological form which increasingly diverges from the actual material relations. Caste in contrast had no necessary connection to production and thus does not exist 'in itself'. At one extreme a Brahman landlord may live side-by-side with a Brahman bonded labourer; or while he may be the king's *purohit* or priest, his wife in practice may be little more than an uneducated domestic labourer or courtesan.[11] Like citizenship, caste mystifies class and gender divisions and exists to further the interests of particular class groups.

The class divisions which underlay caste initially consisted of surplus taking classes based in landed property (landlords from priest and military groups) and commercial capital (traders). Unlike in the Mediterranean, where only slaves and non-citizens engaged in trade, commercial groups enjoyed partial enfranchisement as the lowest of the 'touchable' *varnas*, perhaps because the community did not begin with the land as its seat as in the case of the Mediterranean city state. One possible explanation is that commercial capital had developed as a specialized occupation within pastoralism prior to the entry of the Aryans into the subcontinent and their establishment as landed proprietors. Thus having already arisen as a social interest independent of landed property, commerce had to be given a place among the enfranchised castes. Another explanation is that because production was based on the general subordination of the rural community rather than slavery, trade was not dominated by landed estate holders but relied on relatively independent merchants mediating between communities. In either case, since it did not in general establish itself directly over producers, it continued to remain subordinated to landed property until after industrial capital entered the subcontinent in the nineteenth century, when the indigenous commercial classes took up the upcountry trade of industrial imports and local raw materials and increasingly displaced the foreign merchants during the first half of the twentieth century.

For the labourer, it was another story. Like in Ancient city, both craft producers and agricultural labourers were disenfranchised socially, politically and ideologically according to descent. However, unlike the labourer in Mediterranean cities, the surplus producing labourers in the subcontinent were not chattel slaves. They remained upon their land and in possession of it and their tools. Without the restriction of craft labour and commerce to slaves, there was no creation of an unemployed urban mass of freedmen and landless citizens as characterized the Mediterranean city state. Thus in the Indian cities we do not see the rise of the institution of 'bread and circuses', in which the municipality distributed hundreds of thousands of free loaves of bread and built great coliseums to keep the restive, unemployed rabble fed and entertained. This significant difference between the community under the regime of South Asian caste as opposed to Mediterranean citizenship is a result of the difference in the expansion of the two forms. Industrial capitalism, in contrast, has sought to create such a 'reserve army' in the India subcontinent, which the ruling classes and political parties seek to arouse and inflame with religion, nationalism, communalism and so forth to consolidate and extend their positions.

It must be emphasized that the four *varnas* arose out of the growth of consciousness associated with the various main functions within society and evolved in hand with the increasing complexity of relations. It is unlikely that there was ever an original correspondence between the *varnas* and class as has been assumed by Meillassoux

(1973:92) when he wrote: 'The system of the Varnas (which corresponds to the interpretive concept of "orders") was an attempt to maintain class relations as they existed during the classical period.' In previous periods not only were the relations much less differentiated but the categories themselves lacked a specialized existence, especially as given it by Meillassoux from European feudal conceptions ('seigniorial class', 'clerical class' and 'emerging merchant group'). The categories of landed property, religious priest and mercantile capital only developed a specialized existence with the development of specialized groups in society, and furthermore, this existence was always ultimately defined by the relationship of these to the dominant category in the particular time and place (as they now represent the various manifestations of capital).

The driving forces behind the development and elaboration of a society characterized by an ideology of caste rather than citizenship were the exigencies of a dispersed pastoral people, already transformed from a lineage-based or segmentary to class society, expanding into the South Asian subcontinent among people still organized according to segmentary states (tribe). Their premise was not an established city with a territory divided up among citizen cultivators as private property, which they expanded by conquest and cultivated with the labour of conquered peoples whom they had uprooted as slaves.

The Aryans groups, rather, took as their premise, on the one hand, their own developed productive forces and social organization organized around private property in herds, and subsequently land. They premised themselves also in the intercourse and commerce with urban civilizations of West Asia, which had further augmented the productive forces and transformed the social organization of the segmentary state. And they took as their premise the existing organization of segmentary states they subjected, with their already emerging social differentiation and accompanying ideology and ritual. Given these premises, the invading Aryan groups established themselves as landlords by inverting the clan principle into a caste one, and setting their already relatively well established division of labour, with the developing caste divisions of priest, soldier and merchant, over the lineages of the segmentary state, transforming the members of these into a labouring class. The lineages of the previous segmentary state were themselves increasingly divided among themselves according to the same caste principle, while their ritual leaders were co-opted into the upper castes. Simultaneously, the Aryan groups also introduced more developed productive forces, including irrigation, plough agriculture, metal working and so forth, thereby backing and augmenting ideological and ritual means of control with increasing material powers, providing the basis for military expansion into empires. In a society where control of water and cattle provided the means to augment and control human labour power, both were given a sacred character.[12]

While the cultivator groups were disenfranchised both economically and politically, they were subjected within their communities according to the principles of the pre-existing organization. The caste principle fully developed the ritual subordination to the lineage groups of the segmentary state into a subordination of agricultural and craft labour to landlords. Distribution of subsistence to all groups was framed legally in terms of shares of agricultural product. While ownership of landed property became alienated from the agricultural and industrial producers, these producers remained in possession of their land and tools. Thus where was not the creation of a propertyless proletariat.

Like in assembly of the Mediterranean cities, the democracy of the clan persisted in the community level Panchayat councils, but the franchise was restricted to Brahmans. And these in turn were dominated by the wealthiest among them. At the state level, it persisted in the council of advisers to the king, the Raj Subba, but again limited not just to one caste but to the predominant families of the nobility within it.

The process of expansion of these landed classes can be clearly seen in the subjection of the segmentary political organization identified for pre-Rajput Nepal to a landed property class. The expansion of landed private property into Nepal was associated with the movement of 'populous clans of warrior cultivators' from north India, where they were involved in the same 'slow process of settlement which set the main feature of land-control in modern times from the borders of Awadh to Bengal' (Bayly 1983:17). These warrior cultivators, referring to descent from Rajput lineages as a means to establish their legitimacy, set themselves over the hill peoples and their lineage organized polities, initially subjecting them through their existing lineage hierarchies. The warrior cultivators subsequently established sovereignty through introduction of Brahmanical ideology and ritual and set up leading families as kings to represent their interests. They pushed the villagers from the more fertile rent producing bottom lands up onto dry hillsides where, unable to sustain and reproduce themselves as autonomous communities, they provided a bonded labour force to the new landlord class.[13]

This private property form, in combination with the introduction of productive forces such as the plough, irrigation, oxen, other domesticated plants and animals and associated forms of knowledge, provided the basis for agglomeration of wealth and power, eventually enabling one of these Rajputs, King Prithivi Narayan Shah of Gorkha, to launch in the mid-eighteenth century the war of conquest which resulted in the full 'unification' or subjugation of the present nation state by the end of the first decade of the nineteenth century.

The Kirat areas of Rai and Limbu speaking peoples to the east of the Kathmandu Valley which had not been subjected by the Rajputs were still organized as segmentary states, and land remained under communal tenure. Thus while the Kirat areas provided no match militarily, due to lack of concentration of power, subsequently they have been the most difficult to bring under the regime of private tenure; inversely, while the states to the west were conquered militarily only with great difficulty, their lands were relatively easily re-allocated among landlord interests represented in the state, since these lands had already been subjected to the private tenure of such classes. Indeed, it was the desperate economic condition of the villagers in these same already subjected areas and their ties of patronage to landlords who aligned themselves with Gorkha which allowed Prithivi Narayan Shah and his successors to mobilize them with promises of land and security.[14] For villagers subjected in terms of landed property relations, land ownership seemed like liberation. However, these plots were encumbered with the property class which constituted the state, and the cultivators never emerged as an independent peasantry.[15] Like citizenship and democracy in Mediterranean city states, caste and its assemblies and councils, which have been resurrected and elaborated in the twentieth century in the Indian subcontinent, were and continue to be 'a glorious facade'.

NOTES

This chapter originally appeared in *Contributions to Nepalese Studies*, Vol. 8, No. 1, 1991, pp. 1–18.

1   Thus Southall goes against the positions that advocate a primitive communism prior to the rise of the city and civil society, such as of Marx (1973a) and Engels

(1983), or a 'traditional' classless and acephalic (stateless) political organization of lineage society as advocated by much of early anthropology. He further develops his criticism of the 'tribe' and other anthropological formulations of supposedly 'stateless' societies.

2   Meillassoux (1978a:134) takes this as a characteristic of what he calls 'self-sustaining societies'.

3   Meillassoux (1978b), in a rather mechanistic interpretation of materialism, relates the development of classes with the development of the various 'instruments' of production (which he defines more in terms of forces or even a kind of simplistic notion of capital). In my mind, materialism means that human relations and other aspects of human life are produced by humans and that social relations arise from and therefore must correspond to the array of productive powers available to humans, and not that there exists some direct causative relationship between the material objects of humans, that is instruments, and social and ideological forms in which everything can be reduced down into. Rituals, conquest and so forth which set one class over another presuppose previously developed production relations. The relationship is a developmental and not a mechanistic or directly causative one.

4   A contemporary news story in *The Rising Nepal* refers to an incident about the descendants of such ritual leaders, called here 'rain maker' (Kahl 1991:4): 'A dispute over a buffalo has had far reaching consequences for the people of Karungu, a village on the shores of lake Victoria. Their troubles began one year ago when an old man accused the grandson of a local rainmaker of stealing the animal. Word of the alleged theft quickly spread and the accused George Owuor, went to the village headman to complain of what he saw as a blemish on his character. "If I am really a grandson of the rainmaker, Mze Minot, there shall be no rain here in the next seven years, no harvest and the people shall experience serious hunger during these days", the angry young man vowed.

'Local belief has it that rainmakers are able to do more than move the heavens to open. If they are angry they can also bring on a drought. At first, nobody in Karungu took George seriously. It was only this spring when the time came to sow the fields that they remembered his curse. The rains, which had always fallen at the time the crops were being sown, failed to materialize this year. Alarmed, the village elders demanded to see George. He was not in the village so they questioned his widowed mother instead.

'Three times Mrs. Dorsila Jongo Ogola was called to appear before the village council and each time she was quizzed about why she had brought on the drought. The woman admitted she was the daughter of a now deceased rainmaker, but said the power to make rain or cause droughts could only be handed down to boys, not to the girls. This explanation failed to appease the elders, who argued that other villages in the region had had plenty of rain during crop-planting. Only Karungu and its immediate vicinity were left dry, with the result that drinking water was in short supply and crops and other vegetation were damaged.

'Some villagers pointed out that Dorsila had not bothered to till her own fields knowing full well that no rain was going to fall. People began to ignore her. Some even demanded she be punished. When George returned he went to the elders to complain of the treatment to which his mother had been subjected. There ensued a lengthy discussion which ended with George apologising for his curse and shaking hands with each member of the village council. That same night a hefty rain shower fell on the village, according to a report in the Kenya Times. The allegations against the widow and her son were dropped.'

5   This is the position that Meillassoux (1978b:167–9) follows, except that he goes too far by only identifying the market as gaining a role with the development of capitalism.

6   See Max Weber, 'Religious Groups (The Sociology of Religion)' (1978:399–634).

7   Thus women revolutionaries, such as those in the Sandinista army, have found that to continue to maintain their power in society after a successful armed revolutionary struggle the women's divisions in the army cannot be disbanded.

8   'The Kutchin (Louchoux) of the Yukon river Region [North-east Territories, British North America, southerly from the ex-Russian coastal lowlands] are Athapascans and with them (according to the letter of the late George Gibbs to Morgan): among the Kutchin "3 grades or classes of society (should call totem, which however may be dissimilar in rank) [& in the manner namely how had come to the dominance of the gens principle, could by & by gens to give way to the caste-formation? Where then the prohibition of intermarriage between different gentes completely inverted the archaic rule of the intermarriage within the same gens;]; a man does not marry into his own class, but takes a wife from some other, and that a chief from the highest may marry with the woman of the lowest without loss of caste. [The concept of caste carries the letter writer further & he interprets such that a man cannot marry into his own gens, probably rather into the gens of his other brother—or cousin phratry; this shows but that as soon as a difference of rank between blood relations of the gentes arises, this comes into conflict with the apparatus (geräth) of the gentile principle & the gens in its contrary, caste, can petrify]. The children belong to the grade of the mother [which thus the rank distinction between gents, brothers and sisters of all resign themselves in gentes of each rank. The kindred ranks let no complete aristocracy to arise, fraternity remains in the sentiment of equality]. The members of the same grade in different tribes do not war with each other' (Marx 1983:183; emphasis omitted).

Cf. Hegel (1956:144): 'The next degree in advance of this Unity is Difference, maintaining its independence against the all-subduing power of Unity. . . . that independent members ramify from the unity of despotic body. Yet the distinctions which these imply are referred to Nature. Instead of stimulating the activity of a soul as their centre of union, and spontaneously realizing that soul—as is the case in organic life—they petrify and become rigid, and by their stereotyped character condemn the Indian people to the most degrading spiritual serfdom. The distinctions in question are *Castes*.'

Hegel saw the development of caste as a differentiation of Humans as object of the idea and not in terms of their free will which he used to rank from peoples from east to west. But clearly the same process was happening in the Mediterranean with citizenship, with the same degrading of peoples, and it persists in the modern world with the extension of a global financial and industrial capitalist class over massive populations of people disenfranchised in terms of citizenship between countries and practically through the electoral process within countries.

9   Meillasoux (1978b:167) writes: 'Once we have a social structure where one corporate group dominates and exploits other corporate groups we are dealing with a class system. . . .'

'Kinship is transformed here into an ideology whose "raison d'être" is not so much to express the relationships generated from the growth and organization of the society as to justify and even support a domination imposed from the outside. We could relate this ideology to the new rules of kinship which develop in the aristocratic lineages and which are different because they obey political rather than economic constraints.

'When kinship reaches a religious dimension, it may gain enough strength to be considered as the basic justification for domination and exploitation. The situation is inverted: people, instead of being kin and dependents because of the relations of production they are in, are integrated into such relationships because of an alleged ideological kin relation. Hence the emphasis on "blood" relationship in some cases, or on religion in others.'

For Meillassoux, as kinship becomes more abstract, he sees the ideology as itself as being what determines people as kinsmen. Marx sees that the relations are still being produced and reproduced, but now as class. The political itself premises on production. Meillasoux sees that every element disappears because kinship less and less corresponds to the economic form underlying it. Marx, in contrast, sees a change in the production relations, making the kinship ideology become more abstract and seeming to take on an existence of its own, which is altogether different.

10   'The quadruple division of society is mentioned in some of the earlier (Vedic) hymns, but it makes its formal appearance in the *Purushasukta* which seeks to explain the existing divisions by adumbrating the theory that "when they divided the primeval being (*Purusa*) the *Brahmana* was his mouth, the *Rajanya* became his arms, the *Vaisya* was his thighs, and from his feet sprang the *Sudras*"' (Majumdar et al. 1978:31).

11   Even today in my ethnographic sample from Bandipur, the gender proportions taking the School Leaving Certificate (SLC) examination in the of Bandipur in central Nepal among Brahman men to women (78 per cent *versus* 12 per cent) is no different than other villager groups, despite the Brahmans' positions as landlords. This demonstrates a linkage between property, its ideology, and the disenfranchisement of women, discussed in the previous sections (Mikesell 1988:213).

12   The sacred character of the cow was subjected to a debate started by Marvin Harris in British and US anthropological journals in the late 1960s and early 70s around the question of the functionalist rationality versus economic irrationality of the sacred cow. However, among a herding people, domesticated cattle were property par excellence, and in cultivation, along with prepared land and irrigation, one of the main means of production of surpluses. Thus its sacred character was the means to control the distribution of this surplus within society; as such it is less irrational than the sanctions given to capital today, in which all forms of labour power have been subjected to

the logic of private property in the form of the exchange relation, and in which the lives of millions of people are sacrificed to preserve and expand the division of labour and accumulation of surplus represented within it.

13   Available histories of course describe the process of the establishment of private property merely in terms of the conquest of tribal lands by Rajput kings who replace earlier 'chiefs' or kings without providing any indication of the transformation of the property or associated political forms. However, a good idea of the process as I have described can be obtained from the experience of the Kirat cultivators of Eastern Nepal (Limbu, Rai), who were only conquered two centuries ago, and whose communal forms of tenure are still undergoing a process of transformation, and where the present state was forced to recognize these forms of property and associated interests even as it set about to destroy them.

14   Prithivi Narayan Shah was quite aware of this, as quoted in his deathbed advice to his heirs in 1775 (Stiller 1968). Thus it is the hill people of the western hill kingdoms of Nepal, and not the people of the eastern communally based states who are described as the 'martial races' and who subsequently were recruited by the British Army.

15   The miserable condition of these people is described in Ludwig F. Stiller (1976).

CHAPTER 17

A Critique of Baktapur as Urban Mesocosm

'I quite agree with you', said the Duchess; 'and the moral of that is—
"Be what you would seem to be"—or, if you'd like it put more simply—
"Never imagine yourself not to be otherwise than what it might appear
to others that what you were or might have been was not otherwise
than what you had been would have appeared to them to be
otherwise. "'

—Lewis Carroll, *Alice's Adventures in Wonderland*

ROBERT I. LEVY'S *Mesocosm: Hinduism and the Organization of a Traditional
Newar City in Nepal* (1992) is an exhaustive and daunting study of the
city of Bhaktapur, of the Kathmandu valley, through its symbols,
ideology, and ritual. Levy initially frames the study in terms of a
comparison with his earlier fieldwork in Tahiti, in order to develop
an evolutionary schema in which Bhaktapur represents an
intermediate type between primitive and modern. As the study
develops, it becomes clear that the term mesocosm refers implicitly
to this intermediate evolutionary stage. More prominently, however,
Levy uses the term to refer to the city as representing an intermediate
'organized meaningful world' between the 'microcosmic worlds of
individuals and the culturally conceived macrocosm, the universe,
at whose centre the city lies'.

Reminiscent of the nineteenth century concern for the
relationship of the civil society and the state, the problem is how the
private world relates to the public world and how its activities are
oriented to the needs and purposes defined in the public one. The
private world, used by Levy in the sense of the private religious world
of household rituals, simultaneously is affected by the mesocosm and

provides its output—religious, social, manpower and so forth—to the intermediate religious world of the city. The mesocosm or intermediate world is organized by a system of symbols which in the city of Bhaktapur is Hinduism, given that 92 per cent of the population and all except 60 out of 6,000 households are Hindu— 'this great preponderance of Hindu Newars who are at the centre of our treatment of Bhaktapur's symbolic organization' (p. 92). The kind of city being organized is an 'archaic' city (understood here to be used in the dictionary sense of characterizing 'an earlier or more primitive time'—Webster's), which for Bhaktapur is a Hindu city in its full development.

The main concern of this paper is Levy's theoretical method introduced in the first part of the book, which aims to delineate the archaic Hindu city as a universal evolutionary stage and show how Bhaktapur embodies this ideal in its religious and normative everyday life. To establish his position, Levy makes a series of equivocations between Hinduism, Bhaktapur and ideal types found in the literature. Proper comparative method requires identifying the differences as well as the similarities when making analogies with ideal types, and then explaining these differences; but in favour of his argument Levy typically sets up a conditional relationship—in the manner of, 'if this were the case then . . .'—and thereafter assumes that the condition held without establishing it. The second and third parts of the book provide an exhaustive study of the religious life of the city, which exonerates its theoretical failings without providing substantial support for his earlier arguments. His major mistake is that he wants to make an understanding of the city as a whole while limiting himself to the religious realm and religiously framed normative one, without integrating it into the historically arisen material one—production, reproduction, consumption, distribution, exchange, classes, non-religious forms of representation and orientation, and so forth. Thus, though he claims that his purpose is to know the city and its people, my sense is that the real city as it is actually experienced by its residents is never known.

Levy's position is that symbols, particularly those from the Hindu religious realm, being a function of the intimate experience and mental organization of the residents of the city (assumed, not demonstrated), *are* significant as they make the city known to its residents (and now the ethnographer). This leads him to seeing his analysis as having to address two questions: 'What is Bhaktapur that a Newar may know it, and a Newar so that he or she may know Bhaktapur?' Although Levy refers to the title of a mathematics paper as the source of these questions, they also paraphrase Dumont and Pocock's rendering of Mauss: 'A sociological explanation is finished when one has seen what it is that people believe and think, and who are the people that believe and think that' (Dumont and Pocock 1956:13, quoted in Harriss 1989:127). This position was based on the premise that ideology, particularly caste ideology, ascertainable in large part in texts, constitutes Indian society.

Levy pursues this premise to assert that symbols—that is, the representations of ideology—constitute the city that is known, differing from Dumont and Pocock only in his identifying the operation of many more variables than caste. Although Levy's text repeatedly acknowledges social differentiation, it treats the Newar who knows Bhaktapur as an undifferentiated subject who can be represented by elite religious practitioners. His methodology relies upon two highly educated Brahmans in Bhaktapur and a Vajracharya Sanskrit scholar and art historian trained and employed in a major American university to assist in the interpretation. This approach makes for a complex, interesting and authoritative analysis of Hindu symbols and the city as such, but whether interpretations by high caste, high class religious specialist reflects the variety of understanding and interests of Newars in general—ranging from businessmen, bureaucrats, Jyapu farmers, factory workers, house servants, untouchables, intellectuals, Communists, and so forth—and the real material life of the city is questionable.[1] The analysis furthermore denies the possibility that other forces besides Hindu ideology affect people, ignores individual experience except in the domain of Hindu symbols, and denies significant orientations and actions except in the sphere of ritual. This is *not* to lessen the significance of the analysis, which is an exemplary and important example of the long tradition of collaboration between anthropological specialists in culture and indigenous cultural specialists—all the more significant because Levy gives recognition to the collegial role of his co-specialists.[2] But it *is* to dispute the claim by the study that it can represent a Bhaktapur known and experienced by Newars other than the representations of high priests and religious books,[3] especially low class, low caste labourers or other exploited and depressed status individuals who make up the bulk of the population.

In order to privilege Hindu symbols, it is necessary for Levy to establish that the initial form of the city was a manifestation of Hindu ideas and that contending influences have not subsequently affected it. Levy identified the historical origin of Newars from 800 BC, into whom a north Indian ruling class gradually merged and elaborated into an autonomous and unique Hindu Newar culture from about the fourth century AD. Levy sees the destruction brought by the invasion of the Kathmandu valley by Shams ud-Din Illyas in 1349 as providing the conditions for rebuilding the city according to an ideal urban order, in which Hindu ideas converged with reality. This was brought to fruition by Jayasthiti Malla, who was credited with the city's laws and customs.

Jayasthiti Malla came to represent to Newars the Hindu ordering of Bhaktapur, an order built on an ancient plan. (p. 44)

Jayasthiti Malla revivified, extended, and codified an order that built on preexisting forms and forced them into Hindu ideals of the proper form for a little kingdom, a city-state. Subsequent developments of this order must have been retrospectively credited to him, validated by his name. This order was the mesocosmic order of the Newar cities, which was to last in Bhaktapur for some 600 years. (p. 45)

That laws and decrees were framed in terms of Hindu ideas does not mean that Jayasthiti Malla was any closer to realizing them. Jayasthiti could never have established himself in a strong position unless there were elements in the society that had built sufficient strength to support him and whose interests were represented and extended by these laws. Levy points to Jayasthiti's enactment of laws making 'property in houses, lands and *birtas* . . . saleable' (p. 43, quoting Wright) and allowing 'his subjects to sell or mortgage their hereditary landed property' (p. 43, quoting Padmagiri) as indication of his 'reordering' of the status system. This does not indicate so much that he 'made poor wretched people happy' with the institution of an ideal Hindu order as that he was appeasing certain emergent social interests over old entrenched ones. This possibly implies growing power of state servitor and merchant classes which supported the palace in their nascence but threatened to oppose it as they grew stronger, indicating a dynamic in the society, contradicting Levy's claims of changelessness in the next two pages. By giving custom the force of law, Jayasthiti was recognizing and selecting particular social interests. Most likely, he also thereby put down competing claims which may have been antagonistic towards him, making certain other poor wretches unhappy. Of course contemporary scribes, benefiting from state patronage, praised him in terms of the Hindu ideal of the time. But this is no indication that the reality converged with this ideal. One need go no further than the *Rising Nepal* or the stacks of books formulating, analysing and praising the Panchayat and current multi-party versions of 'democracy' to see how things work, or for that matter, all the high sounding proclamations of the UN agencies on its programs for the Third World. Overall, the laws and decrees of the Mallas were a strategy within a process of competition for and consolidation of power and control over material conditions, not of making life better for the poor or constructing an ideal Hindu society. Proper historical conclusions require critical use of the historical material.

Levy interprets Jayasthiti's grandson Yaksa Malla's construction of a moat around the city as both defence and 'containment of the city at whose boundaries Ananda Malla had long before placed protective goddesses . . . even more concentrated and isolated within its boundaries' (p. 45). With his sons' division of the Valley into three kingdoms, 'Bhaktapur entered on its long period of relative isolation' (p. 46). Levy wishes to establish that the city still pretty much represents Jayasthiti's ideal in support of his 'mesocosm' hypothesis by showing that the city became isolated and changeless soon after the death of Jayasthiti. But he takes the chronicled history which makes kings into the subject of history at face value, forgetting that kings are the faces given to history and not its subject or content. Such content is found in the interplay of the various groups and social interests making up the society—the palace and its retainers, the army, landlords, merchants and especially the artisans and cultivators, who build, shape, nourish, fight and clean up with their own hands, but who rarely get a chance to write the histories and thus do not enter into them except as praising and acclaiming the acts of those who are doing the writing (as exemplified in the popular *Mahabharat* and *Ramayana* Hindi television serials). Levi's analysis in terms of legal forms and personages reinforces representations in terms of symbols, as these forms are secondary and relate through representations. But to identify change or lack of change he must look at why and for whom the moats were built and laws made. That people build moats and laws indicates perception of threat to their order and acknowledgement of change by attempts to prevent it, not changelessness. Because he excluded the countryside from his analysis, he does not show how the relationship of the city to the countryside—key to the definition of the city (Mikesell 1991)—changed or how it related to eventual downfall of the government with the conquest from the countryside.

Levy interprets the conquest by the 'Indianized mountain state of Gorkha' in the eighteenth century as the incorporation of Newar society into an 'enlarged territory and state' bringing the 'long autonomous political history of the Newars' to an end (pp. 14–15). He sees the conquest is a radical transformation because it makes the Newars into just one of many subjected ethnic groups. Yet Levy argues that because the Gorkhalis used existing institutions to build and extend their rule, Bhaktapur remained pretty much changeless throughout the subsequent Rana Rule up to the 'restoration of power to the Shah King' (if 'restoration' can be applied to something that existed only in myth). This allows him to say that Bhaktapur was trying to turn history into 'what might seem a timeless eternal civic order. In 1973, the city, or most of it, was still trying' (p. 15, again the 'city' is made into subject). He adds that 'although under the political control of the Gorkhalis since the late eighteenth century, [Bhaktapur has been] almost untouched by Western influences until the early 1950s'.[4] He finds support for such a view in a government document, as if these are disinterested sources:

as a major governmental development plan for the Kathmandu Valley of the Nepal government put it, Bhaktapur 'has shown very little change throughout the last several decades and thus remains the purist existing documentation of historic Newar towns in the Valley (HMG, Nepal 1969, 76)'. (p. 52)

Hereby Levy attempts to establish that the origins of the present character of the city in the Malla regime and its changelessness since then. Again, the historical process of conquest cannot be understood simply in terms of its outward appearance as a history of regimes and persistence of symbolic and ritual forms. One must ask *what* were the underlying forces and interests represented by the establishment and long preservation of the regime and *how* did these interests change. How was product controlled and distributed? What was the nature of the commerce? What was the relationship of city to countryside? How did these relations change over time and what was the effect of the Shah conquest on them? Does not the removal of the palace from Bhaktapur to Kathmandu indicate an essential change in the character of the city?

The shift of palace activities to the court in Kathmandu should indicate that the content of Bhaktapur extends to Kathmandu as well. Bhaktapur lost its status as what Max Weber calls a 'princely city' with an immense shift of all the functions that go with it—the court, the gigantic job of provisioning the palace and barracks, the large class of retainers and merchants sustained by this. The commercial class in turn must have controlled much of the surplus from the land while at the same time underwriting agricultural production with credit. The subsequent exodus of Bhaktapur and Patan merchants and their establishment in bazaars the length and breadth of the new polity must be taken as a part of Bhaktapur's history as well.

Given that Bhaktapur's symbolic repertoire is drawn from north India, that it grew upon commerce with North India and Tibet, and that following the Gorkha conquest much of the political and economic content of its life shifted elsewhere in the region, I would think that proper analysis should try to locate Bhaktapur within the regional picture of class and urban development rather than attempt to contrive a closed and changeless city for heuristic purposes so analysis can proceed *as if* it were the case. As an example, Bayly's (1983) study of north India is just such an approach to urban development which places it within a regional context, links the household and the urban order, and integrates symbols, ritual and the material world into the analysis without reducing one into another.

Levy, in contrast, attempts to build a Bhaktapur framed as a changeless city into an ideal evolutionary type standing between primitive and modern society. Given the city's changelessness, he defines it in the first of a series of equivocations in terms of Redfield and Singer's 'city of orthogenetic transformation' in which 'local culture was carried forward rather than broken down to be replaced by new means of relation and integration, familiar to us in Western urban history' (p. 19). This gives typological significance to the apparent changelessness, but what of the symbols?

Levy goes on to observe that 'Bhaktapur is to a very large degree characterized by a great deal of a certain kind of symbolism' to such an extent as to be '"extraordinary," of compelling local intellectual and emotional interest'. These symbols are 'in large part, derived from the vast resources of South Asian "religious" ideas and images, locally transformed, ordered, and put to use for Bhaktapur's civic purposes'. When he then compares these 'civic purposes' to the staging of a 'choreographed ballet' in which 'the city space is a carefully marked stage' (p. 16), the implication is that the score of the ballet is found in the symbols. Furthermore, the 'city's conventional arrangements of time' are 'the music of the ballet' (implying that the symbols, as the score, determine the time arrangements). This allows the reduction of the lives of the city's residents to a totally predictable nature so that, 'if one knows what a person's surname [*thar* or clan] is . . . , his or her age and sex, what day of the lunar (for some purposes the solar) year it is, and where the person lives in Bhaktapur, one can make a plausible guess at where he or she is, what he or she is doing, and even something of what he or she is experiencing' (p. 17).

This sounds like the claim of Levy's priestly interlocutors, who have an interest in making the lives of the city's residents subject to astrological charts, rituals and religious texts. Left unmentioned is *who* writes this score, or at least who adapts it. His choice of highly educated Brahmans in the city of Bhaktapur and American universities to assist him in interpreting the score indicates who he accepts as the subject. It furthermore is a highly determined normative order; this would require statistical evidence to verify, which is lacking in the book as it accepts the symbols, ideology and his interlocutors on their own authority. A normative order, furthermore, has to do with *everyday* life. It does not address what people are or have been *making* of their lives—educating their children, expanding their business contacts in India, pursuing posts in the government, affirming, preserving and raising their class and social position, confronting and struggling with the injustice of class and caste, building various kinds of organizations—in short, *producing* their world in the course of reproducing it—which in my mind is what the city with its symbols and rituals is all about. In contrast, Levy's 'significant action' takes us back to ritual activity.

Having made this claim for 'considerable social and cultural order in Bhaktapur' (p. 17), Levy further claims that this is a certain order that can be characterized as an '"archaic city" and "climax Hinduism"' (p. 18). By archaic, he apparently means that Bhaktapur is related to an earlier type of city, given its previous description in terms of an 'eternal order'. For this earlier type of city Levy draws an analogy with what Paul Wheatley described as the 'primary urban generation', or urban civilization as it initially emerged in various areas. He derives this analogy from a need to support his position that Bhaktapur is dominated by symbols, just as the first cities were dominated [not by] commercial relations, a primordial market, or . . . fortress, but rather [by] ceremonial complex. . . . The predominantly religious focus to the schedule of social activities associated with them leaves no room to doubt that we are dealing primarily with centers of ritual and ceremonial. . . . Operationally [these centers] were instruments for the creation of political, social, economic, and sacred space, at the same time as they were symbols of cosmic, social, and moral order. Under the religious authority of organized priesthoods and divine monarchs, they elaborated the redistributive aspects of the economy to a position of institutionalized regional dominance, functioned as nodes in a web of administered . . . trade, served as foci of craft specialization, and promoted the development of exact and predictive sciences. (p. 19, quoted by Levy from Wheatley 1971:225f.)

From this Levy deduces:

Bhaktapur is not an ancient city in terms of historical continuity, but its organization reflects many of the same principles that have been ascribed to otherwise differing ancient cities as members of a certain type of urban community. As a member *in some respects* of such a class it might well suggest, *mutatis mutandis*, something of what they *might have been*, and *may be thought* of as an archaic city. (p. 19, emphasis added)

The question is whether the 'reflection' of the principles of the primary urban generation in the organization of Bhaktapur is one of substance and not just appearance. Levy frames the analogy with another caveat: *mutatis mutandis* ('with necessary changes having been made/differences considered'—Webster's). Instead of following up and actually considering the differences, he goes ahead to equivocate Bhaktapur with the primary urban generation. This again is incorrect usage of the comparative method because it identifies similarities and uses them to equivocate two different things without dealing with the differences or explaining the causes for these differences.

There are real problems in equating modern Bhaktapur with a primary urban generation. (1) The earliest cities in South Asia, of which Bhaktapur was not, arose as a secondary generation from the primary cities of Mesopotamia and west Asia. (2) Hinduism matured within an already advanced urban civilization prior to its entry into the Kathmandu Valley, and its expansion was accompanied by the relations of this civilization. (3) Bhaktapur was never characterized by the highly centralized redistributive economy, 'elaborated . . . to a regional dominance', of the primary urban generation with its assemblage of clay ration bowls. (4) Religion and symbols predominated in the primary urban generation because—in the absence of advanced commercial, industrial and military development and the associated rise of competing classes—priests monopolized power in the city. Kathmandu valley cities, in contrast, arose on the basis of comparatively well advanced regional class development. Certainly by the time of Jayasthiti Malla there could be no comparison between the two. (5) Religion only *seems* to predominate in Bhaktapur because, with the Gorkhali conquest, the monarchy and its associated retainers, barracks, provisioning and commercial activities were transferred entirely to Kathmandu; the religious aspect which seems so predominant when the city is taken in isolation makes up only part of the picture. It is even less significant now when we consider Bhaktapur as a part of a much larger political and commercial framework than even when the palace was located within Bhaktapur. Furthermore, as a result of the conquest, Bhaktapur's well developed and relatively independent merchant sector dispersed itself across the countryside into bazaars or shifted to Kathmandu, while often continuing to maintain friendship, kinship, business, and property links within Bhaktapur.

Given his equivocation of Bhaktapur with the primary urban generation, Levy now allows himself to draw an analogy between Bhaktapur and the ancient Mediterranean city described in Fustel de Coulanges' *La Cité Antique* (1864) in which, unlike in the modern city, the various levels of organization lost none of their individuality or independence.

When different groups became thus associated, none of them lost its individuality, or its independence. . . .

There was a nesting of these cellular units—'family, phratry, tribe, city'— each level marked by its relevant gods and rituals, and in contrast to, say, a Frenchman, 'who at the moment of his birth belongs at once to a family, a commune, a department and a country', (ibid., 128) the citizen of the ancient city moved via a series of *rites de passage* over many years into membership in successively more inclusive units.

Each increasingly inclusive level of structure . . . had its proper gods and cult. . . .

Each unit had its interior and its exterior, and the interior was protected by secrecy. Above all, this was true of the household. . . .

The ultimate unit to which people were related at this 'stage' was the ancient city itself. There was 'a profound gulf which always separated two cities. However near they might be to each other, they always formed two completely separate societies. . . .' (ibid., 201)

What anchored and tied together this structure of cells was its rootedness in a fixed and local space. . . . The city came to define in itself its own proper social unit and was sacred for that group within the city boundaries. . . .

The problem for a summary rejection of Fustel's vision is that the particular formal features of his 'Ancient City' that we have chosen to review here are characteristic of Bhaktapur. (pp. 20–2)

Besides similarity again being taken as unity, there are basic flaws in Coulanges's assumption that previous levels retained their individuality with the development of subsequent ones. Once a form becomes subordinated within another one it takes an entirely different content, and the content of the subordinate form must be explained in terms of the subsequent one. An adequate explanation must account for the full extent of intercourse. Furthermore, the different cellular units did not appear in terms of the order of priority subsequently given them. The Ancient patriarchal family appeared in the course of the development of the division of labour within the clan in the face of expanding intercourse and commerce, and emerged fully as a slave holding institution only with the dissolution of lineage organized society. The separation of various levels has to do with the appearance manufactured by religion from the substance of the relations and life, in pursuit of the ends and purposes defined within the latter.

This perception of the city in terms of autonomous cellular units leads Levy in Chapter 5 to argue,

for the purposes of the city's organization, we may emphasize again that it is the output of the *thar* [clan] that is essential, not its internal affairs and organization—as long as those internal features guarantee that output.

From the standpoint of ritual, this may be true, but from the standpoint of the life of the city and its production, distribution of labour, products, and so forth, for which symbols and rituals are providing the 'orientation' (using Weber's term), the internal organization of the *thar* ('clan-like social unit whose members share the same surname'—p. 774) and family extends from the purposes set for them in the larger life of the city. Changes in the forms of production and reproduction of the city bring about changes in the internal productive and reproductive processes of its elements. Furthermore, the extent and forms of the *thar* and family differ according to people's social status and position within the city—for example, *thars* of low caste labourers may be truncated and insignificant, whereas those of large merchant houses may be extensive, filling an important role in expansion and control of mercantile capital and other properties; similarly, for prominent Brahmans the patriarchal family is the means of expanding the pool of clients that they serve and depend upon for their prosperity.

In addition, Levy's identification of Bhaktapur with the early ancient Mediterranean city also suffers basic problems. First, it contradicts his previous analogy of Bhaktapur with Wheatley's 'primary urban generation' because the Mediterranean cities arose already as a secondary urban form with well advanced class development, industries, commerce, and agriculture. Second, Levy finds himself confronted with the problem of explaining how such a city can persist into the late twentieth century Asia when, as he points out, it had already disappeared by the middle of the first millennium BC in the Mediterranean as

part of a worldwide wave of 'breakthroughs' within the orbit of the 'higher civilizations,' during the first 700 or 800 years before the Christian Era in an 'axial age' consisting in the 'transcendence' of the limiting definitions and controls of these ancient forms. . . . Those who did not participate in this transformation have simply been rejected as ancestors of the modern world. (pp. 22–3)

Levy makes the claim that due to 'the lack of a politically unifying force' the heterodoxies of this axial age, with their 'powerfully transcending attack on the symbolically constituted social order' (p. 23), never succeeded in asserting themselves in India, and thus the subcontinent did not go through such an 'axial transition'.

What did prevail was ultimately the static social order of Hinduism, which, whatever its peripheral inclusion in their proper place of the socially transcendent gestures of renunciation and mysticism, was hardly any kind of 'breakthrough' into whatever the idea of an axial 'transformation' was meant to honor.

All of which is to suggest that traditional India and Bhaktapur, *in so far as* it may be characteristic of traditional India, are very old fashioned places indeed. (p. 23, emphasis added)

First of all, Levy introduces another unsubstantiated conditionality ('insofar as') in order to make an equivocation. The point that he wants to make is that an unchanged Bhaktapur never lost the character of the 'primary urban generation', so that symbols may seen as still constituting the city's social order. It would follow then that an analysis of the symbols will actually allow the ethnographer to discover the Bhaktapur that people know and the people who know Bhaktapur. However, the constituting character of symbols is contradicted by the argument that the existence of a politically unifying force is necessary for making the axial transition. Political unification presumes sufficient development of production, commerce, and industry, along with correspondent development of social relations, to provide a material base for such unification. Herein he contradicts his general position that symbols constitute the social relations.

To complicate matters further, the ancient Mediterranean city states did not experience lasting political unification until the rise of the Roman Empire, several hundred years later than the period attributed to the 'axial transformation'. It was the lack of political unity that provided the scope for innovation and ferment. The subsequent political unification was a period marked by intellectual constriction and reduction of the civil versus the political—a situation from which Europe did not recover for another millennium (Southall n.d.).

As Bhaktapur, like 'traditional India', has failed to make the axial transition to modern society, Levy contemplates the question of what the city is to be. Although Bhaktapur has not become modern, neither is it the opposite pole of the dichotomy—primitive—since according to Wheatley 'the society of the temple-city was neither fully *contractus, civitatis, Gesellschaft* nor organic' (1971:349, quoted on p. 24). Disagreeing with Ernst Gellner's (1974) position that such a middle ground did not make up any sort of distinctive type, Levy sees that Bhaktapur is an intermediate stage which provides

a kind of continent in the Great Divide, which has its own distinctive typological features, exemplifies its own distinctive and important principles in relation to both sociocultural organization and to thought, distinctive features that are blurred and lost in these classical oppositions. Bhaktapur and places that might have been analogous to it in the ancient world are illuminating for this middle terrain. Neither primitive nor modern, Bhaktapur has its own exemplary features of organization and of mind. (p. 25)

Thus Bhaktapur, as an ancient city, is indeed distinctive, representing a sort of missing link between the primitive and modern. The question then is in *what* sense is Bhaktapur distinctive. For Levy, the significant feature distinguishing the ancient city as opposed to primitive society is that, due to the enlarged size and complexity of a society no longer based on face-to-face interaction, 'culturally shaped common sense' is insufficient for integrating the community. Thus in Bhaktapur (and archaic cities in general) people must use '"marked symbols" . . . to solve the problems of communication induced by magnification of scale' (p. 26). Marked symbols are those in which 'meaning must *evidently* be sought elsewhere than in what the object or event seems to mean "in itself"'. They are opposed to 'embedded symbols' which are 'associated with cultural structuring of "common sense"'.

It is untrue that 'primitive' people do not utilize both marked and embedded symbols. The difference between the archaic city and primitive society was not that the former did not use marked symbols, but that a class of specialists which had emerged out of a well-developed division of labour facilitated and controlled the associations of these symbols. These priesthoods elaborated on and developed out of the ritual practitioners of the clan organized societies and priest-kings of the segmentary states (Southall 1956, 1984, 1988), some of which complexly integrated people on continental scale (Wolf 1982)—certainly no longer face-to-face organization. Urban society organized no longer primarily in terms of ranked clans but now in terms of separate strata of families, or classes, within a clear division of labour based on landed property. Although Levy describes the ranked clans as the normative order of the society, these serve as an organizing principle and ideological framework but are no longer the substance of the society. Urban class-based divisions of labour developed on the basis of the domestication of plants and animals and the associated technologies which marked the 'Neolithic Revolution' from 20,000 to 7,000 BC. The role and use of symbols in archaic cities was derived from these developments and the difference between primitive society and the archaic cities must be dealt with in these terms.[5]

Once priest classes had emerged, then the 'marked' character or inaccessibility of symbols (in terms of the interpretations Levi chose to privilege, that is) took on the added character of being accessible only through the interpretation of priests. As symbols in Bhaktapur could not be satisfactorily interpreted (from the anthropologist's viewpoint) by lay people (or elders, medicine women and medicine men, shamans or other rudimentary specialists among them), and Levy, following Dumont, felt he had to go to a trained and certified class of specialists and texts to properly interpret the symbols, he evidently mixed up this control of interpretation of the marked character of symbols by priests with the marked character itself. This led him to deduce that archaic cities were differentiated from primitive society by the dichotomy in the embedded versus marked character of symbols.

He is misled because he was operating under the assumption that the symbols were significant on their own terms (in which a particular Brahmanical interpretation is privileged a priori). He identified political characteristics, more specifically political symbols, in the control and use of symbols in society as being properties of symbols themselves. Furthermore, if he had not stopped his analysis at the ideological sphere, but continued to analyse the social aspects from which the symbols were derived—the class makeup of the city, the markets, the division of labour and so forth—he would have been forced to question the other equivocations that he was making: Bhaktapur as 'archaic city', 'city of orthogenetic transformation', 'primary urban generation', 'ancient city', lack of 'axial transformation'. Instead, he proceeds along an entirely different path.[6]

Bhaktapur . . . can be considered to have . . . typological analogies with archaic cities insofar as it represents a community elaborately organized on a spatial base through a system of marked symbolism. The particular symbolic system made use of is a variant of Hinduism. . . . Hinduism is in many of its features, which we contrast with the 'world historical religions', a system for and of what we have called 'archaic urban order'. (pp. 27–8)

His logic is that if Bhaktapur is organized on spatial base through a system of marked symbolism, then it has typological analogies with archaic cities. Having shown here that marked symbolism in itself is not a distinguishing characteristic of archaic cities, the typological analogies that the city may have with archaic cities are meaningless. Hinduism provides the symbols. Evidently because Hinduism was determined to not have made an axial transformation, it has 'in many of its features, a system for and of . . . archaic urban order' (p. 28): ahistoricity, rootedness in local space, pantheon and inheritance, distributive of godhead into pantheon and sacred in the here and now (p. 27). But many of his 'world historical religions', especially in their orthodox forms with their saints, pilgrimage sites, and so forth, have similar elements.

Accepting that Bhaktapur represents an archaic urban order (disputed here), Levy needs to define the extent of that order so as to ascertain the limits necessary for understanding Bhaktapur and its Newars. For this he utilizes Dumont's 'little kingdoms', which emerge out of and are absorbed into larger polities with the wax and wane of empires, to provide a territorial framework for his conceptual whole. Following Dumont (who was criticizing the use of the *village* as a social whole), he presents Bhaktapur, in another equivocation, with this atomistic unit as the 'social whole' that anthropologists were looking for in the village.

Whatever the shifting historical relations between caste and territorial units might have been, the conditions that allowed for the formation and development of little kingdoms allowed for the fulfillment of Hinduism's potentials for ordering a community. Such little kingdoms seem to have represented, to borrow a term from ecology, 'climax communities' of Hinduism, where it reached the full development of its potentials for systematic complexity, and with it a temporary stability, an illusion of being a middle world, a *mesocosm*, mediating between its citizens and the cosmos, a *mesocosm* out of time. (p. 28)

His argument here is: the Hindu ideal type is a little kingdom; the little kingdom is a social whole of limited extent established within a definite territory and self sufficient; therefore, the little kingdom is a 'climax community' (to borrow a term from ecology in reference to Jayasthiti Malla's Bhaktapur)[7] allowing for the full development of Hinduism's potentials. Defining the community in terms of political characteristics in a city with an important commercial aspect seems to be stacking the deck. An important basis of cities, even primary urban generations, was by definition not self sufficiency but trade, which is a recognition of integration and a whole which transcends the city. Political orders for legitimization purposes usually have an interest in presenting themselves as a social whole, but this must not be mixed up with their substance.

In the last section of the second chapter Levy, believing that he has defined Bhaktapur, returns to the question of 'what is a Newar that he or she may know Bhaktapur?' He approaches this by summing up the differences between primitive society and an 'archaic' Bhaktapur. He describes the primitive in terms of 'mind-forged manacles' in which thought is relatively homogeneous, takes the rural for granted and is directly mediated by symbols which appear as common sense reality—in other words, non-transcendent. This is compared to the complex experience of the people of Bhaktapur, for whom symbols contain many realities. From this he deduces that it is difficult for the primitive folk to engage in critical philosophical thought and discourse and thus they can only be passive subjects of anthropological analysis, while the people of Bhaktapur, being able to engage in sceptical and critical analysis are able to become potential collaborators with the anthropologist (pp. 29–30). Since primitive people cannot engage in critical thought, they cannot deal with incompatibilities—which they consequently relegate to the unconsciousness—and they engage in their actions because they see them as 'natural', although outsiders see them as constructed (p. 30). In contrast, the people of Bhaktapur deal with contradictions, but by providing satisfying answers and enchantment in the form of marked symbols. Only do the moderns free themselves of marked symbolism and relegate it to just being symbolism. Here I think again empirical data contradicts all three pictures. Anyone who has lived through the uncritical stand-off of Communism versus capitalism, as just one example of the complex 'constructions' of 'modern' society, must reflect back on it as an immense elaboration of marked symbolism and self delusion, a complete abandonment of critical thought and sanity by entire modern civilization, and a waste of an entire generation and immense planetary resources. Ironically, some of the most coherent criticism of the constructed character of the moderns' symbols was coming from 'primitives' such as the American Plains Indians more than a hundred years ago when confronted with the genocidal expansionism of industrial capitalism (see Dee Brown's *I Buried My Heart at Wounded Knee*, as an example).

Documentation of extremely critical thought among the so-called primitives negates Levy's position and makes me think rather that the difference he sees in Bhaktapur arises from his choice of elite intelligentsia who, due to their advanced education and western university training, make basically the same assumptions that he does.

Even the Bhaktapur intellectuals, however, he terms 'literati', involved in 'uncritical speculation', as opposed to modern critical intellectuals, since the former have yet to pass through the axial transformation which would allow them to transcend themselves. Conrád and Szelényi (1978) identified these contrasts as two poles of a gradient of roles for intelligentsia as a generic class type. On the one end intellectuals accept the assumptions and purposes set by society, particularly in their role as pure technicians or 'technical intelligentsia' dealing with knowledge concerned with implementation (techné). On the other end they address the premises and ultimate ends (telos) of society as 'teleological intellectuals'.[8] In practice most intellectuals combine both aspects to fall somewhere in between. Being modern does not necessarily make an intellectual radical nor does being primitive preclude a critical consciousness.

In the concluding chapter of the book Levy addresses a similar dichotomy within the symbolic sphere of Bhaktapur between the specialists in 'ordinary dharma' and those of the 'cult of dangerous deities', concerned with political power and operations not produced fully by assent to the dharmic value system, on one side, and the specialists in 'dharma' and 'ordinary Brahmanical religion', concerned with values and norms, on the other (pp. 601–9). Levy identifies the former specialists, involved in direct 'manipulation of materials and force' (p. 603), as the tantric priests and Brahmans serving the role of tantric priests. He identifies the latter, 'manipulators of purity', concerned with salvation, as the Brahmans. Yet as regularizers of dharma, the Brahmans also seem to be technical, while as shapers of the conditions of power, the tantric priests seem to be teleological.

With all this Levy aims to critique Dumont's delineation of secular versus religious spheres, showing that both the 'common order' (dealing with issues of power and force and generally addressing the issues referred to as secular) and the 'strange, mostly religious', order (dealing with religious values and norms) are actually contained within a larger 'religious universe', each with its own gods and religious practitioners as described above. By identifying Dumont's analysis as being too singular, when there are many other oppositions involved which criss-cross the sacred versus secular oppositions,[9] he is able to show that action in both orders is oriented through religious symbols and ritual. However, though he recognizes that the 'common order' addresses issues of concern to individuals other than religious functionaries, because he treats symbols as prior, he ends up circling around and framing the entire issue in terms of gods and symbols, without being able to provide insight into the secular or material realm, or the substance of its relation to the ritual one. I address this issue in a book in preparation:

The fact that an 'ideal' [the symbolic] exists as the determining purpose of activity makes it easy to assume that the ideas or their mediating symbols constitute the material world. People's ideal conceptions, however, arise according to the conditions of their existence, which themselves are products of previous activity. This is not an economic determinism or reductionism as is often made of this perspective. Ideas and institutions *do* orient and determine human life, but always as the products of previous activity and according to the conditions provided by it. Only when ideas are looked at in isolation from the historical context given by previous human activity do they seem to be constituting the material world. (Mikesell n.d.)

The final chapter of the first section of the book attempts to address the question of the material base of the city, what Levy calls 'the other order'. However, Levy's aim is to selectively reinforce his thesis of changelessness with reference to non-symbolic elements— spatial and ecological constraints, production and distribution, demography and so forth. He makes a vague jab at materialist[10] and structuralist approaches for their tendency to de-emphasize symbols as 'epiphenomenal or "expressive" or at best to some modestly supplementary status' (p. 53). The critique is valid, but Levy in turn limits his consideration of the orientation given by symbols to ritual and symbolically framed normative actions rather than relating them to historical action—outside the official history of kings and regimes, that is.

The bent of his argument is to reinforce the position of Bhaktapur's timelessness. Of the physical city he argues that its appearance has changed little from the end of the reign of Malla kings. He finishes with a description of decay, filth, earthquakes, fruit bats and jackals which steal children with the observation: 'All this is a reminder that Bhaktapur was and is still a clearing in a yet more ancient world' (p. 56). Of the demography he concludes, 'All available indexes suggested that at the time of this study Bhaktapur's population was, and had been for a very long time, quite stable' (p. 58). Of the population density he argues that the urban areas of Kathmandu have one of the highest population densities in the world of five to seven hundred persons per square mile, almost twice that of New York City, and Bhaktapur has a population of 117,000 per sq. mile, which is to imply that the city is a more crowded living space.

Without secondary analysis which deals with the two sets of data within their proper context, the comparison is superficial and spurious. New York City has large financial and industrial centers with non-residential industrial and office space. Great amounts of space are given over to the automobile transport system and public parks. And much of the population is dispersed to residences in outlying suburban areas and neighbouring bedroom communities. In other parts of the city very large populations are densely packed into urban ghetto housing and public works housing—'The Projects'—with unrecorded 'doubling up' of poor families (Dehavenon and Boone 1992). On Bhaktapur's side, given the city's largely agricultural population, as documented by Levy, the agricultural lands must be counted as part of Bhaktapur's urban space, which would greatly reduce the population density.

For the relationship with the central government, Levy outlines the formal political organization and stresses its centralized character, implying that 'modern' type politics have not yet entered into the city. 'For the time being . . . at the city level Bhaktapur has little effective local political control. There is plenty of politics within some of the component units of the traditional city organization, but that is another matter' (p. 62). Although the activity of parties, underground at the time of his study, was not in its domain, ignoring the subsequent assertion of Communist Party control over city politics, the conditions and forces that gave rise to it, and the contradictions involved[11] allows Levy to avoid issues that would in many aspects contradict his analysis—that city politics takes an essentially 'traditional' form, the city's changelessness and archaic character, the uncritical character of the city's intelligentsia as a literati, the exclusivity of a symbolic orientation. Even if the Communists were inaccessible to the analysts at that time, adequate analysis requires that the theory must subsequently be remade to account for all the facts and not stick to a certain incomplete and highly selective kind of facts for heuristic purposes.[12]

In dealing with the agricultural economy, Levy observes that as the proportion of farmers is similar to that of rural communities, 'Bhaktapur and its hinterland do not represent the familiar urban-peasant polarization prevalent elsewhere' (p. 62). He argues that the agriculture is subsistence oriented, and that cash comes from nonfarm activities and farm product sales. That 60 per cent of the farming households own some land and pay 25 to 28 per cent of the value of the produce in rents is attributed to the Land Acts dating from 1957 onwards. As a result, citing Acharya and Ansari (1980:113), he argues that the differentiation in income is much less than that found in Kathmandu or Patan (pp. 68–9). Assuming the success of the Land Acts he argues, without data, that the redistribution of land has preserved conservatism by taking the land from the hands of 'traditional landowning classes, the Brahmans and merchants', into those of the more conservative 'farmers'.

The land reforms with their resulting marked improvement in the economic and social position of the farmers in Bhaktapur has [sic] had an unintended effect. To the degree that traditional landowning classes, the Brahmans and merchants, lost their lands and land revenues and the farmers gained them, the newly wealthy farmers have come to be the supporters and clients of much of the traditional religious system as well as important employers of Brahmans. Less educated and less open to modernization than the higher classes, this transition has helped to slow down change and to support and conserve the old system. (p. 64)

This position, which contradicts one quoted from M.C. Regmi that the land reform had little effect, seems to be an apology for the modernization thesis that argues that progressive 'rich' farmers are the agents of modernization; interestingly, his high caste interlocutors come from among the progressive group. In fact, the ownership of 'some land', but not the most productive land, is an integral part of the general system of exploitation. The whole position indicates how the ethnographer can unconsciously become an unwitting collaborator in the class programs of his indigenous interlocutors, who themselves may unconsciously accept it as 'common sense'. By restricting itself to the symbolic sphere, the analysis limits its ability to take a critical stance and leads the anthropologist into the role of Levy's literati.

The whole analysis of 'the other order' comes down to reinforcing Levy's main thesis that the city is changeless, justifying his designation of it as an archaic city stuck somewhere between the primitive and modern.

We have described a city that . . . still retained many of the features which had long characterized it . . . dense but stable population . . . relatively little related to larger economic and political networks. Its economy, which had a large non-monetary component, was still heavily based on internal (including its bordering farms) production and exchange. For the city as a whole it was more of an administered than a political unit, the sources of power and decision were elsewhere, in the non-Newar national government at Kathmandu. That external administration was minimally disruptive, and it was certainly not innovative. *Bhaktapur was then in both fact and ideology 'self sufficient' and turned in on itself.* (p. 68, italics added)

In contrast, I have emphasized throughout this critique that Bhaktapur *appears* to be 'self sufficient and turned in upon itself' because the full urban culture encompasses something wider than just the city itself, particularly a city defined in terms of Brahmanic texts, which Levy mistakenly attributes as being a 'totality'. As he says that it was 'in fact' so, his analysis must also account for facts that argue otherwise.

This dichotomy of microcosm and mesocosm strongly parallels that of civil society and the state, which raises questions of the autonomy of the two spheres and the validity of speaking in terms of a separate mesocosm at all. The nineteenth century critique of this twentieth century argument was that contradictions that appear in the state originate out of the processes, interests and struggles within the civil society, and that not only are the two spheres not autonomous from each other, but that the state is constituted by the civil society rather than the other way around. The same sort of argument may be made here for the symbolic, which for Levy *is* the state in Bhaktapur, as opposed to the material world.

NOTES

This chapter originally appeared as 'A Critique of Levi's Urban Mesocosm Thesis' in *Contributions to Nepalese Studies*, Vol. 20, No. 2, pp. 231–54.

1   On this matter Declan Quigley (whose highly pertinent book I only obtained after completing this essay) writes that a mistake of the colonial understanding of caste 'is the assumption that there is one unambiguous interpretation of the *varna* system which outstanding Sanskrit scholars have access to. The *varna* system is a set of ideas developed to explain an early division of labour, but these ideas have always been interpreted in different, contradictory ways' (1993:16). Even among Brahmans there are 'at least six different Brahmanic personae, with dramatically conflicting characteristics, [which] manifest themselves in the Hindu world' (1993:56). Levi's use of university students and instructors as collaborators and authorities further complicates the picture, as does the existence of Brahmans as prime ministers, party leaders, and promoters of the sale of public enterprises to Indian businessmen and of IMF restructuring and World Bank programs.

2   This should reciprocally highlight the anthropologist's *own* collaborative relation with his indigenous specialist collaborators, particularly when he privileges their particular perspective as having authority over alternative views, statuses, and discourses in society. As Quigley (1993:48) reminds us, giving over authority to a particular view necessarily implies providing legitimacy to power: legitimacy of the class interests and programmes Levy's collaborators extend out of and represent. ['There cannot . . . be status (authority) without power. The very concept of authority is premised on the idea that there is some relation of unequal power which would be problematic if not legitimated.']

3   If he is to refer to texts, it seems that school textbooks, which most young people of all social classes read, or now cable television, would be much more valid.

4   This is debatable; but what is certain is that the city was greatly transformed due to its defeat by Prithivi Narayan Shah, causing it to lose its character as a 'political' city (Weber 1978) and in large part many elements of its commercial character: supplying garrisons, etc.

5   See Mikesell (1991) for preliminary discussion of the process with reference to South Asia and Nepal.

6   Quigley (1993:48) makes the same point: 'But what Brahmanism represents as divine, unalterable truth, sociological comparisons quickly demonstrate to be contingent on a particular conjunction of factors thrown up by particular historical conditions. What Brahmanism cannot do (because to do so would be to deny its own legitimacy) is to explain what these conditions are, and why caste is not timeless as the ideology of Brahmanical purity would have us believe. Any adequate explanation must go beyond its conditional Brahmanical validation.'

7   It seems somewhat inappropriate to apply the term of climax community, which refers to a system of mutually interlinked biological organisms which have filled out the various ecological niches to the extent that they live together in a system of relative stasis—in which the subject is natural laws—to a highly differentiated and divided class society—in which the subject is human activity. As various traditions of sociology and history have addressed this issue and have developed an array of more appropriate terms, there is no need to go outside the discipline for a term.

8   Hegel, for example, was a modern 'critical' intelligentsia to a point, but beyond that he was a literati, serving as an apologist for the Kaiser's regime. Similarly, Lenin was revolutionary until he came to power, then once in power he rationalizing the Soviet regime with his doctrine of revolution in one country.

9   Dangerous deities versus benign deities, tantric religion versus ordinary religion, secular versus religious, conventional versus ritual, king versus Brahman versus other kinds of priests and polluting *thars*, worldly power versus other worldly force, unclean sweeper versus clean Brahman, purity irrelevant to order versus purity relevant to order, bordering/outside city versus inside city, pre-initiation versus after initiation.

10   Specifically the dependency theory variation on materialism which Cameron, Seddon and Blaikie are the early foreign proponents and which is taught as 'conflict theory' in the indigenous social science departments—and which in contradistinction to my own understanding beginning with creative activity or production, focuses on structures such as 'infrastructures' mentioned disparagingly by Levy.

11 For example, the strife between Communist and Congress, and between the CP(M-L) and CP(Farm Labour) parties along the lines of untouchables versus Jyapu farmers, and the patron-client type leadership of the latter by a son of one of the big landowning families despite claims of being a workers' party.

12 At the time of his study, furthermore, there where other struggles brewing, such as the intense fight over the control of the Bhaktapur literacy programs arranged for Newar women between the women's groups and the Panchas (promulgating the government textbook financed and designed by international aid agencies—USAID, UNICEF, World Education, etc.—and accompanying pro-Panchayat reading materials versus locally developed curriculum). The women never gave into this struggle, although they and the program workers were harassed, jailed and beaten by the police. Levi's presentation of his limited analysis as the whole of Bhaktapur does great injustice to such initiatives and justifies reactionary policies against their struggle against repression that continues unabated under the guise of 'preserving' democracy.

Bibliography

Acharya, Rajeshwar, and Hamid Ansari, *Basic Needs and Government Services: An Area Study of Bhaktapur Town Panchayat, Nepal*, Kathmandu: Centre for Economic Development and Administration, Tribhuvan University, 1980.

Alavi, Hamza, 'India: Transition from Feudalism to Colonial Capitalism', *Journal of Contemporary Asia*, Vol. 10, No. 4, 1980, pp. 359–99.

———, 'Politics of Ethnicity in India and Pakistan', in *South Asia*, Hamza Alavi and John Harris (eds.), New York: Monthly Review Press, 1989.

Althusser, L., and E. Balibar, *Reading Capital*, London: New Left Books, 1970.

Alves, Maria Helena, 'Comment on Kerala', *Monthly Review*, Vol. 42, No. 8, 1991a, pp. 25–6.

———, 'The Workers' Party of Brazil: Building Struggle from the Grassroots', *The Future of Socialism: Perspectives from the Left*, William K. Tabb (ed.), New York: Monthly Review Press, 1991b, pp. 233–45.

Archer, David, and Patrick Costello, *Literacy and Power: The Latin American Battleground*, London: Earthscan Publications Ltd., 1990.

Bachofen, J. J., *Das Mutterrecht. Eine Untersuchung über die Gynaikokratie der alten Welt nach ihrer religiösen und rechtlichen Natur*, Stuttgart, 1861.

Baran, Paul A., *The Political Economy of Growth*, New York: Monthly Review, 1957.

Baran, Paul A., and Paul M. Sweezy, *Monopoly Capital: An Essay on the American Economic and Social Order*, New York: Monthly Review, 1966.

Bayly, C.A., *Rulers, Townsmen and Bazaars: North Indian Society in the Age of British Expansion, 1770–1870*, Cambridge: Cambridge University Press, 1983.

Bennett, Lynn, *Dangerous Wives and Sacred Sisters: Social and Symbolic Roles of High-Caste Women in Nepal*, Columbia: Columbia University Press, 1983.

Berktay, Halil, 'The Feudalism Debate: The Turkish End—Is "Tax-vs.-Rent" Necessarily the Products and Sign of a Modal Difference?', *The Journal of Peasant Studies*, Vol. 14, No. 3, , 1987, pp. 291–333.

Berreman, Phillip, *The Religious Roots of Rebellion: Christians in Central American Revolutions*, Maryknoll, New York: Orbis Books, 1984.

Bhandari, Bishnu, 'The Past and Future of Sociology in Nepal', *Occasional Papers in Sociology and Anthropology*, Vol. 2, Stephen L. Mikesell (ed.),

Kathmandu: Central Department of Sociology and Anthropology, Tribhuvan University, 1991, pp. 13–23.

Bhattachan, Krishna Bahadur, 'Sociology and Anthropology Curriculum and the Needs of Nepal', *Occasional Papers in Sociology and Anthropology*, Vol. 1, James F. Fisher (ed.), Kathmandu: Central Department of Sociology and Anthropology, Tribhuvan University, 1987, pp. 11–28.

Bista, Dor Bahadur, *People of Nepal*, Kathmandu: Ratna Pustak Bhandar, 1987.

——, 'Nepal School of Sociology/Anthropology' *Occasional Papers in Sociology and Anthropology*, Vol. 1, James F. Fisher (ed.), Kathmandu: Central Department of Sociology and Anthropology, Tribhuvan University, 1987, pp. 6–10.

——, *Fatalism and Development: Nepal's Struggle for Modernization*, New Delhi: Orient Longman, 1991.

Blaikie, Piers, John Cameron, and David Seddon, *Nepal in Crisis: Growth and Stagnation at the Periphery*, Delhi: Oxford University Press, 1980.

Broderick, Francis L, 'W.E.B. Du Bois: History of an Intellectual', in *Black Sociologists: Historical and Contemporary Perspectives*, James E. Blackwell and Morris Janowitz (eds.), Chicago and London: The University of Chicago Press, 1974, pp. 3–24.

Burbach, Roger, and Patricia Flynn (eds.), *The Politics of Intervention: The United States in Central America*, New York: Monthly Review Press, 1984.

Brown, Dee, *I Buried My Heart at Wounded Knee*, New York: Holt, Rinehart and Winston, 1971.

Collins, Joseph, *What Difference Could a Revolution Make? Food and Farming in the New Nicaragua*, San Francisco: Institute for Food and Development Policy, 1972.

Conrád, George, and Iván Szelényi, *The Intelligentsia on the Road to Class Power*, New York: Holt, Rinehart and Winston, 1978.

Cox, Oliver C., 'The Modern Caste School of Race Relations', *Social Forces*, Vol. 21 (Dec.), 1942, pp. 218–26.

——, 'Class and Class', *Journal of Negro Education* 13 (Spring), Vol. 1, 1944, pp. 39–49.

——, 'Race and Caste: A Definition and a Distinction', *American Journal of Sociology*, Vol. 50 (Mar.), 1945a, pp. 360–68.

——, 'An American Dilemma', *Journal of Negro Education*, Vol. 14 (Spring), 1945b, pp. 132–48.

——, *Caste, Class, and Race*, New York: Doubleday and Co. (rpt. edn, Monthly Review Press), 1948.

——, *Race, Class, and the World System: The Sociology of Oliver C. Cox*, New York: Monthly Review Press, 1987.

Cross, J.P, 'The Gurkhas: As I See It', *Strategic Studies Series*, Nos. 6 and 7 (Winter and Spring), 1985–86, pp. 162–76.

D'Amico-Samuels, Deborah, 'Undoing Fieldwork: Personal, Political, Theoretical and Methodological Implications', in *Decolonizing*

Anthropology: Moving Further toward an Anthropology of Liberation, Fage V. Harrison (ed.), Washington, D.C.: Association of Black Anthropologists, American Anthropological Association, 1991, pp. 68–87.

Dehavenon, Anna Lou, and Margaret Boone, *Promises! Promises! Promises! The Failed Hopes of New York City's Homeless Families in 1992*, New York: The Action Research Project on Hunger, Homeless and Family Health, 1992.

Du Bois, W.E.B, *Against Racism: Unpublished Essays, Papers, Addresses, 1887–1961*, Herbert Aptheker (ed.), Amherst: University of Massachusetts Press, 1985a.

———, 'Colonialism, Democracy, and Peace after the War' in *Against Racism: Unpublished Essays, Papers, Addresses, 1887–1961*, Herbert Aptheker (ed.), Amherst: University of Massachusetts Press, 1985b, pp. 229–44.

———, *Black Reconstruction in America: An Essay Toward a History of the Part Which Black Folk Played in the Attempt to Reconstruct Democracy in America, 1860–1880*, Cleveland and New York: The World Publishing Company, 1964.

———, *The Philadelphia Negro: A Social Study*, Philadelphia: University of Pennsylvania, 1899.

Dumont, Louis, *Homo Hierarchicus: The Caste System and Its Implications*, Mark Sainsbury, Louis Dumont, and Basia Gulati (Trans.), completely revised English edition, Chicago: University of Chicago Press, 1980.

———, 'For a Sociology of India', *Contributions to Indian Sociology*, Vol. 1, 1957.

Dunayevskaya, Raya 'Marx's "New Humanism" and the Dialectics of Women's Liberation in Primitive and Modern Societies', *Praxis International*, Vol. 3, January 1984.

Engels, Frederick, 'The Origin of the Family, Private Property and the State in Light of the Researches of Lewis H. Morgan', in *Karl Marx and Frederick Engels, Selected Works* (5th printing), Moscow: Progress Publishers, 1983, pp. 191–334.

FIPD (Foreign Investment Promotion Division, Ministry of Industry), 'The Other Face of Nepal', *Far Eastern Economic Review*, Vol. 8, October 1992, pp. 37–43.

Fisher, James F., 'Introduction', *Occasional Papers in Sociology and Anthropology*, Vol. 1. James F. Fisher (ed.), Kathmandu: Central Department of Sociology and Anthropology, Tribhuvan University, 1987a, pp. 1–5.

———, '"Romanticism" and "Development" in Nepalese Anthropology', *Occasional Papers in Sociology and Anthropology*, Vol. 1, James F. Fisher (ed.), Kathmandu: Central Department of Sociology and Anthropology, Tribhuvan University, 1987b, pp. 29–42.

Fox, Richard G, *Kin, Clan, Raja and Rule: State-Hinterland Relations in Preindustrial India*, Berkeley and Los Angeles: University of California Press, 1971.

———, 'Pariah Capitalism and Traditional Indian Merchants, Past and

Present', in *Entrepreneurship and Modernization of Occupational Cultures in South Asia*, Milton Singer (ed.), Durkham: Duke University Press, 1973, pp. 16–36.

Fox, Richard G., ed., *Realm and Region in Traditional India*, Durkham: Duke University Press, 1977.

Freire, Paulo, *Pedagogy of the Oppressed*, London: Penguin, 1972.

Frank, Andre Gunter, 'The Development of Underdevelopment', *Monthly Review* (September), 1966.

———, *Dependent Accumulation and Underdevelopment*, New York: Monthly Review Press, 1979.

Frölich, Paul, *Rosa Luxemburg* (Trans. of 2nd German edn), New York: Monthly Review, 1972.

Fürer-Haimendorf, C. von, *The Sherpas of Nepal*, London: J. Murray, 1964.

Gellner, Ernst *Legitimation of Belief*, Cambridge: Cambridge University Press, 1974.

Gervasi, Sean, 'Western Intervention in the U.S.S.R', *CovertAction* 39 (Winter), 1991–2, pp. 4–9.

Gosh, Sunita Kumar, 'On the Transfer of Power in India', *Bulletin of Concerned Asian Scholars*, Vol. 17, No. 3, 1985, pp. 30–45.

Godelier, Maurice, 'The Concept of "Asiatic Mode of Production" and Marxist Models of Social Evolution', in *Relations of Production: Marxist Approaches to Economic Anthropology*, David Seddon (ed.), London: Frank Cass, 1978a, pp. 209–57.

———, 'Infrastructures, Societies, and History', *Current Anthropology*, Vol. 19, No. 4, 1978c, pp 763–71.

———, 'The Object and Method of Economic Anthropology', in *Relations of Production: Marxist Approaches to Economic Anthropology*, David Seddon (ed.), London: Frank Cass, 1978d, pp. 48–126.

Gramsci, Antonio, *Selections from the Prison Notebooks*, New York: International Publishers, 1971.

Gurung, Om, 'Sociology and Anthropology: An Emerging Field of Study in Nepal', *Occasional Papers in Sociology and Anthropology*, Vol. 2, Stephen L. Mikesell (ed.), Kathmandu: Central Department of Sociology and Anthropology, Tribhuvan University, 1991, pp. 4–12.

Habermas, Jurgen, *Knowledge and Human Interests*, London, 1971.

Hamilton, Francis Buchanan, *An Account of the Kingdom of Nepal and of the Territories Annexed to this Dominion by the House of Gorkha* (Rpt., with introduction by Marc Gaborieu), New Delhi: Asian Educational Service, (1819), 1986.

Harris, Marvin, *The Rise of Anthropological Theory: A History of Theories of Culture*, New York: Cromwell, 1968.

Harriss, J., 'The Formation of Indian Society: Ideology and Power', in H. Alavi and J. Harriss (eds.), *South Asia*, New York: Monthly Review Press, 1989, pp. 126–33.

Hegel, Georg Wilhelm Friedrich, *The Philosophy of History*, J. Sibree (trans.), New York: Dover Publications, Inc. (1899), 1956.

Hitchcock, John, *The Magars of Banyan Hill*, New York: Holt, Rinehart and Winston, 1966.

Hodgson, Brian H, *Essays on the Languages, Literature, and Religion of Nepal and Tibet together with Further Papers on the Geography, Ethnology and Commerce of Those Countries*, 2 Parts (Rpt.), Varanasi: Bharat-Bharati (1871), 1984.

Höfer, Andras, 'The Caste Hierarchy and the State in Nepal. A Study of the *Muluki Ain* of 1954', *Khumbu Himal*, Vol. 13, No. 2, 1979, pp. 25–240.

Ignatius, David, 'Spyless Coups', *Washington Post*, 22 September 1991.

Jones, Rex L., and Shirley Kurz Jones, *The Himalayan Woman; a Study of Limbu Women in Marriage and Divorce*, Mountainview, CA: Mayfield Publishing Company, 1976.

Kahl, Hubert, 'Magic Touch Ends Drought', *The Rising Nepal*, 8 September 1991.

Kirkpatrick, Colonel, *Account of the Kingdom of Nepaul, Being the Substance of Observations Made During a Mission to that Country, in the Year 1793* (Reprint), (London: William Miller) New Delhi: Asian Education Services (1911), 1986.

Krader, Lawrence, 'Introduction', in *The Ethnological Notebooks of Karl Marx*, Krader, Lawrence (ed.), Assen: Van Gorcum and Company, N.V., 1972, pp. 1–83.

Lamsal, Yuba Nath, 'The Elections: Misgivings and Messages', *The Rising Nepal*, 20 May 1991.

Leiva, Fernando, Ignacio, and James Petras, 'Chile: New Urban Movements and the Transition to Democracy', *Monthly Review*, Vol., 39, No. 3, 1987, pp. 109–24.

Lenin, V.I., 'Imperialism, the Highest State of Capitalism', in *V. I. Lenin, Selected Works in Three Volumes*, Vol. 1 (1975 revd. edn), Moscow: Progress Publishers, 1977, pp. 634–731.

Levy, Robert I., with Kedar Raj Rajopadhyaya, *Mesocosm: Hinduism and the Organization of a Traditional Newar City in Nepal* (Indian ed.), Delhi: Motilal Banarsidass Publishers Pvt. Ltd., 1992.

Lewis, Todd Thornton, and Daya Ratna Shakya, 'Contributions to the History of Nepal: Eastern Newar Diaspora Settlements', *Contributions to Nepalese Studies*, Vol. 15, No. 1, pp. 25–65, 1988.

Luxemburg, Rosa, *The Accumulation of Capital*, New York: Routledge and Kegan Paul, 1951.

Magdoff, Harry, *The Age of Imperialism: The Economics of U.S. Foreign Policy*, New York and London: Modern Reader Paperbacks, 1969.

Maglaya, Felipe E, *Organizing People for Power: A Manual for Organizers*, Hong Kong: Asian Committee for People's Organization. [Translated to Nepali as *Praaptikaa laagi: janataalai kasari sangathit garne* (Pariwar tankaalaagi-chikitsák Phaundesan), CVICT, Kathmandu, 1992]. 1987.

Majumdar, R.C., H.C. Raychaudhuri, and Kalikinkar Datta, *An Advanced History of India* (4th edn.), Madras: Macmillan India Ltd., 1978.

Marx, Karl, *Capital: A Critique of Political Economy*, Vol. 3, Book Three: The Process of Capitalist Production as a Whole, edited by Frederick Engels, Moscow: Progress Publishers, 1959.

———, *The Ethnological Notebooks of Karl Marx (Studies of Morgan, Phear, Main, Lubbock)*, transcribed and edited, with an introduction by Lawrence Krader (2nd edn.), Assen, The Netherlands: Van Gorcum and Company B.V., 1972.

———, 'Forms which Precede Capitalist Production', in *Grundrisse: Foundations of the Critique of Political Economy*, translated with a forward by Martin Nicolaus, New York: Vintage Books, 1973a.

———, 'Introduction', in *Grundisse: Foundations of the Critique of Political Economy*, translated with a forward by Martin Nicolaus, New York: Vintage Books, 1973b.

———, 'Marx to P. V. Annenkov in Paris, *December 28, 1946*', in *Marx Engels: Selected Correspondence*, I. Lasker (trans.), S. W. Ryazanskaya (ed.), 3rd edn., Moscow: Progress Publishers, 1975, pp. 29–39.

———, *Capital: A Critique of the Political Economy*, Vol. 1, Ben Fowkes (trans.), Ernest Mandel (intro.), New York: Vintage Books, 1977.

———, 'Forms Preceding Capitalist Production', in *Karl Marx and Frederick Engels*. Vol. 28, *Karl Marx: 1857–61, Economic Manuscripts of 1857–1858 (First Version of Capital)*, Moscow: Progress Publishers, 1986a, pp. 471–514.

———, 'Introduction', in *Karl Marx, Frederick Engels, Collected Works*. Vol. 28, *Karl Marx: 1857–61, Economic Manuscripts of 1857–1858 (First Version of Capital)*, Moscow: Progress Publishers, 1986b, pp. 17–48.

Marx, Karl, and Frederick Engels, 'Feuerbach. Opposition of the Materialist and Idealistic Outlook', in *The German Ideology*, Vol. 1, *Selected Works of Karl Marx and Frederick Engels*. 5th ptg. Moscow: Progress Publishers, 1983, pp. 13–97.

Meillassoux, Claude, 'Are there Castes in India?', *Economy and Society*, Vol. 2, No. 1, 1973, pp. 89–111.

———, 'The Economy' in Agriculturally Self-Sustaining Societies: A Preliminary Analysis', in *Relations of Production: Marxist Approaches to Economic Anthropology*, David Seddon (ed.), London: Frank Cass, 1978a, pp. 127–57.

———, 'The Social Organization of the Peasantry: The Economic Basis of Kinship', in *Relations of Production: Marxist Approaches to Economic Anthropology*, David Seddon (ed.), London: Frank Cass, 1978b, pp. 159–69.

Mepham, John, 'The Grundrisse: Method or Metaphysics?', *Economy and Society*, Vol. 7, No. 4, 1978, pp. 430–44.

Messerschmidt, Donald A., *The Gurungs of Nepal: Conflict and Change in a Village Society*, Warminister, England: Arris and Phillips, Ltd., 1967.

Mishra, Chaitanya, 'The Gurkhas: Its Genesis', *Strategic Studies Series* Nos. 6 and 7 (Winter & Spring, 1985–1986), 1986, pp. 155–61.

———, 'Three Gorkhali Myths', *Himal*, Vol. 4, No. 3, 1991, p. 17.

Mikesell, Stephen L., *Cotton on the Silk Road (Or the Dialectic of a Merchant Community in Nepal)*. PhD. diss., University of Wisconsin, 1988.

———, 'Marx's Ethnological Notebooks, Feudalism in Asia, and Strategy in Nepal', *Jhilko*, Vol. 10, No. 3, 1990a, pp. 3–13.

———, 'The Class Basis of the Movement: Historical Origins and Present Significance', *Jhilko*, Vol. 11, No. 1, 1990b, pp. 1–20.

———, 'A Comparative Study of South Asian Caste and Mediterranean Citizenship in the Development of the State', *Contributions to Nepalese Studies*, Vol. 8, No. 1, 1991a, pp. 1–18.

———, 'The Next Step: Cultivating the Roots of Rebellion', *Jhilko*, Vol. 16 (April-June), 1991b, pp. 1–18.

———, 'Dialectical Marxism and the Segmentary State', in *Culture and Contradiction: Dialectics of Wealth, Power, Symbol*, Hermina G. De Sota (ed.), San Francisco: The Edwin Mellon Press, 1992a, pp. 178–92.

———, 'The Local Government Law and Participatory Democracy: A Comparison of Opposites', *Law Bulletin*, Vol. 54, No. 6, 1992b, pp. 14–33.

———, 'The Paradoxical Support of Nepal's Left for Comrade Gonzalo', *Himal*, Vol. 6, No. 2, 1993, pp. 31–3.

———, 'The New Local Government Law: Diluted Raksi in an Old Bottle', in *Anthropology of Nepal: Peoples, Problems and Processes*, Michael Allen (ed.), Kathmandu: Mandala Book Point, 1994, pp. 287–303.

———, *Hill Bazaars and Industrial Capitalism: The History Subsumption of Peasant Society in Nepal*. Unpublished manuscript, n.d.

———, 'My friend, the minister of street dogs', *Everest Herald*, 20 May 1996.

Mikesell, Stephen L., and Jamuna Shrestha, 'The Gurkhas: A Case Study of the Problem of Mercenary Recruitment in Barpak, Nepal', *Strategic Studies Series*, Nos. 6 and 7 (Winter and Spring), 1985–86, pp. 146–54.

Mitter, Swasti, *Common Fate, Common Bond: Women in the Global Economy*, London: Pluto Press, 1986.

Morgan, Henry Louis, *Ancient Society or Researches in the Lines of Human Progress from Savagery through Barbarism to Civilization*, New York: Henry Holt, 1977.

Nepali, Gopal Singh, *The Newars: An Ethno-Sociological Study of a Himalayan Community*, Kathmandu: Himalayan Booksellers, 1965.

Onta, Pratyoush, 'Rich Possibilities: Notes on Social History in Nepal', *Contributions to Nepalese Studies*, Vol. 21, No. 1, 1994, pp. 1–43.

Ortner, Sherry B., *Sherpas through their Rituals*, Cambridge and New York: Cambridge University Press, 1978.

Pahari, Anup, 'Ties that Bind: Gurkhas in History', *Himal*, Vol. 4, No. 3, 1991, pp. 6–12.

Phear, Sir John Budd, *The Aryan Village in India and Ceylon*. London, 1880.

Pignéd, Bernard, *Les Gurungs: une population himalayenne du Népal,* Le Monde D'Outre-Mer Parse' et Présent, Premiere Serie, études 21. Paris: and Lahage, 1966.

———, *The Gurungs: A Himalayan Population of Nepal,* Sarah Harrison and Alan Macfarlane (trans.), Kathmandu: Ratna Pustak Bhandar, 1993.

Prasad, Ishwari, *The Life and Times of Maharaja Juddha Shamsher Jung Bahadur Rana of Nepal,* New Delhi: Ashish Publishing House, 1975.

Quigley, Declan, *The Interpretation of Caste,* Oxford: Clarendon Press, 1993.

Ray, Rajat Kanta, 'The Bazaar: Changing Structural Characteristics of the Indigenous Section of the Indian Economy before and after the Great Depression', *The Indian Economic and Social History Review,* Vol. 25, No. 3, 1988, pp. 263–316.

Redfield, Robert, and Milton Singer, 'The Cultural Role of Cities', *Economic Development and Cultural Change,* Vol. 2, No. 1, 1954, pp. 53–73.

Russell, Bertrand, *History of Western Philosophy and its Connection with Political and Social Circumstances from the Earliest Times to the Present Day* (2nd edn.), London and New York: Routledge, 1961.

Shaha, Suranjit Kumar, Historical Premises of India's Tribal Problem. *Journal of Contemporary Asia,* Vol. 16, No. 3, 1986, pp. 274–319.

Shanin, Teodor (ed.), *Late Marx and the Russian Road: Marx and 'the Peripheries of Capitalism',* New York: Monthly Review Press, 1983.

Shrestha, Kusum,. '"The Constitutional Monarchy" as Defined by the King', Kathmandu: Nepal Law Society (Photocopied typescript), 1990.

Sklar, Holly, and Chip Berlet, 'NED, CIA, and the Orwellian Democracy Project', *CovertAction* 39 (Winter), 1991–2, pp. 10–13 and 59–62.

Southall, Aidan, *Alur Society: A Study in Processes and Types of Domination,* Cambridge: W. Heffer and Sons, Ltd., 1956.

———, 'Reformulating the Segmentary State', paper presented in the panel on The Theory of Segmented Society and State in South India: Challenges and Rebuttals, at the 13th Annual Conference on South Asia, Madison, Wisconsin, 1984a.

———, 'Significance of Marx's View of Urban Evolution for a Theory of the City', paper presented at the workshop on Meanings of the City, at Wingspread Conference Center, 25–7 October, 1984b.

———, 'The Segmentary State in Africa and Asia', *Comparative Studies in Society in History,* Vol. 30, No. 1, 1988, pp. 52–82.

———, *The City in Time and Space,* Princeton: Princeton University Press, n.d. and 1997.

Stein, Burton, 'The Segmentary State in South Indian History', in *Realm and Region in Traditional India,* Robin G. Fox (ed.), Durkham: Duke University Press, 1977, pp. 3–62.

———, *Peasant, State and Society in Medieval South India,* Delhi: Oxford University Press, 1980.

Stiller, Ludwig F., *Prithivi Narayan Shah in the Light of Dibya Upadesh,* Ranchi Bazaar, Bihar: Catholic Press, 1968.

————, *The Silent Cry, The People of Nepal: 1816–39*, Tripureshwar, Kathmandu: Sahayogi Prakashan, 1976.

————, *The Kot Massacre*, Kathmandu: Centre for Nepal and Asian Studies, 1981.

Sweezy, Paul, 'The Theory of Capitalist Development: Chapter I, "Marx's Method"', *Monthly Review*, Vol. 44, No. 7, 1992, pp. 14–27.

Tse-Tung, Mao, 'Analysis of Classes in Chinese Society', in *Selected Works of Mao Tse-Tung*, Vol. 1, Peking: Foreign Languages Press, 1975, pp. 13-21.

Upadhyaya, Bishwonath, 'Sovereignty Cannot be Divided (an interview with Biswonath Upadhyaya)', *Nepali Patra*, 25 October 1990.

Wallerstein, Immanuel, *The Modern World System*, New York: Academic Press, 1974.

Weber, Max, *Economy and Society*, 2 vols., Berkeley: University of California Press, 1978.

Welpton, John, *Kings, Soldiers and Priests: Nepalese Politics and the Rise of Jang Bahadur Rana, 1830–1857*, Delhi: Manohar Publications, 1991.

Wells, H. G., *The Outline of History: Being a Plain History of Life and Mankind* (revd. and updated edn. by Raymond Postgate), London, Toronto, Melbourne, Sydney, Wellington: Cassell and Company, Ltd., 1951.

Wheatley, Paul, *The Pivot of the Four Quarters*, Chicago: Aldine, 1971.

Wolf, Eric, *Europe and the People Without History*, Berkeley, Los Angeles and London: University of California Press, 1982.

Zinn, Howard, *A People's History of the United States*, New York: Harper Perennial, 1990.

Index

slum dwellers, 142; and subordination of women, 189n. 4. *See also* Asiatic Mode of Production; private property
prostitution, 37

Quigley, Declan: ambiguity of *varna*, 300n. 1; authority, 301n. 2; Brahmanism, 301n. 6; methodological assumptions, 63n. 3
quota system, 239, 249, 250

race, 71, 82n. 2
Rajputs, in Nepal, 211n. 8, 273–5; settlement of, 264
Rana, Jang Bahadur, 202
Rana, Juddha Shamsher, 246
Ranas: ascendance of, 90–1; collaboration with British, 202; fall of, 204; insurgency against, 93; opposition to, 92, 203–4; rise and fall, 91
rank, 261–2, 269, 281; exchange as basis of, 263
rationalization, 186
rebellion, 81, 213–28. *See also* resistance
referendum (1980), 100
reflexivity, 34–5, 47, 53
relations of production, 57, 40, 66– 7n. 14
religion: as metaphor for organising, 219; salvation, 265; vs. secular, 296–7; urban, 279–300; world historic, 293
rent, 52, 184
representations: of Democracy Movement, 88; of Democracy Revolution, 185–6; of history, 223; of social groups, 281; sociology as, 76; of struggle, 225–6; of tourism, 226
repression, 111–12
reproduction, 43, 261
research, 53, 174
reserve army of labour, 271
resistance, 92–3
revolution: and class development, 92– 4; communal control of, 215;

dialectic of, 213; initiative of, 166; 'in permanence', 43; petty bourgeoisie in, 207; premise of, 61–2; process of, 160; requirement of, 217–18; and subsumption, 43
Revolutionary Workers Party, 101. *See also* United National People's Front
Rise of Anthropological Theory (Harris), 41
ritual, 261
ritual leaders, 261, 275–6n. 4
ritualization, 162–3, 198
roads, 95, 240
Robeson, Paul, 73
Rohit, Comrade, 107
Roman Empire, 179–83
Rosa Luxemburg (Frölich), 168n. 4
routinization of charisma, 162
rural life, 238–9
ruralization of the city, 180

sacred cow, 197, 273, 277–8n. 12
Sahlins, Marshall, 38
Sandinista National Liberation Front. *See FLSN*
Saraswati Cloth Factory, 246–54
secular vs. religious, 296–7
segmentary state, 262; and caste, 260–4, 269; and cities, 266; and gender, 263; as generic type, 266; expropriation of, 193–200; Gorkha's subordination of, 200–1; in Nepal, 274; modification of, 268; ritual leaders of, 261; ritual suzerainty of, 262; subsumption of, 22, 272, 263, 263
self-sustaining societies, 275n. 2
Sen, Makunda I, 211–12n. 9
Shah dynasty, origins of sovereignty of, 193–4
Shah, Birendra Bikram, and constitution, 125
Shah, Prithivi Narayan: on Bandipur, 235; basis of unification of, 167n. 2; founder of Nepal, 89; and hill people, 278n. 14; and imported textiles, 239
Shanin, Teodor, 189n. 3